Galatoire's

BIOGRAPHY OF A BISTRO

[signature: Marda Burton]

MARDA BURTON

&

KENNETH HOLDITCH

[signature: Kenneth Holditch]

HILL STREET PRESS ATHENS, GEORGIA

A HILL STREET PRESS BOOK

Published in the United States of America by

Hill Street Press LLC 191 East Broad Street, Suite 209, Athens, Georgia 30601-2848 USA

706-613-7200

info@hillstreetpress.com   www.hillstreetpress.com

Hill Street Press is committed to preserving the written word. Every effort is made to print books on acid-free paper with post-consumer recycled content.

The recipes in this book require careful preparation and the use of proper ingredients. Neither the author, Galatoire's Restaurant, nor the publisher assume any liability for the preparation and/or consumption of food prepared using the recipes in this book.

Hill Street Press books are available in bulk purchase and customized editions to institutions/companies.

Our best efforts have been used to obtain proper copyright clearance/credit for the images in this book. If an unavoidable and inadvertent credit error has occurred it will be corrected in future editions, upon notification. Photographers usually hold copyrights to their works.

To protect the privacy of some individuals, certain details in terms of names, descriptions, and situations presented herein may have been slightly altered. If readers are able to ascertain the identity of any character thus altered it is unintended.

Any credits appearing on pages 223-224 of this book constitute an extension of this copyright page.

Galatoire's and Galatoire's Restaurant are registered trademarks of Galatoire's Restaurant LLC.

Editor: Judy Long

Text and jacket design: Anne Richmond Boston

Jacket photos: Front top, ©Joshua Clark; front bottom, courtesy David Gooch

Library of Congress Cataloging-in-Publication Data

Burton, Marda.
    Galatoire's : biography of a bistro / by Marda Burton & Kenneth Holditch.
        p.   cm.
    ISBN 1-58818-071-9 (alk. paper)
    1. Galatoire's Restaurant. I. Holditch, W. Kenneth. II. Title.
    TX945.5.G35B87 2003
    641.5'09763'35—dc22   2003017165

ISBN 1-58818-071-9

10 9 8 7 6 5 4 3 2

CONTENTS

"Make no mistake: Much backstage talent is required to pull off something like Galatoire's. But ultimately this is a show owned by the actors on the main stage, the staff of twenty-nine waiters and their long-time regulars, whose courtly interaction follows a script known only to them. They are the sole reason Galatoire's remains the same world unto itself that it was before the remodel. For these people and those watching them, Galatoire's is New Orleans."

—S. M. Hahn, Restaurant Critic, *Times-Picayune*, November, 26, 1999

FOOTLIGHTS UP
Introduction

*I*n a city where people live to eat rather than eat to live, nobody doubts the importance of food and very special places to indulge in food. They are necessary to the very fabric of the city. All the better if a place also allows indulgence in other, less tangible requirements of the self. Besides nourishment, one needs a place in which to feel cherished; to toast one's friends in convivial ceremony; to celebrate life by breaking bread together— or sometimes just to get all dressed up and go out in public and act foolish. Food and cachet in equal measure are requisites of such a place.

In New Orleans, that place is Galatoire's.

In New Orleans, that place has been Galatoire's for so many generations that by now the century-old restaurant has absorbed the very essence of the city. Within its four walls lingers unseen but strongly felt the unique spirit that causes life to be lived in a certain inimitable style in this most consciously and conscientiously charming of cities.

Perhaps even more importantly, for its regulars Galatoire's creates its own cocoon, a place where ordinary cares are put aside the moment you walk in the door. Much more than simply a place to dine, it is a rare haven from the real world swirling outside—on both the rowdy street named Bourbon and its counterpart in the larger sense, a modern world that assails us with a cacophony of complex problems and pressures. The very fact that this restaurant has resisted change for so many years, indeed epitomizes that Southern penchant for eccentricity and welcomes it, makes it different and special and worthy of our regard. The delicious irony for which New Orleans is noted seems intensified at Galatoire's, making the restaurant all the more beloved.

This book came about back in 1998 when my collaborator and I were having one of our endless lunches at Galatoire's, greeting various friends coming and going at our table—the one also preferred by Tennessee Williams. At some point in the afternoon, after many tales had been told and a copious quantity of alcohol consumed, Kenneth and I looked at each other and said: "Somebody should write a book about this place." So we elected ourselves.

Our waiter was informed, toasts were made, and the project began. Little did we realize that the century-old time capsule would have so many stories to tell us and on so many levels. As a river of stories rolled in, the light soon dawned. "We should have started this when we were in our twenties," Kenneth said with a laugh. When discussing the title with food writer Gene Bourg, I told him we had thought of "Tales from a Bistro" but there were too many tales for one book. "Do a sequel," he said. "Call it "Son of a Bistro." We leave this title to writers a hundred years hence, when Galatoire's will surely be marking the beginning of its third century.

For now, far from being the restaurant's entire feast of memories and tales, this book is what we had time to write between meals.

MARDA BURTON

For Mississippians, New Orleans has always been a magnet, the El Dorado of their dreams, the sybaritic center of the universe where all pleasures of the flesh can be satisfied. This is especially true of young Mississippians, or was for me and my generation when we were growing up, though perhaps things have changed since then. By the end of the 1940s, I had read every New Orleans book I could find in the Tupelo High School library and in the public library and, filled with visions and facts from George Washington Cable and Lyle Saxon, craved more, craved, indeed, the real thing. When my father, who worked for the Natchez Trace Parkway as a civil engineer, announced that he was required to go to New Orleans to survey a drainage canal at Chalmette, the battlefield where Andrew Jackson and his troops routed the British troops and won the city for the United States, I was delighted and prevailed upon him to take my mother and me along.

After we settled into the hotel, I could not wait to cross Canal Street and wander in the French Quarter about which I had read so much that it seemed to loom in my consciousness. My first reaction was a mixture of awe and fear. I recall vividly even now, more than half a century after the fact, a large brutish man of the type one often saw in movies performing the dirty work for Sidney Greenstreet or others, but this one was hauling large stalks of bananas. My breakfast and lunch meals consisted of beignets at Morning Call, but in the evening, the three of us would go to a restaurant, first to Tujague's, an old and honored institution in those days, where Madame Guichet reigned behind the cash register and gave out advertising mirrors to ladies she liked. Every time we were in there in subsequent years, my mother received a mirror, and I now have her collection. The menu was table d'hôte, something totally new for us, but we found it delightful.

The next night we dined at Galatoire's, and once we walked through those front doors and into the mirror-lined bistro, I thought I had found paradise at a very early age. I recall eating Truite Amandine on the recommendation of the aged waiter, who was courteous to us, but a bit put off by the fact that we ordered no wine or liquor. I was too young and my father was a reformed drinker and my mother, who in later years would have a drink with me, did not drink in front of him. Sitting at that table in that magical place, far removed from the clutter and noise of the street outside, I said to myself, "This is where I want to live. I have found my home." Quite a change from Tupelo, but the change I wanted.

It took me fifteen years, but I finally accomplished my dream, for when a position in the English department at the recently founded University of New Orleans opened up, it was offered to me. I eagerly accepted it, although it meant a three thousand dollar a year cut in salary. I have never regretted that decision. I was in the city that I loved and I could dine whenever I wanted on Stuffed Eggplant or Shrimp Clemenceau or Crabmeat Yvonne or Oysters en Brochette, or a variety of other favorites. And I could drink those delectable cocktails that had been invented in New Orleans—notably Sazerac and Old-Fashioneds. (No, I did not share my father's temperance proclivities, a fact that caused some friction in our relationship, I might add.) In a figurative sense, I had taken a Streetcar named Desire, transferred to one called Cemeteries and wound up on the Elysian Fields I wanted: the French Quarter and Galatoire's. My home away from home. Those first few years I actually lived on Elysian Fields, but it was not my ideal place—the Quarter was, after I left my heart there in 1949.

There is a particular attachment Mississippians feel for Galatoire's, a proprietory attitude as if we owned part of it and, own it or not, did not want it changed. One evening I sat with a group of people including fellow Mississippians Marda Burton, Willie Morris, and Philip Carter—publisher, entrepreneur, son of Hodding and Betty Carter—and we planned how to take New Orleans away from Louisiana and give it back to Mississippi, as the original division of the Louisiana Purchase had intended. It was a natural decision on the part of the cartographers, for after all, New Orleans is on the east side of the river and most of Louisiana is on the other, but such was not to be. Only in spirit.

Well, the time, the money, I have spent in Galatoire's, as often as not at Tennessee Williams's table, have been well rewarded. Those long, leisurely lunches that stretch on into dinner and then beyond—or used to—are among my most treasured memories. *Je ne regrette rien!* in the words of Edith Piaf. Although I regret none of my experiences there, however, I do regret changes in Galatoire's that sometimes seem whimsical, but *c'est la vie*, I suppose.

Through the years I learned to like and respect a variety of waiters, indeed, to welcome them into my extended family circle, as well as Miss Yvonne Galatoire, that grand doyenne who for years faithfully guarded the integrity of the establishment into which her father, Justin Galatoire, had brought her to work as a young woman. "My father didn't like change," she said, "and neither do I."

Now so many have gone—Miss Yvonne of blessed memory, Lee McDaniel, Cesar Rodriguez and Gilberto Eyzaguirre, waiters of the top rank, and all the others who have died or left, and for them we grieve. I lift a glass to all of them and they live in my heart.

There is really no way to describe the relationship between Galatoire's and one of its devotees. You have to witness it, watching carefully, listening. Attorney Tommy Keller once called Galatoire's a club, and all you have to do to belong, he said, is to show up there and participate in its bounty. This is an amazingly democratic organization, although the real habitués prefer a dress code, because they look upon dining at the restaurant as a ritual, almost religious in its nature, though far from solemn.

Galatoire's is special. Galatoire's is—Galatoire's. God bless it—and preserve what it was.

Otherwise, to the ramparts!

KENNETH HOLDITCH

DRAMATIS PERSONAE
Authors' Note

Leon, Justin, and Gabriel Galatoire were admired by their children and grandchildren and various family members carry their names. We have chosen to refer to the namesake descendants as I, II, III, etc. to assist the reader in identifying the players.

Justin I	(8/10/1886–12/04/1973)	(Galatoire)
Justin II	(11/02/1952–)	(Frey)
Justin III	(4/18/1989–)	(Frey)
Justin IV	(3/10/1940–)	(Ansel)
Justin V	(9/13/1972–)	(Ansel)
Justin VI	(7/10/1985–)	(Nugent)
Gabriel I	(1891–1944)	(Galatoire)
Gabriel II	(11/29/1917–10/23/1985)	(Galatoire)
Leon I	(6/01/1884–4/17/1961)	(Galatoire)
Leon II	(10/29/1912–6/17/1979)	(Galatoire)
Leon III	(11/24/1954–)	(Galatoire)

Act One

Scene One

Producers
The Family Galatoire

*"The one focal point the family comes back to
over and over again is tradition."*
—Carolyn Frey Rodman, granddaughter of Justin Galatoire I

*T*hree essential components compose the Galatoire's picture: the family, the staff, and the customers, and the relationship between this triad is surely unique not only among most New Orleans restaurants, but also among eating establishments all over the United States. To propose that any one of the three components is the most important would, of course, be to engage in a moot argument, since none of them could exist without the other two. However, first and foremost is the family, the Galatoires, the founders and their descendants, without whom none of us would be making our pilgrimages with the regularity of the devout to that sacred shrine in the two hundred block of Bourbon Street.

Elsewhere in the United States, the term "family restaurant" designates an eating establishment to which one takes the entire family; the term "family restaurant," however, in New Orleans has a special, much more significant meaning, for it denotes an eatery that has been owned and managed by one family for a long period of time. As John Wilds wrote in *New Orleans Yesterday and Today* (1983), "It has been the family owners, rather than individual chefs, who have carried the tradition of New Orleans restaurants and influenced their evolution."

The Galatoires trace their roots to Pardies in southern France, a little over twelve miles from Pau in the foothills of the Pyrenees Mountains, where

1

members of the family were pork merchants ("marchants de porc"). Michele Galatoire, granddaughter of Leon I, relates that Pau, near Basque country in the region of Bearn, "is situated on high bluffs that run parallel with the mountains and is the most elegant of the towns and cities that overlook the Pyrenees." According to Leona Frey, daughter of Justin Galatoire I, her father took the children out of school one year and the whole family went to Pardies, where his oldest brother was still living; indeed there are still Galatoires in the town.

Jean, the first Galatoire to come to New Orleans, was born in December 1854, and lived until September 30, 1919. He was married to Gabrielle Marchal, who was born in October, 1862, and died July 27, 1940. Jean immigrated to America at an early age and settled briefly in Birmingham in 1880, where he ran an inn and restaurant on Twenty-first Street near First Avenue North. Then he opened an eating establishment in Chicago to take advantage of the World's Fair of 1893. He made enough money in Chicago to come south to New Orleans in 1900, obviously attracted by what he had heard about the large French population in the city, where the preparation of food and dining had been exalted to the level of a religion. Jean came to the old Creole city with a treasure: recipes for the wonderful French dishes that would become the staples of his famous eatery.

After the very Southern city of Birmingham and the very American and Midwestern Chicago, Jean Galatoire may have felt almost as if he were back in Pardies as he walked through the narrow streets of the Vieux Carre. Hearing the distinctive New Orleans patois of French, Jean must have noted how very much it was like the language with which he had grown up, and yet what marked differences existed as it was spoken by the natives of the city.

OLD NEW ORLEANS

Over a hundred years ago, when Jean Galatoire came to town, New Orleans was a metropolis of 100,000 or so inhabitants, but functioned more as a small town. The Vieux Carre was already more than 150 years old and had burned down and been rebuilt twice. The wealthy and elegant resided Uptown and on Esplanade Avenue; a few French families clung to their old homes and old ways, but most had moved out of the crumbling townhouses in the Quarter, and immigrants had crowded into the district. The Vieux Carre had become a slum; it was filthy, crime was rampant, and vice flourished. A few blocks from the restaurant, across Rampart Street, were the cribs of Storyville—today told as a romantic story, but in reality sad and sordid.

New Orleans' most lucrative business was shipping, and the riverfront seethed with commerce. Stevedores loaded and unloaded cotton, bananas, and sugar cane, and

Apparently Jean operated a bar near the L and N Station on Canal Street before using the money he had made in his Chicago venture to open his first New Orleans restaurant on Dauphine Street, all the while learning secrets about regional products and recipes of south Louisiana from the local chefs. Subsequently he became associated with Victor's at 209 Bourbon Street, which had been opened by Victor Bero in the mid to late 1800s. It was located in a three-story brick building that had been constructed as a townhouse in the 1830s at a cost of eleven thousand dollars. According to Carolyn Frey Rodman, "The new entrance was a carriageway that went all the way back. The kitchen stands on the site of an open courtyard, and the second-floor walkway where the bathrooms and wine room are were slave quarters." When Victor Bero opened the restaurant, it was a small eatery of the type common in France, with game and hams hanging in the windows. Victor and Jean became good friends, and family tales recount that the younger man was soon so totally involved in the running of the establishment that customers began calling it Galatoire's even before the official transfer of ownership.

When Victor Bero, by then an elderly man, decided to retire in 1905, Jean bought him out, and under his management, Galatoire's was converted into a more modern restaurant: the hams and game were taken out of the windows and the menu expanded. Jean's wife, Gabrielle ("Madame Galatoire"), in the typical French manner, served as cashier. (It seems likely that the couple lived upstairs over the restaurant during that period.) Genevieve Gragnon Stark, who has been a Galatoire's customer for seven decades, recalls that her grandmother, Mrs. Frederick B. Nunn, was a friend of Gabrielle Galatoire's. The Nunns moved from New Orleans, but later their son returned to the city to intern at a local hospital, and Mme Galatoire would often invite him to dine

businessmen bought and sold in the hotels and barrooms. At night drunken sailors prowled the streets, and all manner of licentious entertainments were devised to attract them; ladies never crossed Canal Street into the Quarter without an escort.

However, the enthusiasms of a new century were in the air, and change was on the way. Jean Galatoire had seen the future at the Chicago World's Fair in 1893; he had seen the telephone and the electric light revolutionize life; he had seen medical advances attack the plagues that emptied New Orleans in the summertime. He saw the vibrant potential in a changing society and a glowing future for New Orleans. As he adopted a new country, a new city, and a new society and brought to them his special skills, he began a dynasty that would leave its mark.

209 Bourbon Street, home of Galatoire's

at the restaurant as their guest. Jean brought chefs over from France and set to work to put his own distinctive mark on Victor's, using some recipes from the old restaurant, some of his own creation, and standard French dishes using the best local ingredients.

In 1911, Jean bought the building in which the restaurant was located from a widow, Marie Odile Carr, for twenty-five thousand dollars. The neighborhood was a good one in the early twentieth century. Next door to the restaurant was Mme Marie Rapho's establishment for fine linens and brides' dresses, which had opened in 1863. After her death in 1912, Mme Rapho's son and then her granddaughter continued the business until it closed in 1959. (In an ironic twist, Mme Rapho's upscale dress shop has been replaced by a store that features erotic garments.)

4

Word of the excellent food available at the "new" Galatoire's began to spread far and wide in the early 1900s, and it had soon become one of the most popular spots in New Orleans, well on its way to being one of the most famous dining establishments in America. Stanley Clisby Arthur, in *Old New Orleans: A Walking Tour of the French Quarter* (1936), contends that although there are those who would argue that New Orleans is second only to France in the quality of its food, there are also others who insist that the city is unrivaled, even by Paris. He says of the restaurant that it "has long been an institution in the Vieux Carre. Here Jean Galatoire and his nephews, who succeeded him, have originated many of the special dishes which have lured visitors and home folks in search of perfection in cookery." Arthur cites in particular the Truite (Trout) Marguery, the Crabmeat Ravigote, and Poulet Maison d'Or. In *The New Orleans Restaurant Cookbook* (1967), Deirdre Stanforth describes the upstairs private dining rooms in the early 1900s, where cotton factors—remember, cotton was still king—Canal Street department store owners, and other businessmen had soon become regulars. They could bring their clients and out-of-town guests to the restaurant, and soon the club-like aspect that it retains even now had been established. Stanforth noted that in the 1960s, never had either the standard of quality established by Jean or the enthusiasm of the diners varied, and much the same can certainly be said today.

Chris Ansel Jr., a grandson of Justin I, says that even before Jean, who had no children of his own, took over Victor's, he invited two of his nephews—Justin and Leon—to come from Pardies and join him. Jean's brother had died in Pardies and left his widow with seven children to support. Jean was doing her and her family a favor as well as providing help for himself. Justin, who was only fifteen, was the first nephew to come to the U.S., arriving in 1902 according to his descendant Becky Breitoff. He sailed to New York where he took a train to New Orleans with only twenty dollars in

THE FABULOUS 1900s

When the world whirled into a new century in 1900, people greeted the twentieth century much as future generations did the twenty-first century pre-September 11, 2001—with great enthusiasm and bright hopes for the future. While Jean Galatoire was founding his famous bistro, the scientific and mechanical accomplishments of mankind—cinema, X-ray, automobiles, radium, radios, flying machines, diesels, and the theory of relativity—spiked up and almost off the charts of the past world's relatively flat and predictable trajectory.

With all of these advances happening outside its doors, inside Galatoire's waited the perfect table at which one could enjoy good company and a fine meal.

his pocket. He got off at Mobile to buy a pie from a peddler who, not having change for a twenty, left Justin to get it. When the train was ready to depart, the peddler had not returned, and Justin had no choice except to reboard with empty pockets and a pie.

In New Orleans he worked for his Uncle Jean at his Canal Street bar for twenty-five cents a day, performing a variety of chores. Jean sold the bar and later became associated with Victor's, where Justin joined him. In the meantime, Leon Galatoire, the eldest brother, had come to America in 1906, and he took a job as a waiter at the Cosmopolitan Restaurant before going to work for his Uncle Jean. A few years later, Justin and Leon were joined by their younger brother, Gabriel, and the three of them learned the ins and outs of running the business as apprentices to their uncle. When they arrived in the United States, the brothers spoke French and had to learn English, even though the city still had a large French-speaking population. Clarisse Galatoire Gooch remembers her father, Leon I, as the quintessential French gentleman who stood out from their "American" neighbors because of his accent and his Gallic mannerisms. The brothers remained bilingual and taught their children their native tongue. However, by the time grandchildren came along, Carolyn Rodman says that her grandfather, Justin, was very much Americanized. "Consequently, he didn't want us to learn French. He was certainly not ashamed of being French, but he was grateful for the opportunity that he had here and was very proud of being an American, proud to pay taxes and be able to earn a living in this country."

In 1919, Jean, who was ailing, wanted to retire, and the three nephews bought the restaurant for forty thousand dollars. "Many of the people in New Orleans thought that we had inherited," Clarisse Gooch said, "but my father and his brothers laughed. They didn't inherit it, they worked hard and they paid him for it." After his retirement, Jean and his wife took up residence on Esplanade Avenue, across from Holy Rosary Church.

The new proprietors, Leon, Justin, and Gabriel Galatoire were comanagers, and their heirs continued to own and manage the institution into the new millennium. Ansel recalls that Leon worked in the morning, beginning at 5:30 or 6:00 A.M. and Justin arrived later. "He was there with the people. When the people were there, Justin was high profile." Gabriel, the youngest brother, who was actively involved in the business as well, resided in a luxurious apartment on the third floor of the building at 209 Bourbon in which he had an impressive collection of art. From all accounts, Gabriel, who never married, had quite a colorful tenure at Galatoire's until his death in the mid-1940s. In order for the Galatoires to keep their ties with their Gallic heritage, Gabriel would arrange for members of the family to stay in a villa near Pau, sometimes for several weeks, and visit their relatives. Three decades ago, Stanforth observed in the Galatoire family, as have other writers through the

Jean Galatoire, founder of Galatoire's

Leon Galatoire

Gabriel Galatoire

Justin Galatoire

Opposite top: (left to right) Chris Ansel Sr.; Rene, Justin, Leon, and Gabie Galatoire; and Yvonne Galatoire Wynne at Galatoire's fiftieth anniversary party, September 1955 at Lenfant's Restaurant

Opposite bottom: Galatoire family and staff at Galatoire's fiftieth anniversary party

8

9

years, the "kind of clannish solidarity and devotion" evident in the restaurant's operation that produced "a dependable and unfailing quality that is virtually without equal."

The glue that holds this family together is the work of the three brothers and the memory of them. Imbued with the French work ethic and determination, they spared no time or energy to make their restaurant a success. Without exception, the children and grandchildren seem to have admired Leon, Justin, and Gabriel and still remember them with love, humor, and devotion. Various family members carry their names; there are five cousins named Justin, one Justine, two more Leons, one Leona, another Gabie, and another Jean. (Justin and Leon married first cousins with the same names: Clarisse Houlne, so there are several Clarisses.) The daughters and grandchildren of Leon and Justin spoke of them as "saintly men," religious, loving of their families, and committed to their famous eatery. (Jokingly, Miss Leona said, "My grandmother and my aunt lived with us when I was growing up. Was my father a saint?") A strong sense of honor, integrity, and devotion exhibited by them is to a large extent responsible for the long continuance and success of the restaurant. The *Times-Picayune* (April 19, 1987) quoted Miss Yvonne (Galatoire Wynne): "My father [Justin I] said that the minute you let things get outside of the family's hands, things change. The most important thing is having the family in place." The three brothers, alike in their commitment to the family business, also differed in many respects. Leona Frey observed that Justin "was with all the people in the restaurant; everybody knew my dad." Leon, on the other hand, was "just the opposite. He was a good man, but he was quiet." Another contrast: Gabriel was the social, party-going, gregarious brother. "Gabriel sat at the desk and greeted at the front," Miss Leona said. "That was about all he did—when he felt like it. He was very elegant, fun to be around."

The arduous hours the brothers spent working at the restaurant and their complete dedication to a job they clearly loved are legendary. Leona Frey remembered that her father would go to work in the morning, then come home on the streetcar on Bourbon Street. "I'd run to the corner to meet him." He would take off his shoes and she would shine them for him. "He'd always tell us you weren't well dressed unless your shoes were shined." After an early dinner and a few hours at home, Justin would return to the restaurant and remain there, sometimes until midnight. Chris Ansel Jr. commented on "the grueling hours the older Galatoires spent at work" and suggested that few people nowadays are willing to make that sacrifice. The brothers worked seven days a week, including Mondays, when the restaurant was dark and they would do all the ordering and billing. Unlike members of succeeding generations, Justin I and Leon I did not cook, as far as Leona Frey knew. "I don't think my father knew *how* to cook!" she said.

"If he did, it was when he was young, but he started as a busboy with his uncle, then became a waiter."

The 1938 *WPA Guide to New Orleans* describes Galatoire's as a French restaurant, operated by Gabriel, Leon, and Justin Galatoire, that opened at an astonishing 8 A.M. and did not close until 10:30 P.M. From 11 A.M. to 2 P.M., they offered a "merchants' lunch for sixty cents, and from 5 to 8 P.M., a one-dollar *table d'hote* dinner, with a quarter added if one desired a small bottle of wine." The entry commends the Marguery sauce, usually served on trout, and the delicious handpicked crabmeat. The Dinkelspiel Salad is singled out as "a meal in itself, its base being crabmeat, surrounded by many tempting hors d'oeuvres."

The daughters of both men said that the brothers were determined to keep their family lives and their work separate. The family seldom dined at Galatoire's because their fathers believed that they must be fair in sharing the assets. Carolyn Rodman observed, "I'm not sure my grandmother ever went to the restaurant." Both brothers would bring home some of the fresh seafood and other ingredients for which they were famous—Clarisse Gooch remembered that during the Depression they dined well while others suffered deprivation—but visits to the restaurant that was making the family name famous were rare. Her son, David Gooch, recalled that when he was growing up, the family always had big Sunday dinners at either his Grandfather Leon's or his Uncle Justin's home. In later years, the two brothers worked on alternate Sundays at the restaurant, and dinner each week would be held at the home of the one who was not on duty.

Carolyn Rodman spoke of the Sunday dinners at "Pépère's and Mémère's," with the four daughters, ten grandchildren, and a few great aunts and uncles. Justin I would always say, "Girls, do your duty," and that meant we should be sure the table was set, that the French bread was cut and in baskets, and that the ice had been chipped and put in glasses. "Ten cousins were very close, we were together every week, lived in the same neighborhood. We were a close family, but not necessarily at the restaurant." Lynne Wagner, whose grandfather was a Galatoire cousin, treasures her mother's childhood stories about brunch at the Galatoire home. "I remember my mother telling me how she had to sit up perfectly with napkin in lap having her tea, and how she always left with tea cookies and homemade candies wrapped in tissue." Chris Ansel Jr. reminisced about Sundays at his grandparents' house, where he learned to cook when "I helped my grandmother in the kitchen, making hogshead cheese and sausage."

Justin Galatoire, who continued to manage alone after the death of his brother Leon on April 17, 1961, was, and still is, affectionately known by his descendants as "Popsy." He was thoroughly democratic, his daughters said, and did not want his children to feel superior to others. He used to tell them fondly, "Remember, you're nothing but a bean-seller's daughter, and your ancestors were pig farmers." (According to Michele Galatoire, the family in France actually owned an abattoir.) Although he was self-taught, he always stressed the value of an education.

As a youth, the first Justin had wanted to be a soldier in France, but his father had other plans for him, wanting him to enter the military in the U.S. One of his friends, a military man who grew up with Justin in France, said that it was a shame the young Galatoire did not have a career in which he could have become famous—in the military, for example—because he was extremely well-suited to military life. It is noteworthy that one of Justin's favorite customers through the years was General Claire Chennault, a hero of the Second World War, who had grown up in Louisiana. On one occasion a friend of Chennault's came into the restaurant and told Popsy that the general had requested that he bring him some Galatoire's rémoulade. Justin was so delighted by the request from a hero of his that he sent the general a gallon jar of the distinctive sauce. Even in the 1970s, Justin had not forgotten his early desire to be a soldier, for a newspaper article reported that "every afternoon he salutes his staff as he leaves. They salute back."

Shrimp Rémoulade

1 pound shrimp, boiled, peeled, and deveined	2 tablespoons paprika
1 bunch green onions	1 tablespoon prepared horseradish
1 stalk celery	Dash Tabasco
2 cloves garlic	Salt and fresh ground black pepper
1 bunch fresh parsley	1/3 cup vinegar
5 tablespoons Creole mustard	2/3 cup olive oil

In a food processor fitted with a steel blade, chop all vegetables very fine. Remove to a ceramic or glass bowl and add mustard, paprika, horseradish, Tabasco, and salt and black pepper to taste. Add vinegar and gradually add olive oil while whisking.

Fold in shrimp and let marinate several hours or overnight in refrigerator.

Serve cold on a bed of lettuce leaves.

SERVES 3 AS AN APPETIZER.

Miss Yvonne retained a wonderful glint in her eye and gestures that were distinctly Gallic, although the family has now long been in the United States, and she was born here. Sometimes when she repeated a remark of her father's, she would imitate the French accent with which Justin continued to speak English throughout his life. She said of her father, "He was a wonderful man. He's got a crown in heaven." Her sister, Leona Frey, pronounced the ultimate accolade when she insisted her father "was a saint. I can tell you that." Family members said that he never had an "unkind word for anyone," and attesting to the truth of their statement are the reports of countless customers through the years who were devoted to Mr. Justin. The late Jesse Core, for example, an author, *bon vivant*, and U.S. Air Force officer in World War II, described him as a "true gentleman of the old school," who always looked after his establishment "with affection and attention." Even today, waiters who remember Mr. Justin speak with respect of his pleasant, but firm rule and refer to him as "the Old Man." John Fontenot recalled that "Mr. Jus-tan," as he called him, "was a great guy. He wore these little round glasses—he had a round face like mine." He walked about that restaurant, checking all the food as it came from the kitchen and other details in the dining room. Fontenot recalled that if Justin saw something out of order, he would say, "Waiter, come here," and he'd take you to the kitchen and say to the cook, 'Fix that up, cook . . .'"

Certainly all three of the brothers contributed their share to creating the unique restaurant that is Galatoire's. When Gabriel and Leon were gone, Stanforth wrote in 1967, it was "Mr. Justin" who now truly shaped the character of the place. She described him as "a marvelous, friendly man who loves people," is "sympathetic and congenial," and "communicates equally well with all kinds." It is typical of his nature and his pride in being an American that when integration became the law of the land, Popsy acceded to it, while some other restaurant owners in the city fought back in various ways, for example, turning their establishments into "private clubs." His daughters remembered his response, typical of his democratic nature: "This country has been good to me, and if that is the law, we will abide by it." According to Chris Ansel Jr., when customers were upset with integration, Justin told them, "If you don't like the law of the land, either you try to change it by voting or you leave. Whatever the law is that's what you do, and that's it." "He didn't mince words, I can tell you," Ansel said.

In 1964, William Diehl wrote of the eighty-year-old Mr. Justin in *New Orleans Magazine,* that he was "straight as a light pole, as spry as a Swiss yodeler, as sharp as a French butcher's knife." Having been a manager since 1918, he was an expert at checking every delivery, fish or meat, handling the pompano and shrimp to be sure it met his standards, and, if it did, giving "a quick smile and a short nod toward the fish dealer." At night, he sat behind the century-old desk at the rear of the dining room, "patiently, like a character out of Dickens," making sure that all his customers were being satisfied. Diehl credits "this kind of intense interest in both quality and the customer" with making Galatoire's "one of perhaps the ten best restaurants in the world."

In a 1972 article, in the New Orleans *States-Item*, Harriet Cortez quotes Miss Yvonne as saying, "I'm my father's son by default. He was reluctant to let me work here because I was a girl studying music. But I came here thirty years ago and have been here ever since." (In 1949 she married attorney Doug Wynne, who also worked at the restaurant part-time for about thirty years.) Miss Yvonne said that soon after she first came to work at Galatoire's in 1935, she began to suggest changes. Mr. Justin told her that he had known "too many people who got too big and things went bad," and he always told family and friends that Galatoire's was only "a little chicken place." For years the menus were handwritten, until a friend said that it looked "like a Greek restaurant" and they decided to have them printed. Miss Yvonne suggested to her father on one occasion that they expand into the building next door, which happened to be empty at the time, to which he replied, "I've got just the size restaurant I can manage well." "At the time I thought he was wrong," she said with a laugh, "but now I know what a wise man he was." Whenever some alteration was suggested, Miss Yvonne remembered her father saying, "We've been in business a long time and have many satisfied customers, so we must be doing right."

Miss Yvonne told Cortez that "My father has a head of marble," for example, in his insistence that the restaurant do no advertising. When, periodically through the years, other members of the family suggested that perhaps they should try placing ads in various publications, Justin would decline with a wonderful, humorous rejoinder: "When people complain, we can always say we didn't invite them." Those complaints have been very few, but Yvonne was reminded of her father's own complaints about local people who would call up to say that they were entertaining a "big shot" from out of town and wanted to get special treatment in the restaurant. "It's always big shots," Justin would say, and his reaction to these requests was that "if someone would say he has a poor slob he wanted to feed I'd probably invite them right over!" Justin was apparently shy of publicity for when Cortez arrived at Galatoire's to interview family members, he scurried away, leaving his descendants to provide the necessary information.

Miss Yvonne cites one crisis in the restaurant's history, the 1955 fire, as an example of the strength of her father and his character. Diehl's article quotes her as saying, "I was nearly hysterical," and she feared, with the rest of her family, that the shock would be fatal for Mr. Justin, but he stood across the street until the fire was extinguished, then announced that they would rebuild. A few hours later, the workmen had begun restoring the landmark, because, Mr. Justin said, "We must remember the customers. We can't keep them waiting." That sentiment is perhaps the major reason Galatoire's has remained the acclaimed dining institution that it is after one hundred years.

Much of what is now accepted as "established tradition" at Galatoire's originated in the decisions of Justin and Leon Galatoire and their management. The standards they instituted, the integrity and fairness they brought to their business and personal dealings, and their genuine affection and concern for people—all have left their mark. For example, the restaurant was open for Mardi Gras in its early decades, but on one particularly boisterous Fat Tuesday, a distraught man came in the door carrying an unconscious friend. Popsy told the man, "Bring him in the back," and then instructed the waiters, "Close and lock the door." From that day until the present, Galatoire's has not opened on Mardi Gras, certainly a wise decision these days when Carnival celebrations have become more and more disorderly and attract more and more nomadic street people, especially to Bourbon Street. That sense of obligation to the traditions of the past has been the backbone of the restaurant's continued success. "Tradition" was one of Miss Yvonne's favorite words.

Justin's long and illustrious reign at Galatoire's—a span of almost seven decades, first with his brothers, and later alone—ended in 1973 when he died at the age of eighty-five. His daughters noted that their mother "survived" for seven more years but did not "live" following the death of her husband. His legacy is summed up in Stanforth's observation that he provided his patrons with good food and wine "without pretension," that he did not, as some other restauranteurs did, reserve certain vintages to impress "important" people, but treated all fairly, with no exceptions.

With the passing of Justin I, the second generation of the family that had made Galatoire's an institution came to an end, but members of the third generation were already in place to carry on the family tradition. Justin's successors included: one of his four daughters, Yvonne, who later became president; Christian Ansel Sr. and Jr.; and two sons of Leon, Rene and the second Gabriel, known affectionately by family and friends as "Gabie." Unlike their French-born father, Gabe and Rene, their brother Leon, and sister Clarisse, were natives of New Orleans. All three brothers served in World War II, and afterward Rene and Gabe returned to take their place in the family business, manning the door and desk. Long-time customers still speak fondly of the two brothers, their charm and their wit. Mary Mitchell, another transplanted Mississippi regular at Galatoire's, says of Gabe, the older brother, "Oh, he was a darling. He was a sweetheart." Michele Galatoire, Gabe's daughter, fondly remembers his playful nature, for example how he would "call football plays" in the dining room by sending customers to their tables on a particular yard line. Wally Shelby, Galatoire's cook of longest standing, tells of an afternoon when Gabe raced through the kitchen and out the back, a girl friend in tow, because his other girl friend had just arrived in the restaurant for a surprise visit. Michele remembers that her father loved the good life: elegant clothes, Caribbean cruises, and, like a good Frenchmen, good food, including the delicacies his relatives in Pau would send him—pâté de fois gras and French chocolates—and in true French fashion, his favorite meal: "lobster or steak with sautéed mushrooms, thinly cut French fries, followed by vanilla ice cream and cantaloupe."

Simone Nugent proudly relates that her father, Rene Galatoire, was a supply sergeant in World War II and was awarded the Purple Heart for dragging a fellow soldier to safety. When he returned to New Orleans, he started working in the kitchen of the restaurant, then moved to the dining room in a managerial position, and when his father, Leon I, died, became president of Galatoire's, a position he held until he retired in 1984, after working at the restaurant forty-four years. Like Gabriel, Rene had his own coterie of supporters and was often at the door to greet customers. "Till this day," Nugent says, "waiters talk to us about my father and the way he ran the restaurant. He was very good to the employees, demanded a great deal of them, and also gained their respect." Imre Szalai, who was hired by Rene, recalls his generosity: "When someone in the restaurant was sick or in need Mr. Rene would always help them out. I will always be grateful for the opportunities Mr. Rene gave to me and my family." Following Rene's retirement, Miss Yvonne assumed the position of president and held it until a year or so before her death in 2002.

As members of the fourth generation matured, many of them moved into positions at the restaurant. They included the grandchildren of Leon Galatoire: David Gooch, son of Clarisse Galatoire Gooch; Leon and Michele Galatoire, children of Gabriel Rene; and the descendants of the original Justin: his grandsons Christian Ansel Jr., and the son of Leona Frey, Justin, who is now a vice president. David Gooch served as comanager with Frey and now also serves as a vice president. His brother Jack, an attorney, is the most recent president of the board. Christian Ansel Sr., who was married to Laurence Irene Galatoire, worked at the restaurant from 1947 to 1964, serving part of that time as comanager with Rene Galatoire. Ansel Sr., while accepting a restaurant award from a television station, tragically died of a heart attack. Ansel Jr., Justin's first grandson, came home from France to follow in his father's footsteps, working at Galatoire's for seven years, beginning in 1966. He said that he never worked in the kitchen but did learn how it functioned. He was in the front and back of the desk. "We all did paper work in the morning, ordering on a regular basis." Ansel Jr. left in 1973 to open his own restaurant, Christian's, which is still very successful, although

Gabriel Rene Galatoire   *Rene Galatoire*

David Gooch and Yvonne Galatoire Wynne behind command center desk;
Endre Toth, waiter, at right

Michele Galatoire   *Leon Rene Galatoire*

Cousins Justin Frey and David Gooch

Descendants of Jean Galatoire's three nephews in front of the restaurant, 1997

18

he retired a few years ago. He assisted in the planning process during the Galatoire's restoration, serving as board president for one year.

Most of the other family members working there served their time in the kitchen, learning what makes the restaurant function in terms of cuisine, before moving on to managerial posts in the main dining room, following in the illustrious footsteps of their ancestors. Leona Frey relates that her son, Justin, after earning a college degree in business, told her that he wanted to work in the restaurant. "Justin," she said, "you know the hours your Papere put in," but he responded, "Yes, but I want to." He started in the kitchen, worked there for three or four years, then moved on to managerial duties. David Gooch apprenticed for four years after Miss Yvonne said he was needed most in the kitchen, because "good cooks are hard to find." Leon III worked in the kitchen, manned the central control desk for several years, where he "cut a wide swath," and serves now on the board of directors. Other members of the family have followed a similar path: beginning in the kitchen, learning the business from the ground up, and then moving into administrative positions. Michele likewise served her time in the kitchen before assuming a post at the desk, running the dining room.

When you have several members of the Galatoire family assembled, you realize how close they are because of their association with the restaurant, its past, and their ancestors, and yet what a diverse group they constitute. In addition to the family business, Galatoire descendants can be found working in many professions, among them teachers, lawyers, engineers, nurses, dentists, and computer specialists. Although they are tightly-knit, each has his or her own opinion and usually does not hesitate to express it. Just as the three brothers, Leon, Justin, and Gabriel, were committed to their work but had distinct characters, the same can be said for subsequent generations. Miss Yvonne was shy, quiet, reticent, "not one to leave home," her sister Leona said. "She was a big baby." Miss Yvonne and the other two sisters all stayed home and learned to cook, Miss Leona remembered, except "Me. All the time I wanted to run the streets."

The same distinctions can be seen in the current generations. Some are volubly French-American, eager to talk, while others are reticent. All, however, after they begin to speak, are pleasantly garrulous and willing to communicate facts about the past, especially about the family. Underlying their actions and their words is a commitment, strength, and Gallic determination that continues to preserve what has made Galatoire's a rare institution in the modern age.

Yvonne Galatoire Wynne, at her beloved post

MISS YVONNE GALATOIRE WYNNE

"Madame Yvonne, she was Galatoire's!"
—John Fontenot

In the rear of the charming old dining room in Galatoire's, under the S. Fournier clock, just outside the doors of the kitchen, in front of a large wall mirror on which are two shelves of liquor bottles from which the waiters used to pour the hefty drinks for which the place was famed, stands the U-shaped desk that serves as the imposing command post from which the complicated operation of the restaurant is directed.

At that desk, for almost a century, some major member of the family has sat—overseeing the domain, doing quality checks on the dishes being rushed from the kitchen to the tables by the waiters, collecting and dispensing money.

For years, one stately and elegant woman was the resident genius, reigning behind the desk in imperial silence, her posture erect as ladies of her generation had been trained, her hair always perfectly coiffed, her outfit always fashionable but unassertive. She peered through her large owl-like glasses at the cast of characters in the daily drama in which she was a major actor—or perhaps director. And, like the owl, she was wise, having watched the tragedies and comedies of daily life in a celebrated restaurant being played out before her eyes, year after year, never changing, yet always changing. Before her knowing vision had passed the glamorous and the enchanting, the mundane and the drab, sometimes even the shocking, and she had taken it all in, reacting always with a composure that belied some of the events that had unfolded, an aplomb that rivaled that of even Queen Elizabeth II on state occasions. It was a kingdom that Yvonne Galatoire Wynne loved, the place in which, and to which she belonged, in which she had grown up, her second home, her beloved family restaurant.

When Miss Yvonne had finished her hours at the station, her cherished husband Doug, who worked at the restaurant in the morning, would always join her and they would sit at the small table in the corner to the right of the desk to have dinner before going home for the evening. The next day, she would once again ascend her throne beneath the clock to survey her realm, one day wiser, ready for whatever lay ahead.

Yvonne Galatoire Wynne, born in New Orleans in 1912, spent most of her life in the city. Early photographs of her when she was in a Carnival court, at her wedding, or attending family gatherings, show a striking, obviously vibrant young woman with a twinkle in her eyes and a beauty that in later years remained, mellowed like a fine wine. Her memories of the restaurant in which she spent a large part of her time stretched back to the days when lunch there cost seventy-five cents and even less. She went to work in 1935 when her father begged her to help him out because a cashier was ill. "I couldn't add two and two," she recalled. "I dreamed about it, I was so nervous. But I went and the cashier died a week later, and I've been here since."

Her loyalty to the restaurant was strong and unwavering. Her devotion to her father, Justin Galatoire—Popsy—during his lifetime and to his memory after his death was even stronger. "He was a wonderful man.

He's got a crown in heaven." In 1987, she was quoted in a New Orleans interview as saying that she was not "social," but was "a worker. I'm like my father. I like to stay in the back." Her sister Leona Frey recalled that Miss Yvonne "dedicated her life to the restaurant." Mr. Justin "hated change," she said, "and I hate it too." In the film *Dining and Dynasties,* she asserted, "I always liked the old ways" and proudly pointed out that the restaurant was "the same inside as it was years ago. . . . Of course we have to repair now and then." She cherished the traditions of the restaurant, which "means everything to us. I mean, we try to keep our good name." People often asked why the restaurant did not take reservations, and her father explained, "if you make a reservation you should have a table ready when they come. . . . He believed in fairness, put it that way." She recalled a major change that was accepted when the restaurant became the first in New Orleans to be air-conditioned. With a chuckle and a shake of her head, she remembered that "we had to put diapers under the cooling units to control the dripping."

In those early years, her tasks at Galatoire's were varied and sometimes even taxing. She recalled one occasion when a man delivered his elderly mother to the door, then went back to park the car. Popsy took the lady to her table, seated her, and when he turned his back to walk away, she fell to the floor, dead. She was taken upstairs and placed on a sofa while a young Yvonne sat in a chair nearby. Shortly thereafter the lady's son arrived to ask where his mother was. When he was told that she was upstairs, he asked if someone had helped her get there and was told "two people." He went upstairs to find a shaken Yvonne sitting in a chair near the corpse. "I can tell you," she recalled decades later, "I was nervous."

Into and out of her vision as she sat behind that desk passed the major and minor actors in the continuing melodrama that is New Orleans; she saw and met the great and famous, but was totally lacking in self-importance. To some she seemed distant, haughty, even forbidding, but in fact she was essentially a shy and retiring woman, brought up in the old Creole culture when refinement was the requisite virtue for a lady. "I know many of these people," she once said, making a sweeping gesture with her arm to represent all those gathered now and those who had gathered there in the past, "but I never wanted to intrude upon them."

She was fiercely protective of the privacy of her customers and their personal lives. When a famous photographer, who had been asked to illustrate an article for an international magazine, started moving among the tables and snapping pictures one day at lunchtime, Miss Yvonne beckoned him over and told him to stop. When he asked why, she told him that he would first have to get permission for each and every person who appeared within his frame—and so he did.

Despite her reserve, she had a subtle and ironic sense of humor. Temple Brown recalled giving a brunch at Galatoire's for his close friends on Ash Wednesday when he was King of Carnival. Miss Yvonne told him that he was the "second best Rex ever." When he inquired as to who had been the best, "she named the ultimate Frenchman in town" to which he replied, "Oh, you frogs all stick together." In *Dining and Dynasties,* as she comments on the fact that "everything is the same as it was in 1905," she adds that of course it was necessary to put up new wallpaper and "just like faces like mine it has to be repaired every five years."

Miss Yvonne left her post in 1997 and retired to her other life, the private one with her husband. His sudden death shortly thereafter was a terrible blow to her, and she survived him by only a couple of years. Other than the restaurant, she had several loves: her husband and the rest of her family, and literature. She and her husband had no children of their own, but she looked upon her nieces and nephews as her daughters and sons. "I gave them my heart and my money," she declared proudly, "and it was well spent. They are all mine." The feeling was certainly mutual, for her niece Sally Breithoff recalled, "With Yvonne we felt like we had another mother. She took us all under her wing." Jokingly, they called her "Burn" because she was often smoking a cigarette. When Miss Yvonne was interviewed for the *Times-Picayune* in 1987, she said of her nephews Justin Frey and David Gooch, "I'm the adopted mother for these boys," and a member of the staff chimed in, "For the waiters, too." Only a few people family members and friends knew that Miss Yvonne wrote poetry, which her innate reserve prevented her sharing. She looked upon it as an outlet for her emotions and beliefs, and those who were chosen to share the words she had penned found there a glimpse of an inner life not visible in her outward demeanor. Often she wrote about mothers and their children, fulfilling in verse her own maternal yearnings.

Remembering Yvonne's long years at her post, Temple Brown stated, "That restaurant was Yvonne's life." Food critic Tom Fitzmorris called her "the spokesman of the third generation" of the family, and asserted that "her ideas set the tone" of Galatoire's for more than three decades: "And those ideas went something like this: There's no reason to change anything here that doesn't absolutely need to be changed." Her relationship to members of the staff was close, never that of the grand lady of the manor. Waiter M. C. Emmons remembers Miss Yvonne with affection: "It felt good to come in here, because you knew she was presiding over the place. She really was. People looked up there and waved to Miss Yvonne. Very very nice lady." Angelle Wells, the first female waitress at the restaurant, remembers that when she was invited there by Justin II to have dinner and be interviewed, she met Miss Yvonne, and "I fell in love immediately, she was just so wonderful, just great."

Now Miss Yvonne is no longer at her post, but surely her spirit lives on in the restaurant she kept alive as her father had wanted it; and often if I look suddenly toward the old, weathered desk under the clock, I could swear that I see her there, elegant, silent, and, I hope, approving.

KENNETH HOLDITCH

Act One
Once Upon a Time

Scene Two

Stage Props
Food & Drink

> *"The menu hasn't changed much since
> Teddy Roosevelt was president."*
> —Bill Husted, *Denver Post,* October 2001

*I*n the old days of this food-obsessed city, before Paul Prudhomme and
Emeril Lagasse ushered in the age of celebrity chefs, cults grew up
around famed old-line restaurants such as Galatoire's. Few thought to question or care who cooked their food as long as it was great—and it always
was. An exception to the celebrity rule, however, was Jean Galatoire's friend
and mentor Victor Bero, who, according to the editors of the 1937 *Madame
Begue's Recipes of Old New Orleans Creole Cookery,* was already established
in the Crescent City in 1840. He was "among the earliest chefs of old New
Orleans who achieved undying fame through the dishes he served discrimi-
nating patrons" and his restaurant, Victor's, was "long a rendezvous for
gourmets." (Begue was a famous nineteenth-century culinary genius, whose
cookbook was first published in 1900.)

Victor's again became famed for its table after 1905, when Jean Galatoire
purchased the establishment and gave it his name. Jean brought his own
recipes from home and even hired French chefs, one of whom, Constant
Hippolyte Prouet, brought with him the signature dish known as Trout
Marguery when he came to the United States in 1900 and creolized it in New
Orleans to accommodate available foodstuffs. However, it is reported that
Victor Bero also had a Trout Marguery on his menu, and for many years, an
ancient and grubby volume covered with grease, the *Larousse Gastronomique,*
the Bible of French cooking, was kept in Galatoire's kitchen; it includes a

Welcome to Galatoire's

recipe for Trout Marguery, which would seem to substantiate the story that a chef brought the recipe from France and gave it a local flair.

In their *New Orleans Cookbook,* (1977) Rima and Richard Collin ("The Underground Gourmet") add the information that Galatoire's "benefited from the closing in 1899 of Moreau's famous restaurant, often called 'the Delmonico's of New Orleans.'" The authors indicate that many members of Moreau's staff eventually were employed at Galatoire's. It is noteworthy that in the 1953 film *Missississippi Gambler,* which starred Tyrone Power, mention is made of both Victor's and Moreau's.

In his *Dining in New Orleans* (1945), Scoop Kennedy commended the Galatoire family for resisting "expansion, streamlining, and high pressure salesmanship with the stubbornness of genuine artists. Despite the clamor of ever-increasing trade, the modest seating capacity has remained constant. To add one table they figure would overtax the genius of M. Verges. Four more customers and his omelettes would become commercial projects instead of individual inspirations."

Justin Galatoire with the restaurant's famous fare

By the 1950s and 1960s, restaurants were New Orleanians' prime source of traditional Creole cooking, once done at home. "Unless you can spend hours in the preparation of a single dish, Creole cooking is not for you," writes Pulitzer Prize-winning novelist Shirley Ann Grau in a 1956 article in *Holiday* magazine. She adds a word of warning: "If you do not like onions, garlic, bay leaf and cayenne, don't go to Galatoire's." Clearly, thousands of satisfied customers approved of those ingredients. Kennedy quoted someone identified only as "one of the world's few woman gourmands" as proclaiming, "I don't care if they *are* floating in garlic, Galatoire's Mushrooms Bordelaise are an epic experience."

Devotees of Galatoire's relished the many local Creole dishes on the menu, at least one of which reached legendary fame. Grau told of a friend who said he didn't want flowers on his grave, just gallons of Galatoire's Turtle Soup. Another avowed, "Whenever I pass Mr. Galatoire on the street, I don't really see him. I just see his Turtle Soup." Kennedy began his chapter on Galatoire's saying, "Roll in that wheelbarrow full of adjectives, dump one hundred or so of the fancy ones near the typewriter, and let's get to work on Galatoire's." In 1978, Howard Mitcham noted in *Creole Gumbo and All That Jazz* that Galatoire's was "probably the best seafood restaurant in America today." He praised the Trout Amandine as "widely imitated but never equaled." Deirdre Stanforth in *The New Orleans Restaurant Cookbook* (1967) writes that Galatoire's has achieved "perhaps the highest accolade of all—it is the overwhelming favorite of the citizens of New Orleans." She uses words such as "unpretentious," "modest," and "publicity shy"—in those days the restaurant had never advertised—and says "it exists only to prepare and serve fine food."

According to the late Yvonne Galatoire Wynne in a 1999 interview, through the 1940s, that "fine food"—meaning classic Creole cuisine—was turned out by local line cooks apprenticed to French chefs. Among them was the "mysterious Parisian" named Pierre Verges, cited by Kennedy in 1945, "whose divine recipes are closely guarded by his graying employers, the brothers Justin and Leon Galatoire." Lucette Brehm, Public Relations Manager for the *Delta Queen* Steamboat Company, fondly remembers her grandmother and grandfather, Boulogne-born chef Prouet, who lived on St. Philip Street and raised two sons, one a doctor and the other an engineer. "I remember my grandmother constantly washing and ironing my grandfather's chef's coat and hat. They were starched so stiff that they stood up by themselves."

Another French chef was a member of the Galatoire family—Justin's nephew, Leon Touzet, who began work in 1922. Touzet, now ninety-seven, said that after he finished an apprenticeship as a chef in France, he met Gabriel Galatoire, who was there for a visit. In response to Touzet's request for employment at Galatoire's, Gabriel wrote to his brothers and received an affirmative reply. Touzet left Galatoire's in 1929 to be chef at the Vieux Carre,

Cooks in the kitchen on a break, circa 1940

a restaurant on the corner of Iberville and Bourbon owned by his father-in-law, Justin LaCoste. After a while, all the old French chefs died and only Constant Prouet was left. Then he was gone, and the old order ended to make way for the new, but from those French kitchen pioneers future generations derived the know-how and the recipes that continued to make Galatoire's menu a classic of French Creole cuisine.

Even in 1945, Kennedy was bemoaning the fact that in many of the old French Creole establishments, those magicians of the kitchen took their prize recipes with them when they died, and "in a few instances such recipes of old Creole cookery have been lost for years and only lately recovered." However, at Galatoire's, the recipes endured, since the apprentices who worked with those Frenchmen learned well and carried on the tradition. "The cuisine was passed down from chef to chef," said Miss Yvonne. Rather than chefs trained at culinary schools, cooks often taught by their fathers or uncles even now consistently churn out the timeless recipes to perfection. A bean curd or a sun-dried tomato would not stand a chance in this kitchen. Words like "fusion" or "blackened" are *verboten*. "We have a group of old-time cooks, very hard-working, who do the same thing day after day after day," said David Gooch, who himself apprenticed in the kitchen from 1970–74.

Most New Orleans restaurants once had great black cooks in the kitchen, and Galatoire's still does. "One time in this kitchen it would go from generation to generation," said Gloria Mitchell, "the shrimp lady." "You had to have a cousin or a brother or kin in here. Now anybody can fill out an application and get a blood test." The most senior cook is Wallace Shelby, an employee for almost six decades (since 1947), who began as a porter, worked up to making salads, and became the restaurant's first black cook almost by accident. In the early days, blacks worked as porters and handled preparation and pantry, but the cooks were all white—"old Frenchmen getting up in age and set in their ways," said Wally. After the lunch rush was over, they sat down to drink their liquor-laced coffee; often, rather than bestir themselves to fill the few afternoon orders, they turned them over to Wally (who was in charge of the pantry for fifteen years)—and occasionally the waiters—along with instructions and tutelage. In turn, Wally eventually passed along his expertise to others, including Warren Martin, who later instructed his young nephew, Milton Prudence.

After time took away "chefs" such as George Mansour, the word "cooks" was more often used to describe the Galatoire's kitchen wizards. Charlie Plough, of German extraction, who worked at Galatoire's for more than thirty-five years, insisted on referring to himself as "head cook" rather than chef. Even when celebrated chefs were all the rage, Galatoire's followed tradition rather than the trend. "In this age of rock stars and celebrity chefs it's refreshing that Galatoire's is not in any way chef driven," said food writer Ed Levine. "It's the way it used to be; nobody even knows who the chef is." Gooch told Mark Seal of *Southwest Airlines Spirit* in 1993, "A chef would be frustrated here, doing the same thing," and "not being able to use his creativity." This statement may have referred to Roland Huet, the last truly French chef to work at Galatoire's. Brought in from Paris by Chris Ansel Jr. in the late 1960s, after about a year Huet moved to the West Coast; he returned to New Orleans in 1973 only when Ansel opened his own restaurant, Christian's, where Huet still works a few days a week.

It was not until 1997 that Galatoire's bowed to the fashion and named an executive chef—Milton Prudence, who had run the kitchen since 1976. Levine heard a story that this came about when the owners were talking about doing parties and special events and they thought they could promote the restaurant better if they had a chef. So they decided to name a head chef and Milton was made to order. Twenty-one when mustered out of the Marine Corps in Los Angeles in December of 1968, he came to New Orleans to visit relatives on his way back home to Rhode Island. He liked it so much he stayed, married, and reared five daughters. Although he had intended to be a schoolteacher, his uncle, Warren Martin, who was a fry and sauté cook at Galatoire's for fifteen years, got him a job at Galatoire's instead. (Three or more generations of

Martins and assorted relatives and friends have worked in the kitchen over the years, including Milton's aunt, mother, and grandmother. "Even now, any person in the kitchen whose last name is Martin is my relative.") Young Milton began as a porter, and he said, "I just advanced myself. I learned by assisting Uncle Warren, especially when the kitchen was short-handed," he said. "When I was not busy I was by the stove watching him."

Another chef, Eric Schutzmann, came to work after the 1998–99 renovation, and when he left, Ross Eirich was hired. According to Gooch in early 2003, Milton was in charge of the sauces and dishes of yore; Ross, who was first a sous-chef, did the purchasing and created new dishes for parties and special events. "We have two chefs, and they run the kitchen together," said Gooch. "Our kitchen goes from seven in the morning to midnight, so they both put in very long hours, although usually not at the same time." The two supervised both kitchens. "Ross comes in at 8:00 A.M.," Milton said, "and usually leaves at 6:00 P.M. I come in at 11:00 A.M. and am here until closing. Most of the time I expedite, put on garnishes, do the check, and the second floor person does the same."

Milton began his culinary education by learning how to prepare the standard sauces—hollandaise and béchamel—and making the easier dishes, such as Clemenceau, a combination of sautéed mushrooms, Brabant potatoes, English peas, and chicken or shrimp. As time passed, he learned to concoct the more complicated items on the menu. Through the years, he became adept at all of Galatoire's cuisine, but he, like the others, had his specialties, namely sauces, called by food writer Roy Guste in one of his cookbooks, "the lifeblood of our cuisine" and "perhaps the most complicated and essential part of a dish." Those who master the preparation of sauces are stars in any French Creole kitchen, and Milton performed a once-or-twice-weekly Rockefeller Sauce ritual that was extraordinary to watch, involving myriad ingredients and a kettle about as big as a small room. Indeed, it might be argued that Galatoire's skillful cooks receive short shrift in the media as attention is directed toward the high-profile waiters, but gourmets surely know that back in the kitchen there are talented people working their magic to produce the dishes for which the restaurant is famous.

Another important ingredient in the restaurant's century-old success remains constant as well. "The secret of Galatoire's," Stanforth wrote in 1967, "is their rare insistence on entirely fresh food every single day." They ordered from local places just what they needed that day; chefs inspected the food as it came in the back door and sent it back if it was not up to par. This demand for freshness was backed up by on-the-spot payment in cash. "That's what makes Galatoire's better than other restaurants, because it's fresh all the time," said John Fontenot, one of the long-tenured waiters. "We'd pay cash for everything, so they came here first because they'd get their money here. Other places were credit; Galatoire's was always cash. Galatoire's was 'the old lady.' But we'd run out, because it's all fresh." John shook his head, thinking of "lesser" establishments: "When restaurants don't run out, it's a bad sign."

Of course, seafood was and still is of ultimate importance at Galatoire's, being so abundant in south Louisiana waters that it has always been the basis of New Orleans cuisine. John remembers way back when "Mr. Justin was there early in the morning peeling the shrimp and picking crabmeat" and when "the fishermen would back their trucks up outside and those fish had just come out of the water." An exceptional and well-liked manager for

From left to right, Lynn Mitchell and her mother Gloria Mitchell, "the shrimp lady"

seventeen years, tall, lean Rene Galatoire would stand at the double doors and smell the seafood as it came in. If it was not to his liking, he would simply say, "Out!" This insistence on freshness and daily deliveries remains in force in the Galatoire's kitchen. Just one example: The Shrimp Guys, a father/son company, still bring in their fresh shrimp daily, albeit often netted in more distant waters, such as off the Carolina coast.

Sitting just inside the back door, is "the shrimp lady," Gloria Mitchell, seventy-four years of age, who for forty years has been peeling some two-hundred-fifty-pounds of shrimp a day "and double on the weekends." She has reared eight children—three boys and five girls, who are all "doing fine."

Her hands fly gracefully and are never still; she never bothers to look down at them, instead she watches all the comings and goings. "Everybody speaks, you get to be known—like their mother," she says. "When they look like glass you know they're good," she says of the large shrimp waiting in a huge plastic tub by her side. "I do this because I want to do it. If you don't do it every day, you lose it." After observing Miss Gloria at her task, one will never eat a Galatoire's shrimp dish again without a deeper appreciation of what went into its composition.

"At a certain age, you want to be working around younger people; they keep you young," Miss Gloria says. She saved her big containers of artichoke leaves—otherwise they would throw them away—for one of her young friends, Angelle Wells, the restaurant's first woman waiter. "I ate very well there," said Angelle, "I'd take the scraps off Galatoire's any day; they're some of the finest scraps you're going to get anywhere."

Until recent decades, the meat—beef and lamb—was purchased in large slabs, later to be sliced by cooks, among them Fernando Guiterrez, a native of Nicaragua who has been at Galatoire's for twenty-three years. His first task was to "cut everything they needed—fish and fileting" and he is now known as "a surgeon with the fish." Later he began to stand in for all the stations, one by one—the broiler and the fry and sauté stations—so that now he can perform a variety of tasks, as do most of the cooks, all of whom now cross-train and fill in for one another when needed.

Cooks once worked from those handwritten recipes originally brought from France by Jean Galatoire, his nephews, and the French chefs—recipes

MAKING GROCERIES

An astounding amount of food and fixings is ordered and prepared at Galatoire's on a weekly basis. Manager Melvin Rodrigue supplied the following list:

    600 pounds shrimp
    40 gallons turtle soup
    35 gallons gumbo
    15 gallons oyster and artichoke soup
    600 pounds crabmeat
    50 gallons oysters
    1500 lbs fish, assorted— trout, snapper, pompano, salmon
    500 lbs beef
    300 lbs lamb

In the old days, when the busboys still chipped those much beloved chunks of ice from 50-pound blocks with an ice pick, 500 pounds each day were delivered and chopped.

copied over and over on pieces of plain paper as they became frayed. Now they work mostly from memory (although the recipes are available for them on computers), and each cook specializes in certain tasks and mans a certain station. Although some of the recipes have evolved through the years, many have remained the same. Darleen Carlisle, the daughter of Joseph Pierce, who had been a captain's cook on a boat during World War II and worked at Galatoire's as a cook in the 1950s and 1960s, remembered her father saying that he and another cook created the old rémoulade recipe, the hand-written original of which she still keeps in her safe. Joseph also loved to cook at home with his wife, especially on Mondays, when Galatoire's was dark.

One story well known around the French Quarter, where nothing is secret, concerns a cook who either quit or was fired from Galatoire's in the late 1970s and subsequently was hired by John Thomann for his new restaurant on Rampart Street, John T's. While at Galatoire's, the cook had learned to make the famous Stuffed Eggplant and began preparing it for Thomann's customers, who were delighted. However, when the chef became disgruntled with his new position and left, Stuffed Eggplant disappeared from the menu. When artist George Dureau, a customer at John T's, asked Thomann why he had no copy of the recipe, he replied, "There *was* no written recipe. It was in his head"—and with the cook's departure it was lost, as if it should never have left Galatoire's in the first place.

The war years inevitably brought changes to Galatoire's, including the closing of the second floor dining rooms for lack of waiters to work the floor. Clarisse Gooch said in an interview that although her father, Leon I, had access to food extras during the Second World War because he was a restauranteur, "he and my uncle would never let us put anything on our table that his customers couldn't have." Her cousin, Leona Frey, agreed. "We did not eat meat, just fish," she said. "My father (Justin I) said 'If they can't have it, we don't have it.'" A World War II era menu, signed by Mr. Justin Galatoire, has pages stamped "AVAILABLE" in large red letters. On one old menu dated August 17, 1944, Mr. Justin wrote, "We certify that our charge for cup of coffee during period of Oct. 4 to Oct. 10, 1942, was ten cents per cup." David Gooch observes that "During the wars there were many things we couldn't get, so we didn't serve them." Regular Billy Broadhurst remembers reading placards posted above the mirrors when he was a child that stated in block print "WE DO NOT HAVE REAL BUTTER TODAY." "They were very fastidious about this, always making sure customers knew what ingredients they had." Also, the lack of imported French wines forced the consumption and eventual appreciation of California wines not only at Galatoire's, but in the rest of the United States.

During those years, many servicemen waited in Galatoire's line along with regular customers. This is when the famous line is said to have begun in earnest, after the upstairs was closed and so many military personnel came through the seaport city. One of these, a pilot, dined at Galatoire's after a cliff-hanger landing at the Naval Air Station and was given a small brandy snifter as a souvenir. His friend, Ashley D. Pace Jr. of Pensacola, Florida, recently wrote a touching letter saying that the young pilot had lost his life during the war and how much that act of kindness at Galatoire's had pleased him.

Just as World War II had seen several Galatoire's sons and husbands go off to war and return safely to take their place in the family business, another war did the same. Just out of college (Tulane and LSU), David Gooch was a maitre d' at Galatoire's for six months in 1967 before serving in Vietnam as a combat engineer platoon leader. He returned in 1970, was apprenticed to Charlie Plough, and began graduate school to earn his degree in business. After four years working in the kitchen, Gooch became General Manager of the restaurant in 1974, staying on in that capacity, sharing duties with his cousins, for more than twenty years. "By that time I had learned how to cook everything as well as the other cooks, and I was just married and going to business school. It was time for a new challenge." His great-uncle Justin had recently died and things were changing.

"I'll never forget one of the first changes I made when I saw that the price of butter was five times higher than margarine. We began to make our hollandaise with margarine instead; it was still good but not *as* good." Until then, Gooch recalled, reviews of the restaurant had been great. "'The Underground Gourmet' gave us very high ratings, four stars. But he came back and picked up on a few things like that and gave us a very bad review. So immediately we went back to butter. We worked very hard, but it took a long time for us to get those stars back. So I learned my lesson. I was knocked down hard by butter. I was young and foolish—'penny wise and pound foolish' they say—but I learned." Gooch faced another 1974 crisis when the oyster shells used to present Oysters Rockefeller caused a bacterial problem that affected a group of public health officials in New Orleans for a convention—a quintessential New Orleans irony. The restaurant was forced to close down for a month, substitute new equipment, and use tacky metal shells for two years. Nowadays, real oyster shells are boiled to sterilize, and washed in the dishwashing machines that took the place of the human dish-washers of earlier days.

According to Wally, he has seen astounding changes through the years since 1947. Looking around the place after the renovation, he said, "The only thing that hasn't changed is the dining room; it's a whole different ball game now." He once selected, weighed, and cut steaks on a big butcher block, which has now been banned due to health regulations. Today the steaks arrive already cut, weighed, and packaged. Prior to the renovation, the kitchen was a hotspot indeed, since it was not air-conditioned. Miss

Gloria said that in the old days "we used a fan over ice cubes and we would think cool." Frances Lewis, a twenty-two year kitchen veteran, agreed, "It was a hot kitchen—woooo—we *thought* cool." According to Wally, the summers were hot, but after a while, "it's no surprise. You get your mind prepared. We took salt tablets, and the breeze in that alleyway was our salvation." That alleyway is now part of the new entrance.

Wally still works strictly from memory, and now works a limited schedule, preparing the staff's meals. When the food is ready he calls, "Foooooooood Ooooooooout!" Red beans and rice is one of his specialties. Since the restaurant is closed on Monday, "Tuesday was always our Monday, so I cook red beans on Tuesday"—red beans and rice being the traditional Monday dish in New Orleans. Often regular customers ask for a dish of it.

Wally "came up the hard way," one of six children whose father died when he was twelve. "When I came here, I think I did pretty good. I made twenty-five dollars a week. Now I own my own home, I raised my children and still raise my grandchildren. The Galatoires were a family people, and I had the family man thing about me and they liked that. I was like an adopted son, because they all helped me to raise my kids. I was twenty-one; I'm seventy-eight now, and I learned a whole lot." "Wally loved my Dad, he really did," said Miss Yvonne. And the affection was returned. Wally was there to help out at Miss Yvonne's wedding reception in 1949 at the Galatoire home on Allard Boulevard and for the celebration of the restaurant's fiftieth anniversary at Lenfant's restaurant.

When Milton began, he recalled that learning the names of all the dishes was difficult because, until computers were installed a few years ago, the waiters would walk down the aisles and yell out their orders at each station. "Fifteen waiters at once, and nothing was written down; it was all vocal, so the cook had to have a mind that was quick enough to grab everything coming down the line." Now with the computer and a terminal at each station, the process is simplified and better organized. Fernando agreed that in pre-computer days, when orders piled up, cooks might forget an order, "but now we don't have that problem. We have the orders right there in front of us with the table number and the waiter and everything." "It's amazing that we would get all that food out and get it right," said waiter M. C. Emmons. "What's really amazing is that we had so few errors." In addition to ordering, preparation is streamlined. For Shrimp Rémoulade, for example, the shrimp and sauce stations are set up separately and mixed as each order comes in. In contrast, before the computer days, the pantry people would do the preparation, then the cooks would prepare as many as a dozen orders at a time to be ready for the rush hour. Presently, there are more pantry people than in the past, and the orders are prepared one at a time, when requested by the waiter. The rémoulade sauce is made in advance, Milton said, "because it gets better with time." And pastries, which used to be bought, are made in-house.

A lot of things may have changed in the kitchen, but "the cooks still learn from each other," said Milton in early 2003. "By now, I can tell which of the young cooking apprentices want to stay and want to learn because he comes and asks questions. Cooks here are always looking for that 'jewel,' that one wanting to learn." Like Milton, Fernando said that he is always willing to teach the interested novice. "If somebody will come and ask me, I will work with him and he will learn."

Crabmeat Maison

1/2 cup homemade mayonnaise
3 tablespoons French dressing
   (olive oil, vinegar, Creole mustard,
   salt, and pepper to taste)
3 green onions, chopped fine

1 teaspoon capers
1/2 teaspoon chopped parsley
1 pound crabmeat (jumbo lump)

Mix all together. Fold in with crabmeat.
   Serve over a bed of lettuce with two slices of tomato on the side.
Squeeze lemon juice over salad right before serving.
   SERVES 6 AS AN APPETIZER.

Milton noted that "just about everything is cooked to order today," which involves a lot of preparation of the component parts. Almost anything a diner wants can be combined by kitchen personnel. After reading a Julia Reed food article in *The New York Times Magazine*, a few customers began asking for crabmeat on saltines. "The signature crab salad is Crabmeat Maison . . . I love it on saltines topped with anchovies (a homey and weirdly delicious presentation created by the late, lamented waiter Cesar)," she wrote. Reed titled her article "My Blue Heaven" and went on to say, "Galatoire's is very big on crabmeat," and lists several favorite dishes. If requested, waiters will pile lump crabmeat sautéed in butter and lemon on top of a fish dish, "and for serious crab lovers they will even pile it on top of soft-shells." Longtime favorites are Canapé Lorenzo and the local specialty, Godchaux Salad.

Another specialty, left over from the old days, is the Dinkelspiel Salad— named for businessman Manuel Dinkelspiel—which has the same ingredients as the Godchaux Salad (lettuce, tomato, boiled shrimp, crabmeat, hard-boiled egg, and anchovies), but in a different configuration. In the Godchaux everything is tossed together except the egg and anchovies, the latter crossed on top and the egg crumbled and sprinkled over it all. In the Dinkelspeil, the lettuce and tomato are in the center of the plate with crabmeat on top, and the shrimp are arranged around the perimeter. Then the egg is cut in half and the two halves of yolk crumbled over the top. The anchovies are coiled up and placed in the cavities of egg white and positioned between the shrimp.

Canapé Lorenzo

1 cup Béchamel Sauce (see page 121)	1 tablespoon fine bread crumbs
1/2 cup finely chopped green onions	1 teaspoon grated Parmesan cheese
2 + 1 tablespoons clarified butter	4 slices toast
1 pound jumbo lump crabmeat	1 teaspoon finely chopped parsley
2 egg yolks	1 lemon, cut into wedges

Prepare the Béchamel Sauce.

In a medium saucepan, sauté the green onions in 2 tablespoons of the clarified butter over medium heat until tender. Add the crabmeat, then fold in the Béchamel Sauce. When mixture begins to simmer, remove from the heat and fold in the egg yolks. Refrigerate for 10 minutes. The mixture will become firm so as to mold for canapés as it cools.

During this time, preheat the oven to 350 degrees. Combine the breadcrumbs and Parmesan cheese in a mixing bowl and blend well. Trim 4 slices of toast into 4-inch rounds. Place the rounds on a cookie sheet, then spoon equal amounts of the crabmeat mixture onto each round using an ice-cream scoop.

Sprinkle the bread crumb and cheese mixture over the canapés. Dot each one with an equal portion of the remaining tablespoon of clarified butter, then place into the oven to bake for 20 minutes. Transfer to serving plates and garnish with parsley and lemon.

Optional: Cross each canapé with 2 anchovy slices.
SERVES 4.

Godchaux Salad

1 head iceberg lettuce, cubed
2 large tomatoes, cubed
1 pound backfin lump crabmeat
30 to 35 large shrimp, boiled, and
    peeled

2/3 cup salad oil
1/3 cup red wine vinegar
1/2 cup Creole mustard
3 hard-boiled eggs
12 anchovies

In a large salad bowl, combine the lettuce, tomatoes, crabmeat, and shrimp. In a small bowl, combine the oil, vinegar, and mustard and mix well. Pour the dressing over salad and toss.

Divide salad onto 6 chilled plates and garnish each salad with 1/2 of a seived hard boiled egg and 2 anchovies.

SERVES 6.

A Katz salad, created in the 1920s by Mrs. Gus Katz, contained grapefruit, avocado, sweet pickle relish, and vinaigrette. "It was awful," said Stephen Moses, recalling stories told by his grandfather, Walter B. Moses, founder of Weil & Moses Engineers. The younger Moses also heard about graham crackers being served at Galatoire's. ("They are great with Martinis.") When the treat was discontinued, his grandfather kept a metal box at the restaurant for his own graham crackers, which were brought to the table still in their wrappers. Another regular is so particular about his Old-Fashioneds ("The old recipe calls for two kinds of bitters: Peychaud and Angostura, and it doesn't taste right without both of them.") that he keeps his own bottle of Angostura at Galatoire's, as the restaurant now uses only Peychaud. Unfortunately, so many people request the Angostura that the professor often

SALAD DAYS

Gene Bourg was in Galatoire's in the mid-90s, sitting cheek-to-cheek with Renna and John Godchaux at the next table. When their waiter, Richard Smith, came to take his order Gene proclaimed in a voice intended to be heard by the couple: "Since I'm sitting next to a descendant of a salad namesake, I'm ordering the Godchaux salad."

Richard responded, "No, I don't do the Godchaux salad. I do the Maison Blanche salad." John Godchaux then spoke up, "Get the Stein Mart Salad, it's cheaper." (Note to the uninitiated: The discount house never rated a salad of its own.)

has to replace his bottle, walking six or seven blocks to find one before returning to his seat at Galatoire's. In regard to discontinued customs, Moses remembers David Gooch being asked about a group of men smoking cigars, "How can you let them smoke in here?" His answer: "We sell cigars." But no longer. Along with cigarettes, cigars are déclassé these modern days at Galatoire's, although there is a section in which smoking is permitted.

"Regulars will ask for old dishes that are no longer on the menu," said Milton, "some we can still make and some we can't." He mentioned items that have "disappeared," such as Chicken Florentine, Prime Rib, and Chicken à la King. "We also used to have Roast Beef and Mashed Potatoes and Turkey à la King." According to Leona Frey, other dishes prepared now only by family members at home are Gumbo Z'herbes, made of nine greens and salt pork and served only on Holy Thursday, and Bacalao, a Basque country dish made of dried codfish with either a cream or garlic sauce—a Good Friday specialty.

Oysters Rockefeller

1 stalk of celery	1 teaspoon thyme
1 bunch of green onions	1 teaspoon bay leaf, ground
1/2 bunch of parsley	1/2 cup of ketchup
1/2 pound of spinach	1/3 ounce of Herbsaint
1/4 pound of butter	2 dashes of Tabasco
3 tablespoons of Lea and Perrin	Salt and pepper to taste
3 tablespoons of vinegar	2 cups of ground bread crumbs
1 teaspoon anise	2 dozen oysters, poached

In a food processor fitted with a steel blade, chop all vegetables very fine. Remove to a ceramic or glass bowl and add melted butter, Lea and Perrin, and vinegar. Mix thoroughly. Add anise, thyme, bay leaf, ketchup, Herbsaint, Tabasco, salt, and pepper. Mix well. Add bread crumbs and mix well.

Place each poached oyster on a shell and cover each shell with a spoonful of the Rockefeller Sauce. Broil oysters until brown and serve hot.
SERVES 4 AS AN APPETIZER.

The cherished old Creole dishes that roll out of the kitchen are still much the same. Over the years, the Galatoire family has never lost sight of a great restaurant's most important characteristic. To attract a devoted following consistency is everything—in ambiance and service, but above all, in the food served. In a *Time* magazine (August 22, 1988) feature on New Orleans, food critic Mimi Sheraton proclaimed Galatoire's "the only legendary restaurant in the French Quarter that lives up to its billing." She lauded the "lush Creole seafood: Shrimp Rémoulade with its brassy mustard and paprika-zapped sauce; plump Oysters Rockefeller; Trout Meunière Amandine, fragrant with hot brown butter and almond slices; and eggplant with a gentle, rich seafood stuffing."

Over the years, any alterations to the food at Galatoire's were carefully and subtly introduced, usually in response to outside influences, such as availability of products and changes in trends. "The menu at Galatoire's was almost cut in stone," said Ansel. "The policy was that we didn't want to change any dishes or add or take any dishes off." Although it may appear that the menu has not changed, there has indeed been an evolution of the food served and its preparation. For example, a variation of Eggs Sardou, Crabmeat Sardou, made its way onto the menu in the mid-1980s—crabmeat is used in place of eggs in the recipe.

Leon Galatoire III, right, with alligator—a short-lived item on the Galatoire's menu

Miss Yvonne gave another example. In the 1930s, Spanish mackerel, drum, and sheepshead were very popular fish, but in the 1940s and 1950s speckled trout and redfish took over the table. "In the 1960s Trout Marguery was all the rage," she said. For a long time, this was Galatoire's signature dish. It was so famous that once a Saudi Arabian came into the restaurant, not speaking any English but with "Trout Marguery" written on a scrap of paper. "Ours had a secret ingredient, a black truffle essence," she explained, "then truffles became too expensive and people decided to watch their waistlines so Marguery sauce (a mixture of hollandaise and béchamel) was too heavy. Now we're going back to drum and sheepshead again. It all depends upon what is expedient and upon changing tastes."

Even now, the least change in the food at Galatoire's will cause storms of protest. Old articles about the restaurant show that was always the case; diners not only left with full bellies, but cherished memories of dishes they did not want altered. In 1967 Stanforth wrote: "People have been known to return to Galatoire's after an absence of twenty years, order the same food (very likely from the same waiter), and swear it is still the same." In 1956, long before "fat-free" was a byword, Monsieur Justin pointed out to Grau that "people just don't eat as much now." An old-timer back then groused to Grau, "My dear, now the waiter goes into the kitchen and in twenty minutes you have your order. Years ago it would take two days—if you could just *taste* the things they did!"—proving once again that old-timers of any century dislike change.

Standing: Leon Galatoire III, left, Justin Frey, right; seated: David Gooch, 1987, on the occasion of Galatoire's winning the IVY Award of Distinction, considered the most prestigious prize a restaurant or institution can win as a team

In her article, Grau describes in detail the unpretentious, old-fashioned dining room and writes, "Very little has changed at Galatoire's in the last half century." Almost fifty years later, that statement still holds true in many respects—especially in the comforting cuisine that comes from the kitchen. Devotees still swear by the Rémoulade Sauce, the Trout Meunière, fresh crab-meat dishes, Oysters en Brochette, and delectable Pommes de Terre Soufflé and fried eggplant sticks to dip into powdered sugar or béarnaise sauce. "My friends with leather throats still prefer to mix up a potent paste of powdered sugar and Tabasco," says Jess Johnson (retired and living in Florida), who was a regular in the 1960s when he worked for Texaco, and who still dines at Galatoire's when he and his wife Peggy visit New Orleans.

Gene Bourg wrote in *Gourmet* (1996), "For ninety-one years, this Bourbon Street landmark has managed to reinvent itself continually without abandoning its vital role as a bastion of classicism." The restaurant's unique dishes have well withstood the test of time and evolution. What really matters remains the same: a lineup of delicious French Creole delicacies that keep diners coming back for more.

Milton Prudence at work

MILTON PRUDENCE
The Magic Saucier

The magic Milton Prudence achieves in the creation of the famous Rockefeller Sauce is a ritual that seems almost sacred in its performance. Being allowed to stand by and watch as he works to bring all the disparate ingredients together into a delicious unity is tantamount to being admitted to the inner sanctum to observe the arcane ritual of some ancient secret order. During most of the year, the sauce is prepared once a week, on Wednesdays, but the rush of customers during holiday seasons often necessitates two preparations a week.

Milton is all work, with no time for the chitchat that goes on among some of the kitchen staff as well as waiters and busboys passing back and forth through the immaculately clean area. He is patient amid the frantic activity as preparations are made for the dinner crowd. As he works, Gloria Mitchell, who was employed in 1963, sits nearby peeling a giant mound of shrimp. "When I started off Justin Frey was a little boy," she recalls. She fills one hand with the peeled shrimp, then places them in a container nearby, still without looking.

Three other women are working in the kitchen that day, including Frances Lewis, who has been there twenty-two years, and was "the first and only lady cook, a fryer and sauté cook," until she changed her hours in order to rear her children. Now her work involves preparation, mostly putting Rockefeller Sauce on oysters in pans and placing them in the walk-in cooler; she also still cooks and keeps a check on dishes. Vanessa Scott, who came to work at Galatoire's in April of 2000, helps Frances in her preparations, as does Lashannon Davis, who also began work in 2000. One of them peels and prepares Brabant potatoes, one stirs up the Sauce Maison, and another is removing sweet potato cheesecakes—a new addition to the menu—from the walk-in refrigerator. She releases them from their spring-form pans and returns them to the refrigerator. She washes and dries the pans and lines them with paper to get ready for the next baking. Then she prepares the restaurant's signature dessert, cup custards, for baking—six pans of them, with twenty-two in each pan. Against the wall, there are vats of corn flour, salt, sugar, and in a tall metal stand, trays of thinly-sliced potatoes, already fried once, await the second frying that will magically transform them into les *Pommes de Terre Souffle*. The bustle seems not to affect Milton at all, as he moves through step after step of his complicated process without reference to a list, except that stored in his memory.

When I arrive, Prudence is cutting up and washing twelve bunches of celery, then moves on to do the same with six bunches of leeks, twenty-four bunches of scallions, twenty-four bunches of parsley, and three stalks of anise. The fresh produce is supplied daily by three local distributors. Each of the vegetables in turn is fed into the top of a large food grinder and comes out macerated to fall into a large metal vat on the floor. Milton has an assistant to help with this project, but he supervises every step, checking, for example, to see that not too much water from the celery gets into the mixture, sometimes returning handfuls of the chopped vegetables to the top of the machine for a second grinding if it does not meet his exacting standards. He recalls the time when the food grinder was smaller, so that the preparation took more time, and before they had any machines at all, all the chopping was done by hand: "I'm glad I wasn't here in those days" he says, in his typically understated way.

When all the vegetables are pulverized to his liking, Milton begins swiftly adding the other ingredients to the food grinder, not in any particular order, he says. There are six number 10 cans of spinach, two large cans of ketchup, one-half a spinach can of red wine vinegar, one-half a spinach can of Worcestershire sauce, a cup of salt, a cup of white pepper, a water glass full of green food coloring, two large boxes of seasoned bread crumbs, and an astonishing thirty-six pounds of melted butter! As he adds thyme and anise seed—"I don't have to measure the spices, I've been doing it so long"—he instructs his assistant to go upstairs and get him a bottle of Herbsaint, the New Orleans version of Absinthe.

Meanwhile, the other business of the kitchen continues at its regular pace while Milton moves swiftly and intently from task to task. Waiters and busboys, a vice president, and even a member of the Galatoire family pass through the kitchen, a delivery man arrives, several laundry bags are dragged through and out the back door into the alleyway; Miss Gloria finishes peeling her shrimp and inquires of Milton if there are some large onions that need peeling. There are, he says, and she moves on to that chore before ending her long busy day.

The assistant returns with the fifth of Herbsaint and Milton pours the bottle into the vat, then tears open the large bread-crumb boxes and spreads the cardboard on the floor as a rug on which he kneels like a priest before his altar. The vat is now half-filled with pulverized vegetables, spices, and liquids and Milton thrusts his hands into the mass and begins to mix methodically, making circular motions to be certain that all the ingredients are blended thoroughly.

When he rises from his ritual, the final step completed, he has been at work for almost two hours and produced twenty-one gallons of Rockefeller sauce. The sauce is then placed in pans to be stored in the refrigerator until needed. The outsider, who has just witnessed this lengthy and involved process, is exhausted, but Milton seems unfazed as he moves on to his next chore. For one more week—or a few days at least—Galatoire's patrons can rest assured that Oysters Rockefeller will be available. Next Wednesday, or perhaps before, Milton will once again begin the rite that, like base metal into gold, transforms a few humble foodstuffs into one of the most sublime sauces known to Creole cuisine.

KENNETH HOLDITCH

Act One

Once Upon a Time

Scene Three

Playwrights
Writers & Galatoire's

*"When a lot of people get together in the best places,
things go glimmering."*
—F. Scott Fitzgerald, "Absolution"

*N*ot the least of the charms of New Orleans, both physical and abstract, that have continuously attracted authors and other artists since the city was founded in 1718, is its well deserved reputation as a world food capital. In the 1850s, English novelist William Makepeace Thackeray described the city as "the one place in the world where you can eat and drink the most and suffer the least." Unfortunately, Thackeray was not privileged to add Galatoire's to his cherished New Orleans memories, for it would be almost half a century before the restaurant was founded. Although in recent decades the infectious spread of fast food outlets and such fads as California cuisine, Nouvelle Cuisine, and burned fish and meat passed-off as being chic "blackened" fare has encroached on even the classic food of New Orleans, the city remains a great place not just to eat, but to dine in style. No place exemplifies that tradition better than Galatoire's.

More famous writers than we can even record have had the privilege of relishing the food and drink at Galatoire's, and one, Tennessee Williams, made it immortally famous in his greatest drama, *A Streetcar Named Desire*. A sampling of the experiences of these authors and the restaurant's effects upon their lives and their works gives us a notion of what the eatery has meant to a variety of writers for almost a century. Many of them have recorded their feelings about the restaurant, its cuisine, and its drink in the pages of their books; others have cherished the memories in private. Their reflections serve, in turn, to demonstrate just how much Galatoire's has meant to others not blessed with these writers' facility with the language.

William Faulkner, a Francophile at heart, lived off and on for two years in the 1920s in the French Quarter. One can imagine the response of this sensitive author, newly educated by personal experience in French cuisine, when for the first time he walked into what was essentially a French bistro—Galatoire's—dropped down in the middle of America's most French, and, Sherwood Anderson insisted, most civilized city. In 1926, Faulkner received a small advance for his second novel, *Mosquitoes,* a thinly-veiled satirical portrayal of the life of the bevy of French Quarter Bohemian artists and writers among whom he had lived. He invited several of his friends in the Vieux Carre, appropriately, since he had been enjoying the largesse of many of them during his lean and hungry months, to celebrate his good fortune with him at a Galatoire's dinner.

All of the guests that evening had been subjects for artist William Spratling's caricatures in the humorous collection he and Faulkner published that same year, *Sherwood Anderson and Other Famous Creoles.* The subjects of the drawings were, for the most part, not Creoles at all, but included a cross section of 1920s Quarterites from a variety of places. The guest list included Marc Antony, an interior decorator, and his wife Lucille, who, with Sherwood Anderson's wife, Elizabeth, owned a decorating shop on St. Peter Street. Genevieve Pitot, on the other hand, was a true Creole, whose great-grandfather had been the first elected mayor of the city; she was a classical pianist, who later became a celebrated composer of dance music for Broadway musicals such as *Kismet* and *Kiss Me Kate.* Harold Levy, one of the founders of the literary journal *The Double-Dealer,* was the musical director of Le Petit Theatre, who on one occasion aided Faulkner in completing a poem when, as the novelist wrote in an inscription to Levy, "my muse failed me."

"When we had something to celebrate," Antony recalled in the 1970s, "we often went to Galatoire's. It was and is such a special place." When the guests arrived that evening, Faulkner was nowhere in sight. After waiting a while, they sent an emissary to locate the errant author and bring him back for an evening that was a memorable and celebratory one, but, as Antony recalled, a quiet one "since Galatoire's has always been a rather sedate place." We have no record of the food that was devoured that evening, but given the appetite of the Bohemians, European and American, as portrayed in literature and opera, we can imagine that it was a feast.

A few months after that celebration, *Mosquitoes,* the novel that occasioned it, was published and many of those who had rejoiced in Faulkner's good fortune now read it for the first time and were appalled by what they considered his satirical portrait of the artists and writers of the French Quarter. In fact, the depiction of their lifestyle is not really negative, although most of them seemed to feel otherwise. Even in the 1970s, fifty years after that gala feast at Galatoire's and the publication of the novel, some were still bitter about what they considered a betrayal.

Sherwood Anderson was the leader of the French Quarter literary and artistic community in the 1920s, as well as the magnet that drew aspiring writers to the city. Two members of that group were Lyle Saxon and Hamilton Basso. Saxon was a well-known author, as well as a bon vivant who relished the French Quarter, its architecture, denizens, food, and drink. Saxon wrote in *Fabulous New Orleans* (1928) that "Dining in the cafes of New Orleans quite spoils one for other cities where the food is prepared as a necessity rather than as a rite." Hamilton Basso, a New Orleans writer who achieved considerable renown with his novels, including *Sun in Capricorn,* and *The View from Pompey's Head,* was a protégé of Sherwood Anderson's. When he decided to propose to his future wife, Etolia, in 1930, he wanted to do it in a romantic spot dear to the both of them and so he chose Galatoire's.

Tennessee Williams must first have dined at Galatoire's in the early 1940s, for when he arrived in the city in December 1938 he was virtually penniless, forced, or so he was later to write, to pawn everything, including a typewriter that was not even his, in order to survive. Thus he could hardly have afforded meals in any but the most inexpensive eateries, including the "Eat Shop" opened by his landlady on Toulouse Street, where the meals were all twenty-five cents. For that ill-fated and short-lived establishment, the aspiring playwright created a motto, "Meals in the Quarter for a Quarter," hand-printed it on cards, and gave them out in the Vieux Carre before returning to serve as waiter, cashier, and dishwasher. By the early 1940s, he had made numerous friends in the Quarter, and it is likely that one or more of them would have taken him to what was already established as one of the city's two or three best places to eat. In his biography of the playwright, *Tom, The Unknown Tennessee Williams* (1995), Lyle Leverich writes that among the strong impressions made on the young author by New Orleans was "the sixty-cent lunch at Galatoire's: crawfish bisque, oysters Rockefeller" along with riding on streetcar lines such as Desire and Cemeteries for a seven-cent fare.

During the same period, one writer, who was off and on a friend of Williams's, Truman Capote, first dined at Galatoire's and later expressed one of the few adverse opinions of the restaurant in print. His entire view of the French Quarter cuisine was somewhat jaundiced, and he insisted that coffee and beignets at the French Market were better than the food at Antoine's, "which, by the way, is a lousy restaurant. So are most of the city's famous eateries. Gallatoire's [sic] isn't bad, but it's too crowded; they don't accept reservations, you have to wait in long lines, and it's not worth it, at least not to me."

By the time Tennessee Williams wrote *A Streetcar Named Desire* in 1946, he knew Galatoire's well and even had his own favorite table, in a corner just inside the front door, from which he could survey the rest of the room. Yvonne Galatoire Wynne, the gracious and charming doyenne of the family, would often see him there and said that her father, Justin, would sometimes join the playwright and the two would have long talks. Miss Yvonne also remembers Williams's grandfather, the Reverend Walter Dakin, who sometimes accompanied him. Since Reverend Dakin, who in the mid-1940s was in his nineties, was devoted to good food and good drink (Manhattans were his favorites), Williams saw to it that he dined in the best places, including frequent meals at Galatoire's. Miss Yvonne, recalling their visits, observed, "He really loved that old man, you know."

In 1947 New Orleans achieved a permanent place in the American literary pantheon with the production of *A Streetcar Named Desire*—although many others had written about the city before, it was Williams who brought it to pulsating life on the stage of the world. Williams had just spent his longest sustained stay in the city, living in an apartment on 632 St. Peter Street. In the play, Galatoire's is the restaurant of choice for Stella Kowalski, who wants to take her fastidious sister Blanche DuBois to a place that will impress her. Stella announces to her husband Stanley, "I'm taking Blanche to Galatoire's for supper and then to a show, because it's your poker night." Stanley, clearly not the type for the restaurant—"I'm not going to no Galatoire's for supper"—demands to know what he's going to eat and is hardly placated when Stella informs him that she had put a cold plate on ice for him.

The two sisters would have ridden on the streetcar named Desire from the Kowalski apartment at 632 Elysian Fields to Bourbon and Canal. In those days, the line that the playwright made world famous ran on a loop between Desire Street, along Royal to Canal, thence one block over to Bourbon, where it rumbled right past the restaurant, then back to Desire. What, one cannot resist speculating, would Blanche DuBois have ordered from Galatoire's abundant menu after a few stiff drinks. Seafood, surely, since that was probably her creator's favorite food. Indeed, during his first stay in the city in 1938–1939, he wrote to his mother that the food in New Orleans was the best he had ever eaten in his life, excluding, of course, he added tactfully, the food from her kitchen. Edwina Williams, the playwright's mother, wrote in her memoirs, *Remember Me to Tom*, that her son informed her by letter that he loved New Orleans and its cuisine and was "fulfilling his passion for seafood." In a December 4, 1972 letter from the Hotel Elysee in New York City, where he was accepting the National Theatre Award, to his secretary, Victor Campbell, Williams interrupts his gossipy remarks about Frosty Blackshear, Mary Maude, Jo Healy, Dakin, his Mother, and someone who "shot his wife Gladys dead while cleaning his pistol in the Bronx," to add an aside: "Looking forward to some more of that trout at Galatoire's—how are the noon line-ups?"

Writer Don Lee Keith at a favorite table

In the 1970s Don Lee Keith joined Williams for dinner at Galatoire's, where they were seated at a table for two with Keith's back to the door. They were sipping their drinks when suddenly Williams glanced at the door and said, "Quick, you get over here and let me sit there where you are." After the two switched places, Williams explained that a couple had come in whom he did not want to see. "But you like them, don't you," Keith asked and the dramatist replied, "Not this week I don't. You know I once heard someone refer to that pair as the Agony and the Ecstasy. The problem is that I never figured out who was the *agony* and who was the *ecstasy.*"

Eudora Welty, a typical Mississippian, always had a strong affinity for Galatoire's, its ambiance, and its food. In her subtle and tender short story "No Place for You My Love," a middle-aged man and woman meet while

MIRROR TRICK

Back in the early 1970s, Tennessee Williams's friend, writer Don Lee Keith, went to Galatoire's with Williams and Muriel Bultman Francis to talk over the health situation of a mutual friend. They were waiting in line when it began to rain, and, according to Keith, Williams began to say "Lamentable, lamentable, just lamentable," over and over again. Keith didn't know whether he was referring to the friend's situation or to waiting in the rain.

Finally, inside at a table, "Tennessee told a story about Victor Campbell, a good-looking young man who had until lately lived with him. He said the first time he had brought Victor to Galatoire's that Victor had studied the menu carefully, then asked the waiter: 'Does this mean you don't have hamburgers?' 'No hamburgers,' the waiter replied. Then Victor asked: 'How about pizza?'"

"Tennessee waited for my laugh before adding, 'But before long Victor loved it—once he had discovered the mirrors.'"

(Keith, a renowned journalist and later head of the Journalism School at UNO, was so anxious to record this exchange, that, lacking paper, he went to the men's room and pulled off toilet paper on which to write down the great playwright's remarks.)

dining at adjoining tables in the restaurant. They strike up a conversation and leave together to ride down to Venice, which is more or less land's end in Louisiana. This almost-love-story occurs on a Sunday in summer and the atmosphere of the place, "where mirrors and fans were busy agitating the light, as the very local talk drawled across and agitated the peace," contributes strongly to the narrative. (Of course, Welty was aware that the talk is especially "local" on Sundays, since most of the clientele on that day are residents of the city.) The middle-aged woman in the story—neither of the two main characters is named—glances "at the big gold clock," one of the most imposing features of the dining room, and the "blades of fan shadows came down over their two heads," as the man proposes that they take a drive south of the city.

Although Frances Parkinson Keyes, the author of numerous historical romances, is most connected to New Orleans restaurants through her 1948 novel *Dinner at Antoine's,* she also dined at Galatoire's during her stays in the Crescent City. Keyes includes scenes set in Galatoire's in at least two other works. In *Crescent Carnival* one of the characters, Olivier, drives three friends on St. Joseph's night, 1918, to "a small restaurant on Bourbon Street with the name, 'Galatoire,' inconspicuously displayed in front." Olivier informs his guests that the restaurant has come to be "considered one of the best in the Quarter." Almost as soon as the three are seated, the waiter brings drinks and dishes that "made its reputation easy to understand." With his assistant, a "white-aproned *sommelier,*" the waiter serves the meal "with a Gallic flourish," and soon the proprietor—in 1913, it would have been Jean Galatoire—comes by "to pay his respects," to ask if everything was satisfactory, and to offer them a free drink. According to the narrator, Olivier is not only a regular but also "a natural gourmet, and as such, doubly welcome in a French establishment. . . ." As the "excellent fare" begins to take effect on Olivier, he grows "increasingly amiable" as the "little dinner passed off triumphantly."

In her *Holiday* magazine article, Shirley Ann Grau describes her first visit to Galatoire's in the mid-1930s with her aunt. At the time, she was only

BEING THERE

"A visit to Galatoire's evokes the first time you went to Galatoire's and will undoubtedly prompt recollections, over the Crabmeat Maison and your first glass of wine, of the last time you came to Galatoire's, how much you drank, what you ate, and who you saw there. Unless you belong to that elite set which goes to Galatoire's all the time, in which case all of the above goes unspoken, like a shared joke."

Lili LeGardeur, "Deconstructing Galatoire's"

five or six, but the day made a deep impression, for she remembered "the oyster shells piled in wooden kegs all along the sidewalk (banquette we always said)." The little girl felt very elegant, wearing a large red camellia pinned to the neck of her dress. Inside Galatoire's, she sat on several old, thick books by Honore de Balzac so that she could reach the table and "wondered what those books were doing in a restaurant."

In Ellen Gilchrist's short story titled "Mexico," Rhoda Manning, a recurrent character in Gilchrist's fiction, waits in line at Galatoire's for lunch with St. John, her cousin. A delivery man parks his truck across the street and removes from it "a huge silvery fish" and takes it to the side door of Galatoire's, where he is met by a chef in a tall white hat. As the two disappear into the building with the fish, Rhoda is struck with the almost mythic quality of the scene and its unique significance to New Orleans: "We live in symbiosis with this mystery. . . . No one understands it. Everything we think we know is wrong. Except their beauty." She lives now in another state, far away from this mystery, and cannot fully comprehend it, but the observation of what is now and has always been an everyday occurrence at the restaurant, the delivery of fresh food, a Galatoire's tradition, becomes for Rhoda the catalyst to an epiphany about the restaurant, the city, and, indeed, life.

Soon the maitre d' escorts Rhoda and St. John into the crowded restaurant where the "Friday processional crowd was out in force." Near the door are women seated at the same tables, she thinks, where they sat before she left town months before, and the waiters move through the narrow spaces between tables bearing a variety of drinks and dishes laden with fabulous food. So thoroughly is a Galatoire's experience identified with New Orleans for Rhoda, as for thousands of other people, fictional and real, that she thinks as she observes it all, "I should never have left. . . . God, I miss this town." In Gilchrist's poem titled "Mrs. Cole-McCall," an Uptown lady in a monologue observes that "It is nineteen seventy three, / I'm late to Galatoire's, life lasts forever. . . ."

Two of the best evocations of Galatoire's occur in Sheila Bosworth's novels, *Almost Innocent* and *Slow Poison*. In the film *Dining and Dynasties*, Bosworth said of her writing career that she was blessed by being a Louisianan and having available an abundance of material as a result. Galatoire's is significant to her work because of the restaurant's "history and promise." The "promise" is "that as long as you're within these walls, nothing will go wrong," and by "history," she explains, she means the "tradition of the place," so that the author has a "wonderful framing device" for fiction ready at hand. She explains the fact that Galatoire's has become an important institution in New Orleans by virtue of the fact that "it is predictable in a time when so little is," and it is predictable precisely because of the traditions, "certain rules that always apply."

In *Slow Poison*, while Rory Cade's father is dying in a hospital, Fox Renick determines to "coddle-and-feed" Rory good New Orleans food to lift her spirits. Among the restaurants to which he takes her is, of course, Galatoire's, where, for Sunday dinner, he orders for her Oysters en Brochette, one of their wonderful specialties, consisting of a perfect and ideal combination of two incredible flavors, oysters and bacon, battered and deep-fried. When Rory has finished the dish, Fox tells her that was only the appetizer, and a chef is preparing Trout Meunière for them in the kitchen.

Oysters en Brochette

12 strips of bacon, cut in half	Salt and pepper to taste
2 dozen raw oysters	Flour
4 (8-inch) skewers	Oil for deep frying
1 egg	Toast points
3/4 cup milk	1 lemon, cut into wedges

Fry bacon until not quite crisp. Alternate 6 oysters and 6 half strips of bacon (folded on each skewer). Make a batter with egg and milk and season well with salt and pepper. Dip each skewer in batter, roll in flour and deep fry until golden. Serve on toast points with lemon wedge.
SERVES 4 AS AN APPETIZER OR 2 AS A MAIN COURSE.

It is, however, in her first novel, *Almost Innocent*, that Sheila Bosworth pays her most memorable tribute to Galatoire's with the opening and closing scenes that encapsulate the long relationship between the establishment and many families in New Orleans, in Louisiana, and in Mississippi. In the first chapter of that book, Clay-Lee Calvert encounters her father one afternoon on Canal Street and he invites her for a late lunch, early dinner—at Galatoire's, such distinctions as lunch and dinner are not always apropos. Father and daughter arrive early enough to avoid the dinner crowd and are seated near the counter in the back, which, through the years, in the style of a French bistro, has been presided over by various members of the family and backed, Bosworth writes, by the "little bar where the waiters mix the patrons' drinks."

The Calverts' waiter, almost eighty now, is Vallon, who "generations ago," when Clay-Lee's father was a boy, would take him upstairs for red beans and rice. From their corner table, drinking her Ramos Gin Fizz, a New Orleans specialty, Clay-Lee looks for familiar faces reflected in the mirrors that encircle the room and sees a number of identifiable locals: the scion of a coffee family, afflicted with *anorexia nervosa,* who is eating only a bowl of ice; a surgeon's wife who survived an attempted suicide leap from the Huey P. Long Bridge; and, accompanied by his sister-in-law, a "famous writer who lived in Covington." As a result of this experience of a kind by no means unusual at Galatoire's, Clay-Lee finds herself "smiling at nobody in the mirrored wall. . . ." This mirror phenomenon reflects what often happens in the restaurant when locals, attuned to the various scandals current in the city and the interwoven relationship between people of all classes, peer, as it were, at bits and pieces of local social history as if looking into a unique kind of New Orleans kaleidoscope. Appropriately, the novel ends with the memory of the restaurant, as Clay-Lee recalls, "My father and I, at Galatoire's . . . was it one night we had there together, or many nights, many hours I spent watching his face, calling back the past?" It is significant that she identifies her past and that of her family with Galatoire's and distinctly recalls leaving her father in front of the restaurant "in the early evening lull before the nightly tourist and college crowds converged on Bourbon Street."

Bunt and Walker Percy in front of their favorite restaurant—Galatoire's

The "famous writer" from Covington spotted in the passage from *Almost Innocent,* although he is not named, is, of course, Walker Percy, who, with his wife Berenice (Bunt), often dined at Galatoire's through the years. As a Mississippian, Percy had grown up with an awareness of New Orleans and of its treasures, far from the least of which is the restaurant. In his youth, he would surely have been brought from Greenville to the city by his "Uncle Will," the author William Alexander Percy, since such excursions have always been commonplace among Delta people. In Walker Percy's first novel, *The Moviegoer,* when Binx Bolling sees movie star William Holden walking through the French Quarter, he automatically assumes that "No doubt he is on his way to Galatoire's for lunch." On a houseboat for a fishing trip, Binx's friend Walter Wade asks, "Tell me honestly, have you ever tasted better food than at Galatoire's?" using the standards by which New Orleanians have long measured good cuisine. Binx thinks of the man next to him on the train to Chicago, "no doubt, he had had an excellent meal at Galatoire's and the blood of his portal vein bears away a golden harvest of nutrient globules."

It was in the summer of 1981 that Walker and Bunt Percy first met Elizabeth Spencer, another Mississippi writer, for lunch at the restaurant, and in December of 2002, Bunt Percy and Elizabeth Spencer were reunited at Tennessee Williams's table. "The one thing I like best about Galatoire's," Bunt Percy said on that occasion, "is the feeling it gives you—it's always like a birthday." Spencer's own memories of the restaurant are entwined with recollections of her family. As a child, she heard her uncles speak of New Orleans and the "magic names" of restaurants there: "There was relish in the very sound of them, French and enticing." She was in college when she made her first visit to the city, armed with instructions from her Uncle Joe who told her where to eat breakfast, lunch, and dinner, and added, "don't miss Galatoire's and Trout Marguery." Through the years, Spencer continued to dine there, and on the occasion of her reunion with Bunt Percy and other friends, she ordered Trout Marguery, "because that was what my uncle always had."

In *Pentimento* (1972) Lillian Hellman recounts the story of how, when she first brought Dashiell Hammett to New Orleans to meet her elderly Aunt Hannah, he took them to several leading local restaurants, including Galatoire's, where Aunt Hannah was concerned about the cost. Aunt Hannah was skeptical of his relationship to her niece, but when Hammett told her that "all he had ever wanted in the world was a docile woman, but instead had come out with me, the cost of the dinner at Galatoire's ceased to worry her." She and Hammett agreed that docile women were "ninnies with oatmeal in the head," and the next day, Aunt Hannah told Hellman that she thought Hammett was an intelligent man.

Authors' descriptions of Galatoire's are always varied and evocative. In her 1999 novel *Eleanor Rushing,* Patty Friedmann's eponymous character feels cradled by "the smell of hot French bread and rich people." She remarks that the mirrors "give you nowhere in the restaurant to completely avoid seeing yourself . . . part of the meal would have to do with watching your companion, aware of himself, then watching yourself, aware of yourself." Eleanor likes the way she looks in the mirrors, "their slight smokiness gave me a more ethereal appearance, flawless and very cold."

In the last chapter of Nancy Lemann's *Lives of the Saints* (1985), Claude Collier takes Louise Brown on a Sunday to Galatoire's, where they wait in a line that stretches to the corner. They listen to jazz in the street, watch the "throngs of people," including tap dancers, "tourists, whores, drunks, toothless old men, strippers, bouncers." When they go inside, Galatoire's is "one dazzling blast of light-bulbs and white tile and the light bounces off the mirrors." At the tables are "old judges, society men, their vivacious wives," and the waiters cluster around the "dark mahogany bureau in the back of the room."

Jimmy Buffett has been seen frequently in Galatoire's where Cesar always served him before that waiter's untimely death. In a short story entitled "I Wish Lunch Could Last Forever," Buffett writes of "Caesar," as he spells it, and of the interior of the restaurant, describing the fans turning overhead, as they no longer do, and the mirrors on the walls that "gave an instant view of the entire restaurant from our table." When the main character, Slade, tells Caesar that they plan to stay a long time, the waiter replies, "Take as long as you like, my friend. That's why I'm here." Later Slade invites all his friends to join them for lunch, and when the "wild, motley group" arrives, many of the regulars are displeased because there are "gypsies in the palace." They drink more and more champagne and dine sumptuously on Trout Meunière, omelettes made with crabmeat, soufflé potatoes, and "Pompano en Papillote," which, in reality, is not on the Galatoire's menu. As the meal ends at midnight, Slade's lover Isabella gives him a gift of an old ship's clock and toasts him as "the man who taught me that love could be more fun than work, that music is the voice of the soul, and that lunch should last forever. . . ."

Pompano Meunière

Oil for broiling	1/2 pound of butter
2 (1-1/2 or 2 pound) pompano), cut	Juice of 1 lemon
lengthwise	1/2 tablespoon of chopped parsley

Put a small amount of oil on pompano before broiling.

In a separate pan, melt and continuously whip butter until brown and frothy. Add lemon juice and pour over pompano.

Garnish with chopped parsley.

SERVES 4.

The popular and prolific New Orleans novelist, Anne Rice, has single-handedly made vampire fiction a distinct modern genre. It is, however, in one of her novels about the Mayfair witches that Galatoire's figures. In the first novel concerning that family, *The Witching Hour,* Llewellyn and Aaron dine in the restaurant, and the elder members of the Mayfair family take Rowan there after they have attended a business meeting to discuss what is to be done with the family legacy.

Julie Smith, an Edgar Award-winner who resides in the French Quarter a good part of the year, has written two series of detective novels set in New Orleans, and is yet another literary figure who loves Galatoire's and has made use of it in her work. In *82 Desire,* for example, a councilwoman whose husband has disappeared describes him to detective Skip Langdon in these words: "He's almost dull—goes to work, plays golf, sails. Church on Sunday; Friday lunch at Galatoire's." Her words constitute a litany of the typical activities of many Uptown men. In the same novel, another character refuses an invitation to the restaurant for Friday lunch, saying, "Last thing I want to do is get in that kind of trouble." He thinks as he rejects the offer that all people who went there at noon stayed until six. "It was a place for a power lunch in the networking sense only, unless you were the object of the power play—in which case, it was a great place to get you drunk and friendly toward your host." Any attempt at conducting business, he thinks, is certain "to be interrupted by table-hopping friends" or "single women on a flirting mission."

Left to right, Kristina Ford, Rosemary James, and Julie Smith

Even writers who set their scenes elsewhere make the Galatoire's scene frequently. Galatoire's was always a favorite of Willie Morris, author of *North*

Seated clockwise from the left: Hartwig Moss III, Nancy Moss, Rosemary James, Willie Morris, Joe De Salvo, Marda Burton, and Kenneth Holditch

ADVICE FROM WILLIE

In February 1999, writer Judy Conner went to Galatoire's with Willie and JoAnne Prichard Morris and his son, photographer David Rae Morris. During a wide-ranging conversation Willie asked Judy how her book, titled *Southern Fried Divorce,* was coming along. "I told him I didn't know what would happen," Judy said. Willie then grabbed a cocktail napkin and wrote down the following advice:

2/27/99
Judy
See it through.
See the beauty through:
Also:

I. The brutality	5. The memory
2. The complexity	6. The fun
3. The time passing	7. The fear
4. The resistance	8. The few things which last

"Even after a few cocktails," Conner said. "I readily saw that this was a hefty order for my funny little stories."

Toward Home, New York Days, My Dog Skip, and other works. He loved to gather there with a group including his wife and son and an assortment of Mississippi and New Orleans friends, for a long evening of drinking, eating, and story-telling. Willie was noted as a practical joker and often traveled with several plastic roaches in his pocket that he delighted in slipping into salads or on the plates of unsuspecting friends at the restaurant.

Author Winston Groom never took his Oscar-winning character Forrest Gump to Galatoire's, but he took himself many times. Along with a large contingent of fellow Mobilians, Groom and his family have spent a lifetime in and out of Galatoire's. "It's my favorite New Orleans restaurant, he said. "They're number two for gumbo in the world; I'm number one."

Richard Ford, the Pulitzer-Prize-winning novelist, and his wife Kristina can often be seen at Galatoire's, as can another Pulitzer-Prize winner, Robert Olen Butler. He and his wife, novelist Betsy Dewberry, always dine at Galatoire's with friends when in town for the Pirate's Alley Faulkner Society's "Words & Music," an annual literary festival. On the last day of the 2002 event, Galatoire's hosted a gala luncheon featuring a panel of writers giving their views on "New Orleans Mon Amour: What Gives the Big Easy Its Glamour?" In 2003 the topic for another Monday literary luncheon was "Portraits of Memorable Places: Real and Imagined." Galatoire's itself was one of the real places discussed by the authors of this book.

Rosemary Daniell, poet, novelist, and memoirist, has written that her feeling about being in New Orleans has always been that she has "died and gone to heaven." "But I never felt it more than during my first visit to Galatoire's," where she was introduced to the Sazerac and was charmed by the cuisine and "the ambiance—the long mirrors, the desultory sense of time moving slowly and deliciously, without rush." Ever since, each visit to Galatoire's, which she calls an "event" because "it doesn't seem right to merely call it a lunch or a dinner," has reaffirmed her love of the place.

Daniell's judgment is reflective of the feelings of many a writer and artist throughout the century of Galatoire's existence. How could a creative spirit be anything but inspired by the remarkable atmosphere, ambiance, cast of characters, and ever evolving drama of one of the most unique restaurants in the city and, indeed, in America. Galatoire's is, in many ways, not merely a place to eat a meal or a place to meet people or watch people or listen in on conversations; it is a sourcebook, as Sheila Bosworth remarked, from which an author with any imagination can draw material for myriad stories.

Interestingly, writers—and customers in general—often imagine that "you can get anything you want" at "Galatoire's restaurant," a take-off on the 1960s song by folk singer Arlo Guthrie, "Alice's Restaurant." Certainly, one can find incongruent details in their writings. Sheila Bosworth's central character in *Almost Innocent* orders a Gin Fizz, a drink that is not served at Galatoire's. Patty Friedmann's Eleanor Rushing has a Pimm's Cup, a British concoction that is a specialty of the Napoleon House a few blocks away but has never been available at Galatoire's. In Ellen Gilchrist's short story "Mexico," Rhoda Manning eats fettuccini, which has never been on the menu. Jimmy Buffett describes Slade enjoying Pompano en Papillote (not a menu selection), and the old ceiling fans turning overhead (they have not been turned on in years because the motors are DC current and the French Quarter now runs on AC). Why these factual errors or failures of memory? Perhaps it is simply the fact that since the restaurant seems to be all things to all people who love it, the authors easily fantasize about experiencing there what the heart most desires.

Big Daddy doing a Bourbon Street dance

LEE McDANIEL

Big Daddy Was Here

*W*hen Galatoire's was being renovated in 1998, workmen were disposing of some of the furniture and fixtures that had been stored on the second floor where new dining rooms would be opened. Maitre d' Arnold Chabaud found in the waiters' dressing room an old mirror, which he took home as a memento. "As I cleaned off years of dust, dirt, and fingerprints," he recalled, "it was like a genie's lamp; when you rub it something happens." He discovered etched into the glass the inscription "Big Daddy Was Here." He knew immediately who had written it: Lee McDaniel, who had been a popular career waiter for fifty years, was a portly man referred to affectionately by the staff as "Big Daddy." "I thought of all the thousands of times Lee had looked into that mirror," Chabaud said, "and it was as if he were peering back at me now." He gave the mirror to Nancy Lee McDaniel Galkowski, who cherishes it as a Galatoire's artifact into which her father had gazed. She always wondered why several years earlier he had taken an etcher provided by Neighborhood Watch to work, and now the mystery was solved.

Lee McDaniel was born on November 2, 1920, at Hotel Dieu Hospital in New Orleans and christened Lee Addison McDaniel Jr. He was not expected to live, for he was so small he could fit into a cigar box, but live he did and thrive until his death on February 9, 1998. He grew up to serve in the U.S. Navy in World War II, then to become a waiter at the old Brennan's restaurant on Bourbon Street. He moved to Galatoire's in June 1946 after being recommended to Justin Galatoire by long-time waiter Lucien Thibodaux. By that time, he had married Mercedes Carmel Elgier and they had two children.

Their daughter, Nancy Lee, recalls that every afternoon she and her brother, Lee McDaniel III, would walk from St. Joseph school to the Jung Hotel, where they would drink a malt, then go on to Galatoire's, where they would sit on crates in the kitchen and play cards with the busboys until their father had time to come back and check on them. Then they would catch the streetcar on Canal Street and go to their godmother's house to wait for their mother to come from work to pick them up. "It was just his way of touching base to make sure we were all right," Nancy Lee said. In those early years Carnival parades still rolled along Bourbon Street and Lee and his wife and children would watch them from the second floor balcony with Miss Yvonne Galatoire's nieces.

Lee McDaniel had soon become a popular waiter among his colleagues as well as with his large coterie of customers, his "regulars." In a *Spirit* magazine article Mark Seal described him as "a burly Ralph Kramden type who mixes stout Sazeracs in tall ice-tea glasses and punctuates a customer's every utterance with two words: 'Okay, boss.'" Indeed, Lee called all the men "Boss" and all the ladies "Honey" or "Darling," which typifies the close relationship between the career waiters and their regulars. Nancy Lee Galkowski remembers that only one woman, who was from the North, ever took exception to that familiarity, whereupon Lee assured her that it would never happen again.

Among his regulars were a number of celebrities, including Sebastian Cabot, Phil Harris, Alice Faye, Brenda Lee, Barbara Britten, and Barbara Eden. "Whenever a celebrity would come in," Lee's daughter remembers, "Daddy would call home, put them on the phone, and say, 'Here, talk to my daughter.'" She never knew to whom she would be talking, she said.

Lee had an innate respect for the profession of waiting tables, and Nancy Lee recalls that whenever she or her brother were going to high school dances, her father would give them money and say, "Now be sure to tip the waiter or waitress," because he knew from experience the difficulty of their work. Richard Smith, who went to work at Galatoire's in the 1960s, remembered his colleague as "the best waiter I ever met. Lee knew his job and did it very well indeed."

When Lee had finished work at night, his wife and children would pick him up at the bar and strip club two doors from Galatoire's. Nancy inquired of her father often when he was going to take her in there and show her what went on, and when she was eighteen, he did just that. This was, after all, New Orleans!

He was a man with a love of life, compassion, and a sense of humor large enough to match his girth, and the stories that demonstrate these qualities are legion. One Christmas when Barbara and Sandy Maslansky came to Galatoire's, they asked for Lee, their preferee, and although he had been there earlier, he was nowhere to be found. After a while he showed up, carrying a doll; he had gone all around the Quarter until he found a store that was open so he could buy a gift for the Maslanskys' young daughter. Waiters cited his rich baritone voice that rang out over all the others on the frequent requests for "Happy Birthday" and that he was an avid and expert dancer. One waiter recalls looking out the door and watching him waltz around the street outside. On another occasion, when singer Andy Williams was there with his daughter, somebody paid Lee to sing "Hello, Dolly" to them and Williams joined in, along with the entire crowd.

Lee's humor is wonderfully exemplified in an incident remembered by Evelyn Cox, who, shortly after she and her husband Kyser Cox had moved to the French Quarter, invited out-of-town visitors from Birmingham, Alabama, to join them at Galatoire's for a celebratory meal. The Coxes went early to the restaurant so that their guests would not have to stand in line, and after a short wait were escorted in to a table. They asked for their usual waiter, Lee McDaniel, and promptly ordered Old-Fashioneds. After thirty minutes, Evelyn became anxious about the whereabouts of their friends, so she summoned their waiter and asked, "Lee, could you please go outside and ask 'Are the Hoars in line'?" Lee's mouth, she recalled, "formed a perfect O and he shook his head slowly." Mrs. Cox was incredulous and again urged the waiter, "Oh, Lee, just poke your head out the door and ask if the Hoars are in the line." Lee then simply said, "No, ma'am. I can't do that."

Totally outdone, Evelyn left the table and walked outside where she asked the maitre d', "Have you seen the Hoars from Birmingham?" Before the maitre d' could regain his composure, up walked Emily and Dick Hoar. After much hugging and kissing, introductions were made to the maitre d' and he explained his first thought upon hearing Evelyn's request. Eveyone laughed uproariously and the Hoars said it was not the first time such a misconception had been made. Inside, Lee was introduced to the Hoars, and again there was great laughter. That called for Old-Fashioneds all around.

The career waiters at Galatoire's were often passed down from generation to generation, and Dr. Richard Strub and his wife, Ann, the daughter of Evelyn and Kyser Cox, were *preferees* for Lee until he retired. "Dick and I always ordered the same thing," Ann recalls, "Shrimp Rémoulade and Trout Amandine," and one night Lee remarked, "You two are just like my wife and me, yum-yum togetherness." Then he burst into the laughter that was one of his signatures.

After fifty years at the restaurant, Lee had seen innumerable changes, but he remained devoted to the place that must have been like a second home to him. At the retirement party the restaurant gave for him, he reflected on those changes philosophically. There are stories among the staff of the ghosts who move noisily about on the upper floors of Galatoire's when no one is there. Since none of these revenants seems to be threatening, it is surely possible that one of them is Lee McDaniel, come back for another visit to the place he knew and loved so well.

KENNETH HOLDITCH

Act Two
The Cast

Scene Four

Stars
Waiters

"New Orleans may be the one city in the U.S. that is entirely devoted to pleasure, where the work ethic is blissfully missing and where locals prize a good waiter more than a stock market tip."
—Edmund White, novelist

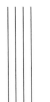 he real stars of Galatoire's are the almost thirty tuxedoed waiters, a sophisticated cadre of friends and servers who treat every day and evening as if it were the opening night of a Broadway show. Their busy, swirling bonhommie is what gives the restaurant its brilliant showmanship and makes every customer feel like a star in his own right.

"They have the best waiters in town," said attorney Peter J. Butler to the *National Law Review*. "They're not pretentious, they're very unassuming, very local, and I love them." For the patrons of Galatoire's, the waiters have always been much more than servers. "Your" waiter is friend, confidant, joke-teller, and kitchen advocate. S. M. Hahn, former restaurant critic for the *Times-Picayune*, wrote, "The waiters of Galatoire's are the last of a vanishing breed, for whom serving is both an art and a life calling. They are your link to the kitchen, and you dine well or not at their whim. Accept these terms, or don't bother."

Julia Reed tried to explain the popularity of Galatoire's waiters in *Southern Accents*. "On more than one occasion I have managed to sit in Galatoire's for upwards of six hours. The waiters are extremely indulgent and entertaining, and they just keep bringing you things so that it gets increasingly hard to leave." "There is never a rush to turn tables at Galatoire's," wrote Curtis Wilkie in the *Boston Globe* on October 17, 1991. "The establish-

Lee McDaniel, left, and a fellow waiter await the crowd, 1979

ment recognizes the markup on wine, champagne and liquor is more profitable than the price of a piece of fish. Glasses that are quickly emptied are just as quickly refilled."

As with top-flight restaurants in European capitals, those in New Orleans have always been distinguished by their career waiters, a tradition hard to find in other American cities, and one that seems to be dying out even in New Orleans. At Galatoire's, service is taken a step further; rather than waiters having regular tables, they have regular customers who ask for them. Rather than customers coming to the waiters' tables, the waiters come to them. This preferee system, in which diners may request their "own" waiter, makes Galatoire's an appealing haven for many. The world over, small but significant comfort is found in being recognized and nourished by a favorite server, and Galatoire's is especially renowned for the custom. "The tradition of Galatoire's is the waiter, the ambiance, and the food. It is that combination that keeps customers coming back. And it is a fragile combination," wrote prominent jeweler Norma Ackley. According to Deirdre Stanforth's *New Orleans Restaurant Cookbook:* "The waiters are an important factor in the enduring success of the restaurant." Thirty-five years later, Errol Laborde wrote in *New Orleans CityBusiness:* "Knowing, without asking, how a customer prefers his Sazerac or how much to spike a Café Brûlot is quite relevant to a world in which dining is not just the mere consumption of a meal, but a leisure activity." There is a unique symbiotic relationship between regulars and their waiters: a reliance for advice and attention on the

*M. C. Emmons and Gilberto
serving Café Brûlot*

part of patrons, and a camaraderie between friends on an equal footing. Some have grown old together. Homer Fontenot's wife, Della, sends homemade fudge and pralines to some of her husband's regular customers, who have come to look forward to those treats.

At most restaurants, in New Orleans or elsewhere, waiters tend to be cut from one fairly standard mold. But this is not true at Galatoire's. Something about the place functions to bring out the inner being. Almost without exception, the waiters tend to be individualistic: some ebullient, out-going, joking, gregarious; a few quiet, subdued, all business; some rather like stand-up comics; others more like attendants at a formal, solemn occasion—but all efficient, knowledgeable, all quick and attentive. "Service is very good to superb," wrote a reviewer. "At its most basic, it moves quickly and efficiently. But if you get someone who's turned up the charm, you may talk about this dinner for years to come." "I'd say the waiters are Southern gentlemen," Cecelia Slatten, a longtime customer, proclaimed. "They are. They really are." The standard was set long ago by Monsieur Justin, who told *New Orleans Magazine* in 1966, "I would rather think of a waiter as a caterer than as a servant. And they are, above all else, gentlemen." The servers represent the epitome of the Galatoire philosophy that a restaurant is a special haven, that preparing food is an art, and that expert service and attention to the dining experience must be given equal billing.

OLD SPICE

"I can still remember the magic of the first time I ever observed the making of Café Brûlot—I fell in love with the scent, the flame and the ritual. It was a winter evening years ago; I sat awestruck between my parents watching the waiter at Galatoire's serve the incredible, incandescent libation with the utmost flourish and pomp. All these many years later, the enchantment remains. There is something utterly spectacular and bewitching about the brew, with its enticing aroma of spice and citrus tinged with alcohol, all bathed in dancing blue flames."

SALLYE IRVINE, *ST. CHARLES AVENUE*, JANUARY 2000

Memorable waiters are legendary at Galatoire's, among them the late Cesar Rodriguez, who could juggle a roomful of call customers (preferees) at one time, and his cousin Gilberto, who made every woman feel as though she were the most beautiful creature ever to walk in the door. From days gone by, customers fondly remember Lee McDaniel, Nelson Marcotte, Joseph Camana, Bill Bordelon, Michel Virrolet, Simone LeMole, Hank LaViolette, Louie Chateau, Frank Tuffin, Russell Barnett, Juba Lebeau, Benny Pastor, Paul Lavagna—those men all put their stamp on the old restaurant. One who is greatly missed by scores of customers is Randy Berkshire, who retired and moved to Greenwich Village, then returned to live in New Orleans where he is rumored to be writing a book about his eventful life.

Back, from left to right, Richard Smith and Imre Szalai; front, from left to right, Charlie Grimaldi, Bryant Sylvester, wine salesman, John, Billy, and Homer Fontenot

The present team is eclectic, composed of twenty-two men and seven women with myriad ethnic backgrounds and winning personalities. Some have served at Galatoire's for decades. Imre Szalai (twenty-nine years), once a Hungarian refugee, usually leads the traditional birthday singing. John Fontenot (almost thirty years) is a Cajun who drives in from New Roads with the latest joke. Cousins Homer (thirty years), Harold Fontenot (forty-three years) and Louis LaFleur (thirty years) provide their own brand of humor and expertise. Dorris Sylvester (twenty-eight years), Richard Smith (twenty-three years), M. C. Emmons (thirteen years), Charlie Grimaldi (seventeen years),

Endre Toth (twenty-five years), Bryant Sylvester (sixteen years) and Billy Fontenot (eighteen years) have all made fine careers for themselves as waiters.

Once waiters are accepted at Galatoire's they usually make it a permanent home, and staff members say they feel like one big family. In fact, some of them *are* one big family. Seven members of the extended Fontenot family are prominent in the Galatoire's dining rooms. Harold Fontenot's son, Billy, and his cousins, John and Homer Fontenot, Dorris and Bryant Sylvester (another father and son) and Louis LaFleur are all waiters of long duration. Bryant often doubles as maitre d'. Bringing younger relatives along as waiters in the preferee system gives them a leg up in the beginning. Their fathers or cousins can hand off customers on their days off, or when they wish to cut back. Having a sponsor is a big help. "When I came here it was hard to get my own customers," said Harold Fontenot, who has been working at Galatoire's since 1960, when he was twenty-two. "I was more like a busboy. I would set up a table and then the people would ask for somebody else. But I helped all the waiters and they began helping me and referring me when they were off, and I started getting customers of my own. Most days I don't wait on anybody strange. I joke a lot with my customers. One man asked: 'Are your soft shell crabs frozen?' I told him: 'Not when you get 'em.'" Now Harold, who is semi-retired and doesn't work nights or on Sundays, has hundreds of regulars from all over the state and elsewhere, even foreign countries. "Galatoire's has been very good to me," Harold said. "They treated me like family, and my family was raised from here. I still wait on the Frey family and Chris Ansel. I'm the oldest waiter; I've been here the longest. Dorris is older in age, but not in service."

Angelle Wells, the restaurant's first female waiter, was on staff from 1994–1998, with a year's hiatus in New York City. Justin Frey was Angelle's entrée through mutual friends. "I never had the feeling that the restaurant was being pressured to hire a woman," she said, "but that it was preventive maintenance, to avoid any problems in the future." From the beginning, Angelle felt at home at Galatoire's, and she valued the assistance and direction of long-time career waiters such as Richard, Imre, and Randy. Some of the waiters, she said, "were a little apprehensive" and "were not sure it was going to work out, but they were never rude. All these men were complete gentlemen, very friendly and very helpful." Similarly, the customers were for the most part cordial and accepting. "I never saw rudeness," she said. "I definitely saw inquiry, curiosity: Who is this person? Why is she here?"

Since she was the one and only female waiter, Angelle tried hard not to "step on any toes." She related an early encounter with a group of businessmen who slipped a substantial amount of money into her hand and said, "Keep it up, honey, because I know how it is to be around these old crotchety men. Don't let them get you down." Angelle received a lot of encouragement such as that, and "I didn't let them get me down. I gave back as good as I got, which I don't think they expected." Whatever animosity she experienced, she believes, was not personal but rather "the nature of the beast of the business. You're in a high energy room and you're working quickly, trying to get everybody served at the same time, and still be sociable."

Soon after Angelle broke the gender barrier, more young women were added to the roster, including Shannon Jones, Rushell Bertucci Chabaud, and Sunny Holliday. Shannon credits Angelle with making life easier for the other female waiters who followed. "If she had been a meek person, the gentlemen might have intimidated her and things would have been different." Rushell remembers well her early days at the restaurant. "At first I was scared and intimidated, and for a while it was touch and go," she said, "but then Richard Smith and John Fontenot showed me the ropes." Now she has a large following of regulars, one of whom, Frank France, told her shortly after her arrival that he never thought he would see a woman waiter at Galatoire's. These days he tells her, "I don't want any of those old guys waiting on me any more!" Rushell is proud of what she has achieved and mentions one recent Friday when she worked non-stop all day and realized at closing time that she had not served a single stranger, only regulars. "Now they call me the Queen of Galatoire's."

Sunny Holliday, daughter of actor/director/producer Billy Holliday of *Fudgeripple Follies* cabaret fame, had worked at a chain restaurant before she came to Galatoire's as the seventh waitress to be hired. Early on in 1997, one of the old-time waiters told Sunny that she would never make it, but now the two have become good friends. "He swears he never said it but he did," she said, laughing. Like the other female waiters, Sunny at first had difficulty with some of the old-line patrons. One night when she and Shannon Jones were sitting at a back table waiting for an assignment, an elderly lady passed by, rapped on their table, and said, "I've got to tell you, I'm not happy you girls are here." Nevertheless, both she and Shannon have now developed substantial followings of their own. Sunny is grateful to her early mentor, Harold, who taught her how the Galatoire's show is staged. She tells her fellow waiters, "You don't know how good you have it here. I love it, I love it, I love it!"

Shannon, the second female waiter to be hired, has the distinction of having been Galatoire's first pregnant waiter. Her son Nathaniel, as blonde as she, is now three years old, and is everybody's pet when he comes to visit. Shannon drew a lot of attention as her tummy grew larger and larger. The wits predicted she would provide Galatoire's with its first on-site birth. That didn't happen, but Shannon did notice that after the birth, her new baby got extremely excited every time he heard "Happy Birthday." She was convinced

From left to right, busboy Manuel Martin, Richard Smith,
Suzanne Rodriguez, and David Gooch

that it was because he'd heard the song so much while in the womb. "Even when he was a tiny baby he knew that song when he heard it."

About the time the first female waiters were being hired, so were the first black waiters: first Shelly Landry, who is now at another restaurant; then John Brown, now retired and working as a barber; then Gerard Beasley, who climbed the ladder from dishwasher to kitchen manager to busboy and finally waiter; and then Steven Charles, who, Angelle said, "started as a pot-washer when he was just a little boy." Working with a variety of waiters as a busboy, Gerard not only learned the trade, but also began to build up a clientele with his easy-going manner, so that when he was promoted, he already had a following.

Although a training program is now in place (newly employed waiters work in the kitchen two days, bus tables for two days, then follow a waiter for two days), the best way for a waiter to learn the ropes is from an older waiter. Bryan Casey's mentor and good friend was the popular Randy Berkshire, and "he taught me all the tricks of the trade. When he retired, I inherited ninety percent of his customers; they were passed to me because I worked with him. He was a classic." Bryan and his brother Scott, who has been a waiter at Galatoire's for about six months, are nephews of maitre d' Arnold Chabaud. "Randy's a great guy and a gambler," said Bryan. "He and Louis LeFleur and I used to go to the casinos in Mississippi every Monday to watch Randy lose his money." Bryan, who began at Galatoire's in 1996, still serves people from all over who ask, "Where's Randy?"

Waiting tables is not governed by the minimum-wage law, so most waiters depend upon tips for their living, and Galatoire's is no exception. ("I made and still make $2.13 an hour," said Harold. "If you make so much in tips, you are not required to get paid minimum wage.") This is called a tip credit by the federal government. For some it can take quite a long time to build up a clientele under the preferee system. But not for newcomer Wayne Brooks, who began in 2001 and who is former chef Milton Prudence's brother-in-law. He worked as a dishwasher for forty-five days and as a busboy for fourteen months before being made waiter. "I had no trouble at all getting regular customers because when I was busing tables, I saw that each waiter had his own routine and I learned how to do one of my own. It's all in how you walk up to the table and introduce yourself."

Homer Fontenot has more than a hundred regulars and also said it did not take long to acquire them. Homer began in 1961, then left for Le Ruth's across the river for a few years. "I missed this place; it was my first love and I still love it. I love the people who come here. I love the food. It has the biggest local following of any restaurant anywhere." The only profession Homer ever had is waiting on tables, and "I made a good living all these years." In the old days business was more seasonal and some of the waiters took summer breaks to work at northern resorts, among them Nelson Marcotte and John Fontenot, who would sometimes go to the Palmer House in Chicago. "The summers were rough here," John said, "we used to draw unemployment because people didn't come in for conventions like they do now." So the young waiter would get other jobs, "any way to make money. I would paint. Go to Mackinaw Island in Michigan and work in summer resorts like the Greenbriar." But always he returned to Galatoire's.

Tall, suave Richard Smith also left for a while—"For twenty years (1964–1984) I had a little vacation in San Francisco by way of Chicago and Houston." He worked at Fisherman's Wharf for a while until a strike in July and August, then "I picked up and came home." Back in 1960, the twenty-one-year-old French Quarterite was greatly impressed by his job interview with Monsieur Justin. "It took a grand total of fifteen minutes."

"(French accent) Yeah, young man, can I help you?"

"Yes, I'm looking for a job."

"What kind of a job?"

"I'm a waiter, sir."

"Where you work at?"

"I was at Brennan's for a long time, and at Arnaud's. I'm working at Commander's now."

"Do you know how to make drinks?"

"Yessir, I do."

"Do you drink?"

Not wanting to get trapped, Richard replied, "I am a waiter, sir," which might imply, of course, that all waiters drink.

"You know how to mix drinks. You're a waiter. There's the bar. You fix your own drinks, and do not stagger in my dining room. If you drink beer drink local, not premium. Come in on Tuesday."

Richard recalled another thing he loved about Mr. Justin: "You were thrown into the pond to sink or swim—no following somebody around to watch. You took the next party in the door." Richard's return after twenty years' absence was like a time warp. Nothing, not even the kitchen had changed. "I walked out of here in '64, walked back in '84 and it was like I'd never left."

Known for his dry wit (writer Julia Reed called him "the driest man in Louisiana"), Richard and other long-time waiters have built up client lists of hundreds of satisfied customers who never go away (five-hundred-plus, he said, of whom at least two hundred are local), often becoming close friends with them. "My first visit to Galatoire's was with my mother sixty-three years ago," said one of Richard's regulars, Leonard Parrish. "She told me: 'You must get to know and trust your waiter.'" Others of Richard's customers who "never go away" are Coleman Adler, Joe Sevier, Norman Scott, Jack Gordon, and Paul and Joanne Ippolito. Another, stockbroker Lee Murphy, tells of a colleague who knew about his Galatoire's habit and said to Richard, "I guess Mr. Murphy is in here every day of the week." Richard answered very seriously, "while looking her straight in the eye, 'Positively not, we are closed on Monday.'"

Harold Fontenot goes hunting with E. J. Caire on his sugar plantation in Edgard, Louisiana, and waits on Caire's table when he dines once or twice a month at Galatoire's. In another venue that camaraderie would have never developed, but this is Galatoire's, where things are different—and egalitarian. Caire has been going to Galatoire's since 1940 when he was ten years old. He remembers his first trip with his grandfather, coming from their plantation and sugar mill forty miles upriver. "My grandfather had stock in D. H. Holmes and Hibernia Bank and after his board meetings we came to Galatoire's and his chauffeur waited outside on Bourbon Street. I was very impressed because my grandfather left a ten-dollar tip and that was a lot of money in those days. I couldn't believe that anybody would tip so much."

Attorney William "Billy" Broadhurst, who lived in Crowley until about ten years ago (and now lives in the French Quarter), first came to Galatoire's with his parents at the age of five. Their waiter was Joseph, who had been a cook/chef at Galatoire's until he realized he could make more money being a waiter. "They made so much money in tips back then," said Broadhurst.

A waiter arrives in style, circa 1940

"Joseph had a good clientele with a lot of money. I know people who would tip one hundred dollars in the 1940s, because the waiters would cook your food and make your drinks and it was just like coming home." Joseph gave Broadhurst's mother, Marian (now ninety-three), many Galatoire's recipes, "but the quantities were huge." As a treat when her son didn't go to New Orleans with the family, Joseph would send his mother home with a cup custard in a brown ramekin. "Now I have a great collection of Galatoire's custard cups," Broadhurst said.

Once upon a time waiters would go into the kitchen and cook a dish to special order for favorite customers, and many of them were excellent cooks with their own specialties. Michelle Heidelberg still talks of the dish her waiter Michel made one time when she could not decide between Trout Amandine and shrimp. "He made Shrimp Amandine which was never on the menu but should have been. It was divine!" Another time he served her favorite soufflé potatoes stuffed with chocolate ice cream for dessert. "It was a much better dish than it sounds," she said. One night Cesar went into the kitchen to smoke such delicious steaks for some of his regulars that memories still linger. The delicious Crawfish Etouffée on the menu is said to be Nelson's recipe. "He was Cajun like me," said John Fontenot. "We had times in the afternoon when there were only two cooks on duty," Harold Fontenot explained. "From two to five o'clock, it was like a skeleton crew back there, and we might not get more than ten orders during those hours. The guys would go sit in the back yard, and the chef would say, 'Look I'm going to show you how to do this but don't bother me anymore because I'm on my break.'" So it was understood that the waiters would learn how to cook everything. "But now it's different," said John. "We're bombarded with customers all the time, at least three cooks stay behind the line, and a lot of the young waiters come in and don't even know how to cook." "When I first started here, the waiter was doing everything," said M. C. Emmons. "I had never seen a place like that before. We had a one on one with the customer so anything a customer needed, we were there for him." Regulars are still pampered with their special orders—off-menu items—but these dishes are mostly cooked to order by kitchen personnel, not their waiter.

A waiter's advantage lies in making sure that every detail, from drinks to service to the meal itself, is exactly to a customer's taste. They know their clients will be returning, unlike most places where you will never see the same diners twice, especially in restaurants that cater to the tourist trade. Reynard Lavigne, a former captain at Windsor Court's Grill Room, points out that "A hotel's visitors return in seasons." But in contrast, "at Galatoire's you see them weekly, so it's much more important to be consistent and remember their habits and wishes." Reynard is still working on his call list. "It usually takes five years, they say. When I got my very first call customer I found out what it was all about here. It took time; you're not just walking in the door; you're walking into a family."

That family feeling is not exclusive to locals. Many out-of-towners are addicted to the preferee system and for years have asked for the same waiter when they come to town. "We always ask for Louis (LaFleur)," said Judy and John Sargent, former residents of New Orleans who now live in Delaware. John Sargent first learned to love Galatoire's as a child when his oil-patch parents brought him over from Corpus Christi at least three times a year. "We always had that big table 22 and it was a gala occasion. My father always asked for Louis, so I inherited him." For Sargent, Galatoire's "typifies

BICYCLE GUY

Jim Vanderhoeven, a customer of M. C. Emmons, flies down in his plane every week from Alexandria. He has been coming to Galatoire's for thirty years and in good weather often rides his bicycle from his French Quarter apartment to the restaurant and locks it to the hitching post outside. One day when he couldn't catch M. C.'s eye, he allowed newcomer Reynard Lavigne to serve him. "Reynard told me, 'I'm glad to see that you save up to come here.' Why do you think I have to save up? 'Because you come on a bicycle.' He thought I was too poor to buy a car."

New Orleans and I wish that all of New Orleans was more like that." His wife added: "I like the fact that things stay the same: fans, mirrors, white tile floors, waiters in tuxes. And they are all so friendly—they want you to have wonderful food and a good time."

Camaraderie among waiters is exceptional, and most of them have at least one trait in common—almost all of them believe waiting tables at Galatoire's is the best of all possible jobs. ("I felt it was such a privilege to work there," said Angelle.) According to Assistant Manager and Maitre d' Jacques Fortier, who was hired in 1999, the wait staff includes self-styled philosophers, football coaches, theologians, national security advisors, and the like. Gene Bourg remembers when his sautéed trout

Louis LaFleur napping

strips were accompanied by "a brief but enlightening lecture on the current economic situation in South America." A recent addition to the wait staff is a bona fide racetrack announcer, Tony Bentley, who also sings in the opera chorus. "We cover all the bases," said Louis LaFleur. "We wait on people from all over the world, and from them we learn so much wisdom," said John Fontenot. "We pick up advice from them, and we learn how to read people." He laughs his Cajun-joker laugh. His eyes glitter. "To be a psychiatrist you need to

DUKING IT OUT

A story related by Betty DeCell illustrates the waiters' aplomb. "Two elderly gentlemen in seersucker suits were lunching on a busy Friday, when suddenly they began punching each other across the table—a real fist fight. The room got deathly quiet. Eight waiters surrounded the table so nearby diners would not be disrupted and just let them duke it out. One man fell under the table and a waiter pulled him out and sat him up at the table again. It was handled so discreetly, with such finesse. We all wondered what would be a waiter first." John is famous for his routine in which he describes to new customers the soft-shell crab, "so fresh they're playing the piano," which he demonstrates with his fingers. "It was great just to hear some of the conversations," said Angelle.

Most people know the waiters by their first names, a good thing because having so many relatives on staff can get confusing. For example, when a lady came in and asked to be waited on by "Mr. Fontenot," Fortier asked, "Which Fontenot?" She replied, "The one from Ville Platte," and Fortier informed her, "That could be either John or Harold." "It's Harold," she said. Until recently, there were no bartenders and the waiters mixed all the drinks. Once a customer insisted that Harold had not made his Scotch and soda with the Dewar's White Label he had ordered, and said he could tell the difference. Harold brought a brand new bottle right to the table, opened it, and poured and mixed the drink on the spot. Another time TV personality Jeanne Nathan told him once too often that her soda-on-the-side was flat. Fed up, Harold brought her a new bottle, unopened but shaken, "and when she opened it, it fizzed out all into her lap. She took it good-naturedly and laughed and said: 'Well, I won't tell you that again.'"

Almost forty years ago, Deirdre Stanforth wrote that the family believed "if waiters are to enjoy work, you must treat them well, so they receive a great deal of loyalty from their staff." One of the things that has made Galatoire's work through the decades is the mutual devotion between the staff and family members, a symbiotic relationship that is rare in business. The old-time waiters speak with affection of "Mr. Justin" ("Jus-tan," those who speak French called him, and in the old days, most of the waiters were bilingual) and "Mr. Leon," "Mr. Rene," and "Madame Yvonne." The ratio then was seventeen waiters to forty tables. It has remained essentially the same, although the wait staff now numbering twenty-nine also serves the new upstairs dining rooms, where a total of twenty-six tables await special parties and customers who are primarily from out of town. "Upstairs is a little quieter, more settled down," said Gerard Beasley. "With most of the locals downstairs, it's louder."

happen next, but nothing did. The two completed lunch, then left together, fast friends again. One was bleeding from his nose all over his shirt and tie. After they left, waiters surrounded the table again, and one crawled underneath to retrieve the silverware they had knocked off." Later, one man's son was told by his father that the fight began when one called the other "an epithet," but he wouldn't reveal what it was. The next time the DeCells came to Galatoire's they asked to be seated in the non-fighting section.

Stanforth also noted the fact that many Galatoire's waiters know instinctively what their customers desire. "The waiter has an importance that is unparalleled elsewhere," she wrote. Obviously, her words are still true. "I always take the advice of my waiter," said Wendy Fisher from Chicago, when she was in town on a consulting job. "I thought I wanted fried oysters today, but my waiter, Endre Toth, said, 'No, they're too small today.' He recommended the Crabmeat Yvonne. It was perfect." Fisher dines at Galatoire's every time she comes to New Orleans, and "I have yet to see a menu and I've always had a marvelous meal." Many others invoke the same tale. "Cesar was an amazing character," said Ken Solis. "He would never write anything down and bring out anything he wanted, and his customers loved it." Francis X. Bege (called "Bege"), a newcomer who calls himself "the oldest rookie in the U.S.A.," likes Galatoire's because "The waiters are pros. They know about food." A longtime restaurateur and food consultant from Philadelphia, Bege came to New Orleans to retire, but instead landed at Galatoire's as a waiter. "Where else in the world is being an older waiter an asset?" He told his wife twenty years ago, "Someday I'm going to work at Galatoire's. It's such a classic; it's food-driven; it's not pretentious; its ambiance is just its ambiance. It just is what it is."

Crabmeat Yvonne

1 pound fresh mushrooms, sliced
1/2 cup + 2 tablespoons clarified butter
2 pounds fresh backfin lump crabmeat
Salt and white pepper to taste
6 fresh artichoke bottoms, boiled and
    sliced

6 toast points
2 tablespoons finely-chopped parsley
2 lemons, cut into wedges

In a large skillet, sauté the mushrooms in the clarified butter for 10-15 minutes. Then add the crabmeat and season with salt and white pepper. Add the artichoke bottoms and sauté gently until heated thoroughly. Serve over toast points and garnish with finely chopped parsley and a lemon wedge.
SERVES 6.

There was a time when Galatoire's waiters were pampered like fine race horses. The custom was for a different waiter to open up each morning. When Mr. Justin arrived, he would take a tray, fill it with shot glasses full of liquor, and take it to the kitchen for everyone to make a drink if they chose. "Give my boys a shot to prime their pumps and get them started," he would say. Not every waiter drank, but those who did could take a drink when they felt like it. "Just don't wobble in my dining room," Mr. Justin would tell them. Each waiter had space in the refrigerator for his own drink, usually in an iced tea glass. "Now waiters don't drink on the job," said John, who never drinks himself, "but back in the old days, they could drink, boy, iced tea glasses full. They could put it away." When smoking in the back, the waiters would place their cigarettes in a certain way that was their own so they could come and go. After closing time, when customers were still finishing up their late dinners, according to the 1966 *New Orleans Magazine* article, waiters were sitting in the back ordering from the menu without restriction. "Just don't waste it and don't order the prime beef," warned Mr. Justin. Today, with a hundred employees, two special meals per day are prepared for the staff by long-time cook Wallace Shelby and served at 10:30 A.M. and 4:15 P.M. each day.

Many favorite Galatoire's tales concern the waiters. For example, there was the time the fresh-from-Peru Gilberto was asked if Galatoire's served sweetbreads. Still shaky with his English, he answered, "No, no sweet bread, only French bread." Or when John Fontenot's sauce dish got knocked into the air and the sauce landed in a lady's wig. And the time Louis LaFleur was standing out in front of the restaurant and was asked by a camera crew if he used Dr. Scholl's Foot Pads. Yes, he said, and was invited to make a TV ad for which he received residuals for years. Everyone still laughs about Clarence ("Red"), a busboy for forty years who was known to nap in odd corners and got locked in the restaurant one night. When he was rescued, he was completely snockered, having helped himself to the liquor supply. "He was the one with false teeth that always clattered," someone remarked.

Jackson Browne, former maitre d', tells of another funny LaFleur named Jeff, who was fond of teasing tourists. His standard line when asked what was good on the menu was: "If it ain't good, it ain't on there." During Jackson's tenure (1984–1990) a police detail always came in with the person who opened the restaurant and waited until the full staff arrived. (This custom began long ago when Doug Wynne was pistol-whipped and the safe robbed early one morning when he was opening up.) At night an officer would come in about 8:00 or 9:00 P.M. and wait for Galatoire's to close. The locals all knew this procedure. One night some tourists noticed the uniformed policeman sitting in back and asked Jeff why he was there. Jeff replied: "They got a bad bunch of waiters here at Galatoire's, and the police is here to protect the customers from 'em."

There was a waiter known in some circles as "Gloria Swanson," who was at Galatoire's for a brief time. One night he went home with a customer, but when bidden to climb into an open coffin, "Gloria" left the scene rapidly. This is New Orleans, after all, home of the Vampire Lestat. And then there was the Spanish busboy who left work early years ago, only to reappear on TV as the hijacker of a plane to Cuba.

The waiters still laugh about the longtime waiter who was getting old and somewhat senile, so the Galatoire family decided that rather than retire him they would make him a maitre d' and put him on the door. A group of Hollywood people came in and after they were seated—because in those days jackets were always required—he went and got one of the Salvation Army jackets kept for emergencies and insisted that one of the women put it on because he thought she was a man. A waiter called "Cupcake" would often crawl into a corner and fall fast asleep when business was slow. Leander Perez Jr., the District Attorney of Plaquemines Parish, came every day for lunch. ("He always drank green chartreuses, but he never got drunk," said M. C. Emmons.) He liked to play practical jokes, so one day Perez decided to give the peacefully sleeping Cupcake a hotfoot. A shoe on fire definitely woke him up, but later Cupcake sent Perez a bill for his shoes and he paid up and laughed about it.

An oft-told tale is one Paul Lavagna told *New Orleans Magazine* in 1966. A young man ordered Crawfish Bisque (then served with stuffed crawfish heads) and told Paul he had "come 3,000 miles just to have a plate of it." When Paul returned to remove the soup plate, there were no shells left in or under the plate. Paul was so surprised he even, discreetly, looked under the table. Back in the kitchen, he told Mr. Justin that his customer had eaten all the bisque, heads and shells, too. "Well," said Mr. Justin, "let us hope he either has very strong teeth or a very strong stomach."

Many stories circulate even now about the politically-incorrect joke-teller Nelson Marcotte. "He had an unbelievable call business. Everyone called for him," said John, who inherited Nelson's position as chief Cajun. Once Nelson told Gilberto: "Gilbert, every time you talk your English gets worse." After taking a look, Nelson said to someone who called his attention to a bug in her salad, "Better than half a bug." Nelson thought nothing of telling jokes that were too risqué to put into a book, such as the famous Five Reasons You Don't Want To Be An Egg. "One of the greatest waiters Galatoire's ever had was Nelson," said stockbroker Lee Murphy. "He is now serving drinks to Donald Stephens (a longtime Galatoire's devotee) at the Galatoire's in the sky."

Carroll Regan from Tallulah, Louisiana, described Nelson as "an Archie Bunker type" and as an example selected a day when Nelson was waiting on a table where two children were seated with their parents. When their food arrived, the young boy asked Nelson, "Would you please bring me some catsup?" "Without changing his expression, Nelson simply said 'No!' There was an incredulous silence; I then noticed that the father had a slight smile on his face, as if to say, 'Son, you just learned a valuable lesson: you don't put catsup on your food at Galatoire's.'"

Nelson had a heart attack one day while at work in the restaurant; Leon III took him to the emergency room. From then on, he only worked nights. When Nelson died in 1989 it was a sad day for many of his friends among the staff and customers. "Having Nelson watch over my group made me feel so cared for!" said Laura Bayon Reichard. "I came to feel, as the years went by, that Nelson watched us all grow up and enter the adult world. When I saw the notice in the paper, I felt I had lost one of my special friends. I wrote a note to his widow and daughter, never having met them, and got a wonderful letter in return. They told me that they were Nelson's family, but he had another family—and it was people like me, people he waited on for all those years. I 'inherited' Harold, who was Nelson's cousin, as my new waiter."

The preferee system has always been popular with waiters and customers, but it sometimes falls apart if a waiter has too many of his or her preferees coming in at the same time. There is a method of scheduling to insure that waiters serve no more than five tables at one time, this being the maximum that management believes can be handled well. "But some customers get very upset when they can't have their favorite," said David Gooch. "All the regulars want to be served by their preferred waiters, so on busy days it is a hard thing to cut the waiter off at five tables." Although some regulars have a shortlist of favorite waiters for that eventuality, others have been known to make their displeasure known none too subtly.

One of Richard Smith's regulars, Wayne Garrett, is known to all as the Tall Man because he stands at six feet, eight inches. When he came in one day for lunch, he was told that Richard had his quota of customers and he would have to take another waiter. The Tall Man obligingly agreed to do so and sat down at a table, whereupon a new young waiter came up and asked him what he would like to drink. "I'll have my usual," the Tall Man said. "What is your usual, sir?" the newcomer asked. "My usual waiter knows," answered the Tall Man. Shaken up, the young man went to the desk and asked who the man's usual waiter was, and when told, he sought out Richard to find out the name of the man's usual drink. Richard replied: "I don't know what it is today; I can always tell by the expression on his face."

The quota method is simple. The desk tallies requests for specific waiters and if no specific request is made or if the preferred waiter already has his or her quota, a rotation system kicks into place. But to avoid offending regular customers, there are other, less direct, methods of keeping everybody happy. One way to get around the five-table limit was related by former maitre d' Ken Solis. For example, if regular customers arrived to find their waiter already fully booked, the waiter could bring the check to one of

Galatoire family members, David Gooch, left, lifting a toast, and Chris Ansel Jr., seated in front of him with loyal Galatoire's staff members

his tables, "even though those customers had no intention of leaving," tell them to pay the bill, and then they could stay as long as they wanted, receiving a second bill at the real end of their meal. "As long as a check was on the table, the waiter could take another table," said Solis. "The older waiters all knew how to play the game."

A great deal of a waiter's success, indeed, of the restaurant's success, is working in cooperation with an on-the-spot busboy—sometimes an under-

GHOSTS IN THE GARRET

Former longtime Maitre d' Ken Solis recalls the strange noises that sometimes emanate from the restaurant, even when it is empty. Before the renovation, the second floor had not been used for half a century. The building was constructed with two sets of doors. One opened onto the alleyway; the other opened onto stairs that led to the second floor and third floors. Owners and employees could go up to the third floor, where Gabriel Galatoire had his sumptuous apartment for a number of years, without going through the dining room. Ken recalls that after Gabriel died, "I used to have some waiters and busboys on the third floor say you could hear something moving." He would always tell the new busboys who went up the third floor to get linens from the cabinets there that it

study for a job of waiter. Galatoire's is known for its excellent and unobtrusive service, its hot bread delivered almost before the first loaves cool down, its water glasses always filled, and its cocktails and utensils close at hand at all times. Busboys play much more than bit parts in that reputation. Just as customers have their favorite waiters, so waiters have their favorite busboys. M. C. Emmons explained that a new system is in place for the assignment of busboys. "We used to pick our busboy," he said, "so a busboy would work with three or four waiters. I had Linzie or I had Manuel or others, but now they rotate. We pay them a certain percentage of what we make, so they are on a pool system. Often the customers give side tips to the busboys." Because the waiters liked him, before being promoted, Gerard Beasley worked with five or six of them, and said "the more waiters you had, the more money you made."

The busboy of longest standing, Linzie Brown, has long been called "Mr. Galatoire," since Dr. Victor Chisesi started doing so because the restaurant's name was embroidered on Linzie's white coat. By now Linzie has earned the nickname, as he's a local favorite recognized by regular customers everywhere he goes. "You take care of them, they take care of you," he said. Linzie, who has reared two sons, got his job after being recommended by a brother-in-law in March of 1963, "the year Kennedy was shot." He was seventeen at the time, and it was his first job. "This place has been like my family," he said. In the nineties, when offered a position as waiter, Linzie turned it down, feeling that he was perfectly cast in his busboy role. Linzie is renowned as a man of very few words but very good service, and waiters commend the fact that he never has to be told but always seems to know intuitively what is needed. Despite the broad smile on his face and the friendly response to any remark or question, he is all work. One thing you can count on when he buses your table: before your French bread can get cold, a fresh pair of hot loaves wrapped in a napkin appears on your table as if by magic. Your water

was haunted "and they would laugh at me. Then I would send them upstairs and sneak up behind them and stand in the entranceway they couldn't see and say, 'Boo.' Yes, that caused some commotion, believe me!"

During construction on the second floor, workmen often heard noises on the unused third floor and would grab hammers and rush up the stairs thinking somebody had broken in, but they could never find anybody up there. "But all said they heard noises up there," Solis recalls. "I got to go up into the attic on the old iron ladder, and the place is full of old spittoons and things." Things perhaps including a few noisy ghosts?

Longtime busboy, Linzie Brown, known as "Mr. Galatoire's"

glass is always filled to the brim from your table's water carafe. "Mr. Galatoire" has an eagle eye and is taking expert and hugely comforting care of your table in every respect. He keeps a watch not only on the tables to which he is assigned, but others. Always, Linzie is there, quietly, efficiently, providing what is needed—and has been for forty years.

Surely no other restaurant in this country has a more efficient, individualistic, or dramatic wait staff than Galatoire's. With a plaintive look on his usually smiling face, John said, "We got older. We grew up with the restaurant, you know." Through the years, waiters have died, retired, or moved away from the city, and new faces have appeared to replace them; but the uniqueness of the restaurant, to which waiters contribute a large share, remains unaltered. If you arrive early, before they begin seating customers, you will see the waiters calmly folding napkins, setting up their tables, preparing for the hubbub of another day—another show. It will be very much like all the others and yet anticipation is there, because, as always, this is a play without a script—a theater of improvisation. Anything might happen, and often does, so the actors must be good. At the end of that day, no matter how hard they have worked or how tired they may be, their good humor is still intact, their patience, though tried, still functioning, their faces perhaps strained but still capable of smiling, for they know they have played their roles, extremely important roles, very, very well.

Imre celebrating Parish Sullivan's birthday, December 14, 1992;
from left to right, Loren Remsberg, Imre Szalai, Parish,
Genny Hardison, and Loren O'Connor

IMRE SZALAI

From Hungary With Love, March 19, 1998

❖❖❖❖❖

*A*s Imre Szalai rolls out his fractured English at warp speed,
his merry eyes open so wide his eyebrows almost disappear into his receding hairline. When he laughs, the bright eyes
close until the slits almost disappear into his cheeks. It's so much
fun to watch him, I almost forget to listen. His accent meets and
conquers my slow Southern drawl; I catch perhaps a third of the
exciting story he tells me—a story that begins in a far country many
years ago.

With a short, pouter-pigeon physique, he stands ramrod
straight, and clicks his heels in greeting—a leftover from his military

training many years ago in Hungary. Imre has called Galatoire's home since March 11, 1974, when he came to New Orleans as a refugee and without knowing a word of English.

"Mr. Rene Galatoire give me job and I speak no English," he says in amazement. Chris Ansel recalls that Imre, after receiving a phone call telling him he was hired, immediately came a long way across town by bus to thank Ansel for arranging the interview with Rene. "Mr. Rene Galatoire fix drinks for me until I learn how. His whole family help me; all his friends still ask for me as waiter. The other waiters help me; take my orders; Mr. Rene give me thirty-two dollars a week in envelope; I carry the plates."

At some point during his apprenticeship Imre began holding his own—"all day long I listen and memorize"—although writing up the tickets has always been, and still is, a trial. "I hate that computer." He points over his shoulder to the big machine now looming over the old-fashioned desk in back, and shows me the pink pad on which he has scratched out his own version of a table ticket. It is incomprehensible to me, but then so is Galatoire's new computer to Imre. Imre's customers often keep those tickets to show their friends from out of town.

"After first day, I understand nothing, but I stay to eat. I eat everything for fat. Mr. Rene he say, 'eat and drink everything, but don't steal.' I weigh one hundred pounds when I get to America, and now the good life it is killing me." He laughs and pats his round little stomach.

Times were hard in Hungary for those not Communist party members. "My brother and sister and I all good students, but no university for us because not Communist." The Communists confiscated the prosperous Szalai farm that had been their home since 1726 and the family was forced into a hand-to-mouth existence. "It is terrible, but we have to steal food from the pigs," he says.

How did he manage to get out? "When I am drafted into army and become border guard, they teach you how to escape. Always two guards, each guard the other; never know which guard; never the same guards together. I decide to go into Yugoslavia. In Austria they can shoot you, but in Yugoslavia they catch you and bring you back, but can't shoot. I send other guard into building to look for noise and then I disappear in woods. In fifteen days I walk across Yugoslavia and cross into Italy; I sleep in haystacks; I have to lose uniform so I take clothes from—you know, wood cross they put up to scare birds away." He flaps his arms out like a scarecrow. "I give up in Trieste police station. I speak other languages, but no English, so I think to live in Germany; but friend tell me that America is best place to be and taking not so much time to get in. I wait seven months for Germany; when I change to America, I wait just two months and I am here." He was twenty-eight years old.

Now he is the second oldest waiter at Galatoire's—not in age, but longevity. "Seven or eight have died," he says. Among them, Nelson Marcotte was one of his main mentors. "Nelson and Harold take care of me," he says, remembering Nelson's well-known penchant for jokes. "He was always telling jokes. One day he tell me to bring two big serving spoons to his customer's table—a lady with big (his hands mimic big breasts). He say to her to use the big spoons so she won't spill on them." Imre shakes his head and we laugh at Nelson's cheek. "Nelson teach me what to say when people ask 'What comes with food?' I say, 'The check!'"

While learning English, Imre had his own way of being agreeable. One of his recurrent and enduring comments is "Good choice! Good choice!"—whatever the customer has ordered. "I say 'thank you, thank you, thank you' all the time (he still does this); and 'yes, yes, yes' to everything people say. Customers they tell me 'Imre, you should not always say yes; you should sometime say no.'" He laughs and clicks his heels together. "But I am very good listener."

Imre calls earlier times "the good oil times," when Galatoire's line began before 10:00 A.M. and often reached around the corner and halfway down the block. "Before Godchaux and big Canal Street department stores closed we had so many lady shoppers on Saturdays and holidays. And many people from Natchez and Baton Rouge. When New Orleans had many shows and symphony and opera, many old time people come—all nice families, even children."

Imre's own children are his pride and joy. He and his wife since 1971, a Spanish señorita named Carmen Davila whom he met on Valentine's Day in 1970, have a boy and girl, both of whom speak five languages. His daughter, Marcella Del Carmen, went to Stanford University as an undergraduate and graduated in 2003 from Boston University Law School. His son, Imre Stephen, was valedictorian at Jesuit High School, then did his undergraduate work at Yale and graduated from Columbia Law School. "Smart kids," he says.

"I never say they have to be best, but I say to do best they can," he says. "I tell them 'You have to study for me.' I show them old suitcase I keep in attic. It has what I bring from Italy: two pants, two shirts, two shoes, two socks, two underwear—all I have then. They have no family here, but friends who know me here better than family. Customers so good to me; always giving me something, they say, 'Is for the children.'"

Imre tells me of a few Galatoire's regulars who were particularly generous to his family, but asks me not to use their names because he might inadvertently hurt the feelings of someone he has overlooked. One is an Uptown grand dame who for many years has been coming to Galatoire's for dinner. He has never forgotten "so beautiful was the dress" she gave him for his baby girl. Another is a prominent local judge who helped Imre's son get into Columbia Law School.

"Everybody so good to me, even customers of other waiters. New Orleans people most kindest people in the world. Sometimes I was crying."

MARDA BURTON

Act Two
The Cast

Scene Five

Costars
Customers

"More than a place to satisfy one's hunger, Galatoire's is a place where time and the outside world fade from consciousness."
—Gene Bourg, *Gourmet Magazine,* October 1996

o its regular customers Galatoire's is much more than a restaurant. It is a haven, a club, a stage. In the simple rectangular room, each table is a setting for its own script and its own stars. Wall-to-wall mirrors reflect high glee and melodrama with equal clarity. The naked light bulbs overhead illuminate brightly because, as career waiter Bryan Casey said, "customers want to be seen and to see other people. It's a big laid-back party, and I have the best job in the city." In a social milieu that regards good food and good fun as good reasons for living, party-loving New Orleanians dine out on stories about the goings-on at Galatoire's; and regulars feel it incumbent upon themselves to remember it all.

Galatoire's is in the genes for New Orleanians," said Doug MacCash in the September 1, 2000 *Times-Picayune,* and artist George Dureau is a good example. "I was eight or nine the first time I came here with my father," he said. "I would have been the adorable child in the seersucker suit. It was in 1939 or '40; World War II hadn't been invented yet. People grow up in this place." And with the passing of time, they age. One of the most enduring and endearing sights at Galatoire's is the entrance of very elderly people, who are obviously longtime customers and persist in returning to their favorite restaurant, despite the difficulties involved. Surely it would be much simpler to go to a good restaurant in their neighborhood, thus spared the trouble of driving or being driven into the French Quarter, finding a parking lot that is

*From left to right, actress and chanteuse Becky Allen,
Andre De Labarre, and George Dureau*

*From left to right, Michele Galatoire, Mickey Easterling, and
Leonard Parrish, enjoying a meal*

not filled, and getting into Galatoire's, but they persist. After all, as Tennessee Williams wrote, when one "has an appointment with grandeur, he dares not stoop to comfort. . . ."

"Galatoire's is my idea of what heaven must be like, to have a wonderful party going on all the time, seeing people who are dear to you," said Laura Bayon Reichard, the Natchez-raised child of New Orleans natives. "There was a sense of feeling I had come home when I went to eat at Galatoire's. After my parents died, I had a fantasy that they must be enjoying such a party together, with all their friends from years gone by." Paul Greenberg, columnist and editorial page editor at the *Arkansas Democrat-Gazette* writes: "I can think of no better way to spend an evening or eternity than to dine at Galatoire's with good company in the real dining room, repeating stories that get better with every telling."

Uptown B&B owner Dan Fuselier is a big fan, too. "The time-honored magical place possesses that certain *'je ne sais quoi'* . . . Galatoire's has an energy that may not exist anywhere else in the Western world . . ." His wife, Mary Ann Weilbaecher, has a favorite name for the restaurant—"Gal's." Her problems and inhibitions shuffle happily away once she enters the door and becomes "Gal-vanized." Others sometimes call Galatoire's "the Big G." However, most regulars seem to relish allowing the old French name to roll off their tongues in an oh-so-luxurious Southern way: "Gal-a-twaaah's."

In the same way, Galatoire's has a name for its regular patrons—they are "customers," rather than "diners," the usual name affixed to those who visit a restaurant to enjoy a meal. The tradition began when career waiters of long-standing referred thusly to their particular patrons, who would call for them by name—as in, "Mr. So-and-so is my customer." Not "my patron," not "my client," but always "my customer," and less frequently "my regular" or "my preferee." Oddly, the French word "preferee," or "one who is preferred," should denote the waiter, not the customer; but according to David Gooch, Galatoire's staff has always used it in the opposite way, just one more example of the restaurant's quirky customs.

The simple egalitarian premise that all customers are created equal lies at the heart of the establishment and permits the benevolent toleration of diners' foibles and eccentricities. Returning the favor, "the pampered diners of New Orleans love Galatoire's in spite of—or maybe because of—all the restaurant's quirks and demands," wrote Richard Nalley in *Vis A Vis,* December, 1987. Nalley also described going to Galatoire's as "stepping inside a private party;" and while that statement sounds elitist, one must remember that anyone can attend. "Contrary to what the newspapers often say, there's no air of elitism," said Kim Sport, a regular. "Because it's an equal opportunity place, the first people who get there get served and it doesn't matter who you are. I admire and respect Galatoire's for having that policy." "I feel that Galatoire's is really a club-like atmosphere, but it's an especially wonderful club because anybody can get in," Attorney Thomas Keller said in *Dining and Dynasties.* "There's no exclusive membership, so all you have to do is present yourself at the door and you join the party."

The restaurant has always been protective of the privacy of its customers, and it is surely safe to say that in the century of its existence, members of the Galatoire family and staff must have learned a great many secrets. Customers come from all strata of society—the wealthy and socially elite, politicians, celebrities, and the masses—and in the French tradition, the Galatoire's cast has learned the value of discretion. If a councilperson or senator dines with someone other than his or her spouse and proceeds to become openly amorous, the staff must keep it to themselves. Regarding the other customers, of course, secrecy is problematic. The gossip mill often runs overtime at Galatoire's, especially when the ladies who lunch also table hop. Just one example: "I'm not dating so-and-so anymore; I got tired of paying for all our dates," said a woman stopping by Mary Flynn Thomas's table of friends. "He said his wife cleaned him out and he's temporarily strapped."

"How sad, darling; do sit down."

"The breakup was frightening. We were in his apartment, with the gas logs lit and the champagne poured, and I told him I thought it best that we stop seeing each other until his divorce was final. You know what a big man he is. He loomed over me with fire in his eyes, yanked me up from the chair and yelled, 'You bitches are all alike!' Then he shoved me back down and threw his glass in the fireplace; it bounced out, rolled across the floor and stained the carpet."

Complete shock. "You mean it wasn't crystal? Thank God you're out of *that* relationship!" Ah, the perspective of the ladies who lunch.

During the century of protecting and indulging its customers, Galatoire's established its own protocols without paying the slightest attention to prevailing trends. In the process, its own arcane customs became

LUNCH BUNCH

The peripatetic socializer Joe Mizelle often documented the goings-on at Galatoire's and other favorite haunts of the *beau monde.* His column in *New Orleans Business* (July 1986) listed the regulars dining on a summer day: "Martha Radelat of D. H. Holmes, lunching with Jean Mills and Arlene Mmahat; Cammie Kock Mayer with Ann Crounse; jewelry-expert Norma Ackley, in a statement-making summertime print dress; Mary Ann Weilbaecher, proprietor of The Josephine Guest House, with Judy and Connie Dahmes; Mo Provosty with business associates; and gorgeous Cassandra Sharpe with three other beauties."

ingrained in the city's culture. Old-line New Orleans families hand down the Galatoire's tradition in a native rite of passage. They bring their offspring to the restaurant straight from the cradle, often to Sunday dinner, and eventually present them with their own house account and their own waiter. Even though credit cards are now accepted, signing a house account tab is still the ultimate Galatoire's status symbol, the lower the number, the more status. Today the list of house accounts still numbers more than seven thousand.

After the death of Saul Stone in 2000, New Orleans doyenne Ruth Katz became the restaurant's oldest living house charge account customer. "I have a very low house account number," she said proudly. (It is K-53.) Mrs. Katz has been coming to Galatoire's for eighty of her ninety-five years, at first every Saturday night with her date, husband-to-be Nathan Katz, whose family manufactured clothing and uniforms for World War II at 123 Magazine Street. "I was a flapper," she said. "I don't remember who was here then or who our waiter was. When you're young and in love you don't care who's there. I do remember one time after two Galatoire's drinks, I went to bed with my hat on." She and Nathan married in 1926, continuing their Saturday night tradition at Galatoire's. Often the couple had to take a cab home and come back the next morning for the car. She remembers when they would have Thanksgiving dinner at Galatoire's. The cost: fifty cents.

Her husband died in 1975, and during his final illness Galatoire's provided takeout. Then Mrs. Katz began going to Galatoire's on Saturday nights with her youngest son Gerald and his friend David Gibson. "I never liked to hop the line," she said, but after she had a heart attack and was recuperating, her waiter allowed her to come inside and sit down. Then she and her two escorts were given the next available table. "People would say, 'Oh, that must be Mrs. Galatoire,' but it made me unpopular with the line," she said with a laugh. She loves to tell the story about the time Gibson was standing outside waiting for their table to be ready and someone handed him a dollar bill, thinking he was the maitre d'. Mrs. Katz always remembers the night she met diva Joan Sutherland at Galatoire's after a concert. "She was at least six feet tall, huge, and was with her husband, the conductor Richard Bonynge. We had a long conversation. She was fascinated with the food, particularly the fresh crabmeat which she could not get in New York City at that time."

Her son died in 1996, but now Gibson continues to take Mrs. Katz to Galatoire's on Saturday nights for her favorite Trout Amandine and his favorite Shrimp Clemenceau, served by their favorite waiter, M. C. Emmons. Occasionally Gibson might opt for his special "eccentric" crabmeat omelette with mint jelly, specially cooked for him. "I come over at 5:30 from the shop (Katz Antiques on Royal Street), and the car picks Ruth up," he said. Mrs. Katz smiled. "Justin promised me a one-hundredth birthday party, and if I live that long, I'm going to remind him."

Shrimp Clemenceau

Vegetable oil
2 Idaho potatoes, peeled and diced
Salt and freshly ground black pepper
1 cup frozen petits pois
5 tablespoons butter
1 pound large shrimp, peeled, and
   deveined

2 cloves garlic, peeled and chopped
1/2 cup button mushrooms
2 tablespoons parsley, finely chopped
4 cups mixed lettuces

Heat about 1 inch oil in a deep heavy-bottomed skillet over medium-high heat. When oil reaches about 350 degrees, add potatoes and fry, stirring occasionally, until golden, about 10 minutes. Drain on paper towels and sprinkle with salt.

Bring a medium pot of salted water to a boil over high heat. Add petits pois and cook for one minute. Drain, refresh under cold water, and set aside.

Melt 4 tablespoons of butter in a large skillet over medium heat. Add shrimp and 1/2 the garlic and cook, stirring occasionally, until shrimp are opaque, about 3 minutes. Transfer shrimp to a plate.

Remove and discard mushroom stems, then thinly slice the caps. Melt remaining 1 tablespoon butter in skillet over medium heat. Add mushrooms and cook until golden.

Increase heat to medium-high. Add potatoes, peas, and shrimp to skillet. Mix well, then add parsley and remaining garlic and season to taste with salt and pepper. Cook, stirring frequently, for 1 to 2 minutes. Arrange lettuces on 4 plates, top with shrimp mixture, and serve.

SERVES 4.

Likely candidates for the male version of "doyennes" are six elderly gentlemen ("None of us will ever see seventy-nine again.") who prefer Wednesday lunches impeccably served by the debonair Richard Smith. One recent Wednesday, it was lawyer Henry Read's turn to pick up the tab, so he was introduced as "the rich one." At that moment at Galatoire's the definition of rich was the one whose turn it was to pay. Later on, someone said that the definition of a rich man in New Orleans is one who comes to Galatoire's twice a week, and the group's wealthy person was identified as Chadwick Winslow, who described himself as a "lay-about." A. L. Jung, of Jung Realty (the Jung Hotel family), was absent that day, but the rest of the group was in attendance: Read; Winslow; Dr. David Bradley, father of Ann Gooch and father-in-law of David; Frank Purvis, retired CEO of Pan-American Life Insurance; and lawyer Louis Jones, who now lives in Covington. The group began forty-five years ago as a gathering of Tulane grads, but according to Purvis, age eighty-eight, the group allowed him to join even though he is a graduate of LSU. Although the men have lived in the city since the 1920s, he describes most of them as "move-ins," meaning they are not originally from New Orleans.

From left to right, Frank Purvis, Henry Read, Dr. David Bradley,
Chadwick Winslow, and Louis Jones sharing lunch

Winslow wears the group's signature tie: a navy affair studded with tiny pink pigs and the initials MCP (Male Chauvinist Pig) with a lining sporting a painting of a nude woman. Jung had the ties made up and presented one to each member of the group. Mr. Purvis declines to wear his because he is partial to bow ties.

Forty years ago, Purvis's firm hosted a group of lawyers from New York City, Washington D. C., and Chicago. They invited the late Mrs. Purvis (Winston) to lunch and sent her an orchid corsage to wear. The lawyers sat ten at a table with Mrs. Purvis as the only invited female. Frank Purvis relates, "Along came one of my old college girlfriends, who saw Winston with nine men and an orchid corsage and asked me 'What is going on here?' I answered 'Nothing, this is just a normal day at Galatoire's.'"

The Galatoire's tradition also infiltrated neighboring states. Generations of Mississippians consider Galatoire's their personal gustatory fiefdom, as do visitors from around the country. Physician Jimmy Royals from Jackson, Mississippi, went to medical school at Tulane and remembers going to Galatoire's for many a meal over the years. "Back then Galatoire's was famous for its Martinis. The waiters mixed all the drinks, and to make a Martini they took a chilled glass, not a stemmed Martini glass but a regular drinks glass, and put in an olive. Then they filled the glass to the top from a chilled bottle of Beefeater's Gin. That was it, nothing else. Best Martinis I've ever had, but if you had more than two you couldn't walk out the door. Even with two you staggered out." After Dr. Royals married his wife Edrie, she would go shopping after lunch while he went back to the hotel and took a long nap. "I think she'd take me to Galatoire's on purpose, so I'd have those Martinis and she wouldn't have me underfoot when she wanted to shop."

The family of Ginger Shands of McComb, Mississippi, has been eating at Galatoire's for five generations. "I love to take care of little kids—future customers," said John Fontenot. "Now I'm waiting on the third generation." John has customers from San Francisco, New York, and Chicago who also send their friends to him. "I wait for them to come every year at a certain time; it's like they migrate." "People who come from out of town have heard that if there's only one place you have a chance to eat it should be Galatoire's," said M. C. Two who agree are Ann and Bill Neblett from Tucson, Arizona, who first came to Galatoire's in 1962 when he was an engineer in Houston. Galatoire's was on a list of twenty restaurants he wanted to try. "Galatoire's was rather simple and unimpressive; it was small, but it had a

FAMILY AFFAIR

As Karl Ewald grew up, his parents not only ate at Galatoire's, but always were seated at the same table in the right front corner. "The first meal that my father ever ate in a New Orleans restaurant was at Galatoire's," said his daughter, Bethany Ewald Bultman. "It had a profound impact, on awakening his senses to the cultural sensuality of dining in New Orleans. From the time I was old enough to hold my fork properly, my parents would allow me to dine at Galatoire's when we came to New Orleans from Natchez, where I was born and raised. It never occurred to me that the restaurant had a menu, or served anything but Trout Amandine and Crème Caramel." The Ewald family came to New Orleans "to do all of our clothing, liquor, and fancy food shopping," and always went to

Customers enjoying Galatoire's, among them, Peggy Wilson, second from left, seated with hat; Rise Delmar Oschsner, standing, with hat

giant reputation," he said. "Of all the restaurants we went to, Galatoire's was the best because it was so different from everything else, and, of course, the food was superb. Now when I come back, I always say if I only have time for one place, Galatoire's is the place I want to go."

"Even the restaurant people eat here," said M. C., naming Tony Mandina, Cindy Brennan, and John Amato, owner of Mother's Restaurant, among others. According to John Fontenot, "All the judges come here, the well known lawyers, the brokers, John Schwegmann and his son used to sit at table 10, the

Galatoire's for lunch on Saturday at 1:30 P.M. (Their routine also included the Pontchartrain Hotel, Kreeger's, D. H. Holmes, the Blue Room, Christ Church, and Sunday brunch at Brennan's.) After she married New Orleanian Johann Bultman, the two raised their family in New Orleans, and the tradition continued. "By cosmic culinary magic," even though no one ever requests it, family members, including the present fourth generation, are always shown to the same table in the right front corner. "In the winter of 2002 my father came to New Orleans for the final time," said Bultman. "I will never forget that we ate at that same corner table. Each time I walk in the restaurant I feel that my father's spirit is dining on crispy, hot bread and a wonderful legacy of happy memories."

Coca-Cola Freemans—every Sunday they would come, like clockwork. We have a helluva clientele, one of the best clienteles in the city."

"You can never go anywhere and find a place like this," said Dr. Dale Archer Jr., a neuro-psychiatrist who lives in Connecticut, but is a New Orleans native. "We lived on Soniat Street thirty years ago with our children Adrianna and Trey, and we keep coming back once or twice a year," said his wife Angela. "We order exactly the same thing each time: pompano and potatoes." Recently, their daughter flew in from New York City to surprise her parents at Galatoire's. Rather than pompano, Pat Glorioso has trout loyalty. "Never in forty years have I ordered anything but Trout Amandine," she says. "I sit down at the table fully intending to order something different, but at the last second the same words come out of my mouth."

When he was a child, oilman and developer Bill Huls' parents would take him on the L & N train from Biloxi to the railroad station at the foot of Canal Street. He remembers back in the 1920s and 1930s when his Uncle Bill Stevens— "my drinking Uncle"—would often take him to Galatoire's. "The Desire streetcar still went down Bourbon Street, and he would just park the car right in front of Galatoire's and go in. I would say, 'Uncle Bill, don't you want to park the car somewhere else, not in the way of the streetcar?' And he would already have had a couple of drinks, and he would say, 'No, they'll come and take it off and we can go get it later on.' Of course, he would have to pay a fine, but when you're drunk, you're rich. The streetcar would come along and clang and clang, and sure enough they would come and drag the car off. But we would be inside waiting to get served. If they did not come and wait on us immediately, Uncle Bill, who was very impetuous, impatient, and imperial, would push a glass to the edge of the table and let it fall off. It would break, of course, on the tile floor, and then they would come over in a hurry and wait on us."

David D. Duggins and his wife coached their two sons, five- and seven-year-olds, on their best manners before going to Galatoire's one Sunday after church so the boys could have "their first dining experience in a class restaurant." The boys were told they could have anything they wanted for lunch. "Our older son ordered a 'sirloin steak, cooked medium rare, and a dozen escargot,'" said Duggins. "The waiter, whose name is long forgotten, nearly fell on the floor. He looked at me for assistance and I nodded my acquiescence in the order. My son got his dozen snails and proceeded to devour them with gusto, as well as the strip sirloin. He is now the chef/proprietor of a New Orleans restaurant, and so this budding chef got his inspiration from Galatoire's."

Residents of neighboring cities also consider Galatoire's their dining room away from home. Bob Miller from Baton Rouge brings his entire family for French Quarter Festival and eats at Galatoire's every night and sometimes lunch, too. "They are the first ones in line at 10:30," said M. C. The parents of Charlotte Norman and Toni Haynes, Arthur and Thelma Norman, made sure their daughters shared their love of Galatoire's, with frequent trips to New Orleans from Abbeville, Louisiana, where they were in the sugar and rice business. In the early 1950s, after big sister Charlotte moved to New Orleans and was working at D. H. Holmes Department Store, the twelve-year-old Toni visited her and was turned loose in the grand Canal Street stores to shop. "I decided on my own to take myself to lunch at Galatoire's," Haynes recalled. "I was greeted warmly, and, after asking for a table for one, was seated at a deuce near the kitchen. I ordered my favorite dish—Trout Marguery—I was treated like the lady I am sure I thought I was. No one talked down to me or asked why I was alone. I am quite sure I did not understand about tipping, but this caused no concern. It was a wonderful example of the epitome of good service, and I will never forget it, even though it has now been over fifty years ago. I have been in the catering business for over thirty years, and have always remembered this as a prime example of service at its best, and have tried to emulate it in dealings with my clients." "It was pretty gutsy for a twelve-year-old to walk into a restaurant like Galatoire's all alone," said Norman, who is now Senior V. P. at Mignon Faget, Ltd. In those days, even older young ladies, such as frequent customer Ruth Ellen Calhoun of Elgin Plantation in Natchez, hesitated. "When I was a single working girl living in the Quarter, I was tempted to stop by for dinner—but it wasn't 'proper' in 1959 for a young woman to enter alone."

Art dealer Walker Ronaldson, who now lives in New Orleans, grew up in Baton Rouge and recalls that during his high school years (1955–1959) "it was a regular rite of passage for all the children who needed braces to go to Dr. George B. Crozat ("Dr Zat") who owned Houmas House Plantation on the River Road and also a huge house on Broadway." The Saturday drill began at 8:15 A.M. when children and mothers and aunts left Baton Rouge on the *Southern Belle* routed from Kansas City. After orthodontist appointments, the group would always lunch at Galatoire's. "Our mothers would sip Old-Fashioneds or a Martini; I always had the Trout Meunière and green salad, and our waiter was always Otto, a round, stoutish Germanic man."

Then the children would be sent to a movie or the famous penny arcade in the first block of Royal Street while the ladies—who would never appear on Canal Street without hats and gloves—shopped at Godchaux, Kreeger's, and Gus Mayer. At 4:00, the group would meet in the lobby of the Roosevelt Hotel (now Fairmont) and go to the Fountain Lounge for an ice cream soda for the kids and coffee for the mothers. Then they took a taxi to Union Station to catch the *Southern Belle* and arrived back home around 7:00, "just a divine day."

The same was true in other "country parishes." Opelousas ladies in the 1960s and 1970s loved to go to the city on Saturdays, "dressed to the nines," to dine at Galatoire's and shop. When they had drinks at Galatoire's they couldn't drive themselves home, so Mrs. Josephine Moseley (mother of New Orleans lawyer Madison "Matts" Moseley) and her three friends often rode the Greyhound bus to New Orleans because Opelousas was not on the train line. One day, in hats and white gloves they boarded the bus, introduced themselves one by one to the bus driver, and chatted non-stop to Baton Rouge. There they disembarked for a fifteen-minute rest and coffee stop. Still chatting, they boarded the bus again and rode along having a wonderful conversation. Suddenly Mrs. Moseley looked out the window and said, "I could swear we just passed my cousin Emily's house." But she was assured that no, that couldn't be, because they were almost to New Orleans. However, a few minutes later, they arrived back at the bus station in Opelousas, as they had boarded the wrong bus in Baton Rouge and made a round trip home. So no drinks and lunch at Galatoire's for the four ladies that day.

On another occasion, the ladies were driving home from New Orleans a little after sunset. At that time the Interstate I-10 Bridge was being built across the Atchafalaya Swamp and it was a mass of construction with many detours. The driver mistakenly pulled the car into the wrong lane and the ladies were startled to see headlights coming toward them. Mrs. Moseley said, "Ladies, get out your handkerchiefs!" They rolled down the windows and waved their white handkerchiefs madly at the approaching headlights. This device evidently worked, as they avoided a head-on collision and eventually arrived safely home, just as Galatoire's customers always arrive safely home.

John Sullivan has lived since the late 1960s in New York, where he runs his own catering business, The Butler Did It. Growing up in Baton Rouge and Lake Charles, he frequently came with his family to "the City, as I thought of New Orleans all my life—at least until the Big Apple." He relates that his grandmother, Josephine Champagne Hoisington Roberts, affectionately known as "Baba," was the mistress of a jeweler in Baton Rouge and also one of the jeweler's wife's best friends. Baba's husband was frequently away on hunting and fishing trips, and she and the jeweler would go to New Orleans to shop, the young boy acting as "the beard for the lovers who would pack me in the back seat of the jeweler's huge black car with a pile of newly purchased comics and say, 'We're taking Johnny to "the City for a little shopping. . . . "'"

"The ritual seldom varied: the car would ease up to the Monteleone Hotel, we'd stroll around the corner to Galatoire's—have a wonderful lunch (the favorite waiter was a Cajun gentleman who remembered everything— and it makes me sad I don't still have his name in my memory—dark, handsome. He knew I loved the Stuffed Eggplant and the Crabmeat Ravigote." When lunch was over, Sullivan's grandmother and her friend would retire to the hotel for a nap, giving him money to spend at D. H. Holmes, Maison

Blanche, or "wherever my fancy compelled me in the wonderful downtown of those years." He was instructed to be back at the Monteleone for four o'clock tea after which the "family" would return to Baton Rouge.

Crabmeat Ravigote

4 green onions, finely chopped	1/4 teaspoon white pepper
3 tablespoons clarified butter	Salt to taste
2 cups Béchamel Sauce (see page 121)	1 teaspoon finely chopped parsley
1 pound crabmeat (jumbo lump)	1 cup Hollandaise Sauce (see page 189)
Pinch cayenne pepper	

Sauté onions in butter over low heat until tender. Add Béchamel Sauce, then fold in crabmeat. Add cayenne and white peppers. Salt to taste. Simmer mixture 5 minutes. Add parsley. Remove from heat.

Fold in Hollandaise Sauce until well blended. Serve in small casserole dishes.

Note: This dish can be difficult to reheat as it may separate. It is best to add Hollandaise just before serving.
SERVES 4.

In the mid-1990s Dr. Brobson Lutz, something of a practical joker, brought two Mississippi ladies to Galatoire's for lunch, after having first set up a little surprise for them. He insisted they must try the turtle soup, and the waiter brought to the table a covered soup tureen containing small live box turtles that Dr. Lutz had brought in his pocket from his French Quarter home and slipped to his waiter to "serve." Recently, Dr. Lutz pulled his turtle prank again, in honor of Gary and Cathy Smith of Nashville. This time his two alligator snapping turtles, named Gilberto and Julia (for writer Julia Reed), scrambled out of their soup bowl and disappeared.

Nutria figured in another practical joke arranged by Joel Fletcher, a native of Louisiana who now lives in Virginia. Fletcher had told a Philadelphia scientist about nutria, the creatures introduced by the McIlhenny family to control the water hyacinths on Avery Island that had gotten out of control and endangered the wetlands. The scientist insisted that no such animal existed, since he had not learned about it in his studies in biology. When he made a trip to New Orleans, Fletcher urged him to go to Galatoire's and ask for John Fontenot, Fletcher's own waiter, who would be expecting him. When the scientist and his party arrived and were seated, John came to their table, greeted them, and when the time came to take their order informed them, as Fletcher had instructed, that the specialty of the day was "Roast Nutria."

A more domesticated animal caused a ruckus one day at lunch. The six-foot-two Carl Cleveland stood up from his table in front of the desk, held a tiny fuzzy white dog high over his head, and called out: "Who belongs to this?" The place went into an uproar, and an attractive young woman way off in the front corner claimed the dog. The dog had been hidden in her handbag, which she placed alongside her chair in the corner. Unbeknownst to her, the little dog had jumped out and made its way down the length of the dining room, running beneath tables and between feet unnoticed until it reached Carl Cleveland. Of course, David Gooch made the woman leave with her dog, strictly verboten for a restaurant. Word spread from table to table identifying her as a dancer from the "gentlemen's club" next door. When she returned a few minutes later sans doggie, the entire restaurant burst into applause.

When he presided behind the desk at Galatoire's, Leon Galatoire loved to observe. "For twenty years, every day a motion picture," he said. Leon remembered the man from New York City who used to come in with an inflatable doll. "He would blow it up and set it across from him. It was his companion. It would

Singer Mimi Guste defying the anti-smoking rule

just sit there with its mouth open." And then there was the man who always ordered two of everything. "Every time he came in, he ordered two fish, two filets of beef, two bottles of wine, two appetizers, two desserts—and he would sit and eat it all. Everyone's question was: How could he consume so much food? But he did." Leon and the staff had pet names for some of the customers. "Mirror Man," the handsome jewelry salesman who came in once a month from New York City, always sat on the side, having conversations with himself in the mirror. "One day he began taping a little mirror to the top of his shoe and every time a woman would walk by on the way to the ladies room, he would stick his foot out and look up her dress." Another man polished his shoes to a high gloss so he could do the same thing. One man treated the restaurant like his home. He would bring his daily pills to lunch—a great many pills—then sit there cutting them up into smaller pieces and washing them down with Sazeracs. Afterwards he would practice karate moves. Then there was "Squeaky" (because she had such a squeaky little voice), who carried a shopping bag containing only paper. All the waiters dropped their empty wine bottles in it as they went by her table; it probably weighed twelve or fifteen pounds by the time she left. She was allowed to charge her food, but she never paid the bill. "Then she had the audacity to complain about things," said Leon. "We gave her a break. She obviously had dementia, but we all loved her."

According to Leon, closing up was not always easy. "One man drove me crazy when we were trying to close up because he would just sit there and never leave. With a friend or by himself, he would just sit there until midnight or one o'clock. He was a brilliant historian, but cuckoo. So we called him 'Sitting Bull.' Very often I would turn out the lights on him and say, 'Look, I'm going home.'"

Annalee Jefferies, actress noted for her portrayals of Tennessee Williams's heroines, and Bob Salazar, on the closing day of the downstairs dining room

Diners regard Galatoire's with the utmost proprietorship. Regulars act as if they are dues-paying members of an elite private club, and in a way they are. You could set a clock by the regularity of their attendance, where they sit, and the waiter they request. For example, Mrs. Lucille Blum, who is ninety-nine years old, has been sitting at her father's table since she was six years old and her father has long since passed away. Dr. Ed Lazarus who has been going to Galatoire's since he was a little boy during World War II, says "I've never *ever* had a bad meal at Galatoire's." When Elva Weiss, widow of Seymour Weiss, the famous manager of the Roosevelt Hotel and pal of Huey Long's, came to town she would often lunch with Leonard Parrish. "When the ladies room was upstairs, Elva wouldn't go up the steps," said Parrish, "so she always made me stand guard at the door of the men's room (downstairs) and went in there instead."

Dentist Richard Reinhardt says about Galatoire's: "You only have to go there once and you know that something's going on. You pick up the energy." Even in its earliest days the energy was there. In 1956 Shirley Ann Grau told the story of her uncle who decided to try the new Galatoire's when it opened in 1905. "As he walked down Bourbon Street, he stepped into the middle of a shooting scrape. He left fast; he didn't want lunch that badly. And it was a couple of weeks before he thought of trying the restaurant again. He liked it so much that he's been going back once or twice a week for fifty years."

Why does Galatoire's inspire such devotion? An attorney friend of Dollye Jordan had a clue. He was just home from doing business in a Northeastern city where a poll was conducted for the city's favorite restaurant. The winner was the chain restaurant Olive Garden. "The Olive Garden!" he exclaimed with a laugh. "No wonder I live in New Orleans!" Some cite such special characteristics as the restaurant's generosity to its old customers as they age and grow infirm. When Marc Turk's mother died, Galatoire's sent over fried chicken. Patty Friedmann remembers that after her grandfather's "liver gave out at age eighty and he couldn't go there anymore, they sent over lamb chops every day until he died." And there are many more, unreported stories. After Richard Cushing Bell died in 1996, his eulogy by Bryan Bell included the following:

"He kept his sense of humor to the very end. In his final days his appetite sagged, something we thought would never happen. But when asked what he would most like to eat in this world he asked for 'a cup custard from Galatoire's,' the restaurant where he and his special cronies had so many wonderful Friday lunches. The manager of Galatoire's personally delivered to his home a supply of cup custards." The handwritten note to Galatoire's from Bryan Bell said: "Thank you so much. Hundreds of people have heard or read of your generosity."

Laura Reichard put it this way: "There are so many of us who have that sense of returning to our past when we go to Galatoire's. And knowing too of all the dear people we have known in our lifetimes who ate there as well. It is impossible not to be happy there, not to feel connected to days gone by. New restaurants may come and go—but the feelings about Galatoire's are deep in our hearts."

Maurice H. Joseph of Jackson, Mississippi even wrote a short poem:

When in New Orleans I am in New Orleans.
When at Galatoire's I am at home.

Marian Patton Atkinson escorted by Rendon Francis

MARIAN ATKINSON
Elegant Lady of the Old School

Marian Atkinson was an elegant lady of the old school, and as such, devoted to rituals. New Orleans, where she was born and spent all of her ninety-eight years, provided her with the perfect stage for such a dramatic existence. She resided in splendor in her grand mansion on St. Charles Avenue among family antiques, attended by a retinue of servants. She was blessed with a lifestyle that many would have envied. Indeed most people would have been loathe to leave such a setting any more than was necessary, but one of Marian's rituals took her out of her home two or three hours a day, when she dined at Galatoire's every evening except Monday, when the restaurant was dark.

In preparation for her visits to this temple of cuisine, she always mixed herself a daiquiri, using a recipe that she had learned in Havana, then, elegantly attired in a stylish suit, a perky hat, and white linen gloves, she would be driven in her black Fleetwood Cadillac by her chauffeur—first there was Rendon, whom she outlived, then Nathaniel—from the grandeur of Uptown to the two hundred block of Bourbon Street. *Times-Picayune* writer Bill Grady, who was her guest on one such visit, reported that Marian called ahead to make sure that her table was ready for her, then arrived promptly at 5:00 P.M. at the front door of Galatoire's, where the maitre d' greeted her and escorted her to table 10 against the front wall. Ken Solis, a former assistant manager and maitre d' says that it was good Marian came early, because she usually got her table. "We'd tell them all kinds of stuff, it's a little cold here, you'd be more comfortable over there, to keep them away from her table." Occasionally, despite her advance call, she found the table occupied, but if the diners were regulars, they knew and honored Marian and her ritual and were glad to allow themselves to be reseated elsewhere, with waiters and busboys scurrying to move drinks and plates and napkins, rather than to interfere with one of the restaurant's long-standing traditions.

Janet Westerfelt, Miss Marian's cousin, says the Galatoire's ritual was established by Marian's husband, Eugene Atkinson, a cotton factor. Marian worked in the 1930s and 1940s in the Whitney National Bank's bond department and met Eugene when he came in one day. He courted her over malted milks at Solari's specialty food store and delicatessen on Royal Street and proposed in the famous Blue Room at the Roosevelt Hotel—like many New Orleanians, their lives seem to have been inextricably entwined with dining places. Years later, when he decided to retire, Eugene came home one afternoon and told Marian to get her hat and gloves because he needed to get out of the house and they were never going to dine at home again.

Tuesday through Sunday, they would dine at Galatoire's, but on Mondays, when it was dark, they opted for either Antoine's or the German restaurant Kolb's. After her husband's death in 1980, Marian continued to honor their tradition, in the process becoming one of the legendary doyennes of Galatoire's, where she had first dined in 1916. From 1980 until a couple of years before her death, she usually invited a relative, such as her stepdaughter, Alice Atkinson Milton, her cousin

Janet Westerfelt, or one of her friends, such as Mrs. Henri (Peachy) Villere or Mrs. Gladys Maginnis, to accompany her.

At Galatoire's, the ritual rarely varied, as Marian began the evening with two Old-Fashioneds ("A bird can't fly on just one wing," she would say). When the first drink arrived, Bill Grady recalled, she would lift her glass and offer the toast she had learned from a friend of her husband's: "Whatever you wish me, I wish you twice more." Through the years, most of the old-line waiters must have tended her, but her preferees were Randy Berkshire, Gilberto Eyzaguirre, and Richard Smith—in that order.

During the course of the leisurely meal, several regular patrons would make the requisite visit to Miss Marian's table to pay homage to one who through persistence had become the living embodiment of their own devotion to Galatoire's. After a couple of hours spent over drinks and three or four courses, she would depart, again escorted by the maitre d', and in her last years leaning on a metal walker. On the side-walk, she would signal for Nathaniel, who would be waiting in the lim-ousine in the nearest available parking space. Then home to rest and wait for the next day, when the ritual would be repeated.

She was such a regular fixture at the restaurant that it is not sur-prising that stories of legendary proportion would be circulated among the staff and regulars about the grande dame at table 10 and that, in the course of the years, these stories would be altered and amended. One such tale concerned the evening when her false teeth fell into her half-eaten soft-shell crab. One version of the story has it that Nelson, her waiter at the time, stood by the table for a while, assuming that Miss Marian would notice the problem, but instead she said in some pique, "Nelson, get this plate away from me!" whereupon he replied, "I'd be happy to do that, Mrs. Atkinson, once you get your uppers out of the crab." In a variation of the story, the waiter was Dorris Sylvester, who replied to her demand by saying, "Well, I will, Miss Marian, if you'll put your teeth back in your mouth." Yet another version has it that the waiter responded to her demand with the quip that he would clear the table "if you remove your upper plate from your plate."

Marian Patton Atkinson was born January 22, 1902 to Rose Voorhies and Mercer Patton in their home on Esplanade Avenue. Her paternal grandfather, Isaac W. Patton, a plantation owner and a general during the War Between the States, was from Vicksburg, Mississippi, but later moved to New Orleans where he became mayor. Marian took pride in her ancestors and family connections; one of her ancestors was a doge of Venice, and she was a second cousin once removed of General George

Patton, whom she entertained when he visited New Orleans. She was, nevertheless, without pretensions in discussing her family's history. She told Bill Grady that she had been "a society belle . . . but not a wealthy one," and consequently had no debut. After her father's death, her grandparents and her mother opened a boarding house Uptown, where they employed so many servants to help run the establishment that, Marian recalled, she grew up without knowing "how to do anything."

She was a student of New Orleans history, having grown up in a French-speaking family in a city that was still very Gallic in its attitudes. Her longtime friend David Baker recalled that when she was still physically able to do so, she would serve as hostess during Spring Fiesta at the French Quarter home of her friend and decorator, C. M. Davis. Marian always wore an Empire dress rather than the more dramatic hoop shirts, favored by the other hostesses, which she insisted were not authentic to the period being celebrated. Stephen Harrison, an assistant curator for the Dallas Museum of Art, recalled that he first met Marian when he was researching his thesis on New Orleans furniture and visited her to examine some of her antiques. Harrison, who would later be invited once a month to accompany Marian to Galatoire's for dinner, referred to her as "the genuine article in that wonderful house on St. Charles."

Toward the end of her long and rich life, Marian Patton Atkinson became gradually more feeble, her hands gnarled with excruciatingly painful arthritis—it took hours for her to get dressed for the daily trip to the restaurant—yet she remained the gracious lady, generous and considerate to friends and strangers alike. She looked upon the wait staff and managers at Galatoire's as family, and when she was gone, the drama that is Galatoire's had lost one of its most legendary stars.

MARDA BURTON
KENNETH HOLDITCH

Act Two

The Cast

Scene Six

Guest Stars
Celebrities

*"Galatoire's is just one of those places where everybody thinks they
are famous, and a lot of them, locally, really are."*
—Larry Hagman, January 1, 1997

*B*ecause Galatoire's is a legend in its own time, the celebrity set finds its classic and unchanging French-bistro setting especially appealing. Actors act here. Singers sing here. Politicians politic here. Henry Kissinger, Dwight Eisenhower, and the Shah of Iran stood in line like ordinary folk. Alec Baldwin, Jimmy Buffett, and Ed Bradley make the scene whenever they are in town, and the roster includes a lengthy list of celebrities past and present.

In the early days, when the Blue Room at the Roosevelt Hotel was *do rigueur* with café society, all manner of celebrities adored Galatoire's. "On many occasions my father would call home and say that he was bringing home someone for a drink after work," said Simone Nugent, daughter of Rene Galatoire and Rosemary Bombich. One night his guest was Harpo Marx; another night Rocky Marciano. Waiter John Fontenot cracked jokes with Jackie Gleason. Singer Brenda Lee welcomed her regular Galatoire's waiter Lee McDaniel to her performances as a special guest.

A popular French waiter during and after World War II, Michel Virrolet, told his daughter Jacqueline about asking Tyrone Power and Robert Taylor for autographs on behalf of his table of "swooning" ladies who were too much in awe to make the attempt themselves—and how the two matinee idols graciously complied. Michel also met Shirley Temple Black and made friends with Lloyd Nolan, who ate at Galatoire's often when he was in town appearing in the *Caine Mutiny.*

Actor Charles Laughton greatly relished dining at Galatoire's, which he did several times during his stay in New Orleans. One day when Sir Charles occupied the table next to a pair of Uptown ladies, their waiter noticed the interaction. "The ladies didn't realize who it was, but they thought it was someone they knew—so they nodded and smiled. Laughton smiled back and graciously said, 'So good to see you again.' When the actor finished his lunch he asked, 'What time is dinner served?' When I told him, he said, 'I shall return.' And so he did."

While in town for an appearance at the Saenger Theatre as King Arthur in Camelot, Robert Goulet belted out "Happy Birthday" to a customer at Galatoire's—a decided improvement over the usual raucous chorus led by the wait staff. Lunching on the same day were former Congresswoman and Ambassador to the Vatican Lindy Boggs, who strolled in from her house down the street, and musician Charles Neville of the famous New Orleans Neville family. Another local musician of international fame, Allen Toussaint, was spotted at lunch recently with his friend B. J. Powell, sitting at the Tennessee Williams table. "It's a guaranteed New Orleans tradition," said the pianist and composer. "The hospitality is impeccable and they will always try to accommodate, even if it's something off the menu. They can do so many different things with shrimp." Touissant loves seeing "the ladies in their hats," and says his favorite Galatoire's meal is "the last one I had."

Tommy Tune loves Galatoire's and has been spotted around Mardi Gras time on the frantic Friday, with his good friend Leo Montegut and an entourage of local people. They make a late afternoon gustatory stop without standing in line, simply pulling up chairs to sit with the group that has already acquired a table and plans to stay for the evening. Anthony Herrera, a Mississippian who has played villain James Stenbeck on the soap opera *As the World Turns* for twenty years, dines at Galatoire's with Mickey Easterling and other friends whenever he is in New Orleans. He is usually besieged by ladies and even waiters seeking autographs. Britney Spears ate upstairs at table 72, "looking plain and quiet, not her flashy self," said Sunny Holliday, her server.

The maitre d' always has the first contact with famous people, and sometimes the last. Galatoire's dress codes and old-fashioned queue are the first rules celebrities question at the door. It is usually the maitre d' who must joust in the verbal battle that ensues when a celebrity is disinclined to believe that all seats are taken. John Fontenot recalls an occasion when he was at the door and Anne Bancroft and Mel Brooks came in and Bancroft announced that they had reservations. When John responded that Galatoire's did not take reservations, the actress, most famous for her portrayal of Annie Sullivan in *The Miracle Worker,* and a personal friend of Gabie Galatoire,

From left to right, George Dureau, Robert Maczewski, Ann Mahorner,
Leo Montegut, and Tommy Tune at their favorite haunt

became extremely annoyed. "I felt miserable," John said, and after the couple was seated, "I felt like daggers were shooting at me with her eyes." Even since the late 1990s when dress codes were relaxed and limited reservations taken, things still get iffy on occasion.

A friend of actor Richard Gere left in a huff after maitre d' Jackson Browne refused to admit him because he was wearing blue jeans. "You don't understand," the man said, "I'm here to meet Richard Gere and we have a reservation. Browne answered: "I'm sorry, sir, but we don't take reservations, and even if we did I can't seat you in blue jeans." Browne thought that would be the end of the story, but two nights later, wearing his other hat as Special Events Manager at Tipitina's, he escorted Gere upstairs to a private area for a Neville Brothers concert. On the way up, Browne identified himself as maitre d' at Galatoire's and told the actor that he had only done his job. "Gere answered: 'My friend said you're the rudest S.O.B. on earth. I can't wait to tell him what a nice guy you really are.'"

Another time, on a hot Sunday afternoon in August, ninety-eight degrees with ninety-eight percent humidity, Browne had tables for two available although there were three parties of four waiting on the extremely hot sidewalk. Browne had just explained to them that if a party of two arrived they would be allowed to walk right in. A couple walked up and each one carried two full shopping bags. The man was not wearing a jacket, and on Sundays coats and ties were required all day. The lady, who was clearly in charge, asked how long the wait was. Browne told her, "On Sunday we require coat and tie all day." She indicated that her companion had a jacket in the bag. "Would you put it on please sir?" Browne asked. "Then she went ballistic, really mean: 'He's not going to wear a coat to wait in line in this heat!' 'Yes, ma'am, but he needs a coat on to go inside.' Another attack. I finally got to explain that if he would put on the jacket we could go right inside and to a table, so he did and we went in. While walking down the aisle she said to me at least three times: 'I'm not usually like this,' and kept on apologizing." Browne rarely watched television so he didn't know any of the TV sit-com stars. "After the couple was seated an elderly lady grabbed me and whispered: 'Is that Cybill Shepherd?'" Never having seen *Moonlighting,* Browne had no idea who the lady was—but it was Cybill Shepherd.

Of course, not all celebrities are difficult. Galatoire's had a long line down to the corner one rainy night when Michael York poked his head in the door and asked Browne how long the wait was. The entire line that night was composed of couples except for York's party of four. Parties of two could not be seated at tables for six, and two were available. Browne said: "I understand your position, and I have to ask you to get in the line." York said with a wry expression: "My position is a very comfortable one." His group went down to the corner to stand in line, and then Browne went down the line asking if anyone had a party of four. Being the first and only party of four, York's group was seated promptly.

John Fontenot enjoyed serving Pernell Roberts of *Bonanza* fame ("he still calls me sometimes"), Bob Hope, Phil Harris and his wife, Alice Faye ("she was a honey"), and Jackie Gleason, when he was king of the carnival Krewe of Bacchus. Gleason ate Trout Marguery and "two servings of ice cream with chocolate sauce on top. I said, 'You're on a diet, huh?'" John confused actor Matt Dillon with his *Gunsmoke* character, but "I got on good with him, him and his family." When Raquel Welch came in one night, "everything went quiet. The man accompanying her was coatless, and he was so tall and burly that none of the restaurant's spares would fit him. Of course, they had to leave. "Boy, the customers got pissed because they wanted her to come in and sit down and eat so they could watch her." John first waited on Lauren Hutton many years ago when she was a cocktail waitress at Al Hirt's and came to Galatoire's to eat when she got off work.

The first credit card, Diner's Club, was introduced to America in 1950, but the new-fangled idea was not accepted at Galatoire's until 1992, forty-two years later. This eccentricity surprised and often displeased the famous from out of town, who, naturally, had been among the first to use them else-where. One world celebrity, in 1965 at the height of his golfing career, was the A-R-N-O-L-D P-A-L-M-E-R of the well-known American Express Card TV commercial. Nonetheless, waiter Bill Bordelon had to tell him "We don't take credit cards." Thinking he meant HIS credit card, Palmer said "You don't understand, I'm A-R-N-O-L-D P-A-L-M-E-R. Bordelon stood firm, however, so young Billy Broadhurst from Crowley saved the day by signing the ticket to his own house account, which he had acquired when he was in high school. "Palmer was just flabbergasted," Broadhurst said, "here was this kid just out of college and he was a national hero flying in on his private jet."

Trout Marguery

2 cups Béchamel Sauce (see page 121)	Water to cover trout
1 cup Hollandaise Sauce (see page 189)	16 large shrimp, boiled and peeled
4 (6 ounce) trout filets	6 large mushrooms, blanched

Prepare Béchamel and Hollandaise Sauces and set aside.
Roll trout filets and secure with toothpicks. Place in a medium sauce pan and cover with water. Poach over medium heat for 3 minutes. Cover pan and turn off the heat.
    Chop shrimp into large chunks and slice mushrooms. In a large sauce pan, pour in Béchamel Sauce. Add shrimp and mushrooms and simmer over low heat for 5 minutes.
    Place one trout roll on each plate and remove toothpicks. Remove Béchamel Sauce from the heat and fold in Hollandaise until well-blended and spoon over trout servings.
    SERVES 4.

In the 1960s, John Fontenot waited on Jim Taylor, an ex-football star from LSU who tried to pay for his meal with a credit card. When he was told that Galatoire's did not accept plastic, he demanded of John, "Do you know who I am?" John replied that he did and had seen him play football on television, but that did not alter the fact that they could not accept his card. Taylor became more and more upset, saying, "You know I'm president of a bank?" Finally his wife told him, "You'd better behave." John diplomatically suggested that he speak to Mr. Justin, who told the angry customer, "Put your name and address on this paper and we'll bill you."

    Jason Robards had the right idea: Go in with a regular. Photographer Louis Sahuc met Robards on a movie shoot in the early nineties, and the actor told him that he had always wanted to go to Galatoire's but could never get in because there was always a line. Sahuc said "Not a problem," and took him over there. "That day there was no line," Sahuc said, "so we waltzed right in." Nancy Moss (Mrs. Hartwig, III) joined the two and told Robards that *A Thousand Clowns* was her all-time favorite play. So he got up and acted out about fifteen minutes of the drama, playing all the parts. "There were only a few people in the place, and nobody knew what was going on," said Sahuc. "Some probably didn't even know who he was. But it was truly an extraordinary performance."

Stories about Jimmy Buffett and Galatoire's are legion. During one Jazz Fest in the late eighties Buffett played an outdoor concert in Woldenberg Park by the river and it went on until 4:00 A.M. At Galatoire's the next day about noon Buffett had nine people waiting for him, led by his usual New Orleans gang of Parrotheads: Robert Alford, Louis Sahuc, and Ed Bradley. The phone rang, and Jackson Browne answered it. "Jackson, is that you?" said Jimmy. "We rocked with you until about 4:00 A.M. this morning," Browne answered. "You were there?" "Yes." "You made it to work?" "Yes." "I was going to tell everybody I couldn't make it, but I guess I'll have to come on in then"—and he did. After another late night performance, Buffett came into Galatoire's the next morning looking tired and unkempt but still ready to act outrageous with

Leon Galatoire III and Jimmy Buffet enjoy a laugh

FANS OF GALATOIRE'S (PAST AND PRESENT)

Jessica Lange, Alec Baldwin, Kim Basinger, Ed Bradley, Mick Jagger, Rex Reed, Jimmy Buffett, Richard Thomas, Lee Meriwether, Bob Hope, Bernadette Peters, Robert Duvall, Phil Harris, Alice Faye, Rocky Marciano, Rob Reiner, Carl Reiner, Carroll O'Connor, Steven Segal, Caroline Kennedy, John Kennedy Jr., Bruce Springsteen, Arnold Palmer, Justin Wilson, Bob Barker, Edwin Edwards, R. C. Gorman, Judy Collins, Julia Child, Tennessee Williams, David Brinkley, Jason Robards, Natalie Wood, Robert Redford, Cybill Shepherd, Richard Gere, Patricia Neal, Stephanie Zimbalist, Elizabeth Ashley, Michael York, Mel Brooks, Anne Bancroft, Charles Laughton, Sidney Pollack, Lauren Hutton, Harpo Marx,

Sahuc and artist Peter Yokum, who were called "The Wild Men of the Quarter" in the eighties because outrageous behavior at Galatoire's was their specialty. Before Buffett got to the table, he spotted a gorgeous woman in their party. He left hurriedly, telling his waiter he'd be back, and when he returned, he was all cleaned up and wearing fresh clothes, obviously out to make a good impression on the lady.

Bridget Kramer Balentine, a Galatoire's regular who now lives in Aspen, is an active member of the New Orleans Parrotheads. She was on hand when the Eagles performed at the Superdome, and she took band member Glenn Frey and his wife Cindy to lunch at Galatoire's. "I told Glenn he should try the Café Brûlot, but he said no, he would just have regular coffee," recalled Bridget. "I ordered it anyway, and he liked it so much, he just dumped his coffee out and dunked his cup in the bowl." Bridget also remembers a lunch during the time Pope John Paul II was in town, September 11–13, 1987. His Holiness did not dine at Galatoire's, but no matter, Buffett and Bradley wore Pope masks and soap on a rope and went around the dining room with palms upraised blessing the tables in faux Latin.

Ed Bradley wearing a favorite pair of glasses

Secrecy is virtually impossible where rock star Mick Jagger is concerned. "One Sunday Ed Bradley called and I said bring him on in, but keep it quiet," recalled Leon Galatoire. Although Bradley dutifully kept it

Raquel Welch, Brenda Lee, Fanny Flagg, Steve Allen, E. G. Marshall, Natalie Schaeffer of *Gilligan's Island*, President George W. Bush, Diana Ross, Pernell Roberts, Rowan and Martin, Terry Bradshaw, David Schwimmer, Rosie Greer, Oliver Stone, Mike Wallace, Natalie Portman, Dick Van Patten, Laura Bush, the Bush twins—Barbara and Jenna, Willard Scott, Dan Rather, Francis Ford Coppola, Dennis Miller, Britney Spears, Jeff Foxworthy, Lena Horne, Lloyd Nolan, Shirley Temple Black, Robert Taylor, Tyrone Power, Johnny Unitas, Laurence Fishburne, Courtney Cox, David Arquette.

quiet, Leon called his girl friend and she alerted her friends, so there were numerous fans in the dining room waiting to see Jagger, who dined on the Grand Gouté and Grilled Pompano with Crabmeat. "The girl from the next door lingerie boutique brought in a Mick Jagger poster and he signed it. He was very nice." M. C. Emmons, who waited on the party with Cesar Rodriguez, recalled that a birthday was being celebrated at the next table, and when Imre began to sing "Happy Birthday," Jagger joined in. The celebrant kept saying, "Wow, what a rare treat. I had Mick Jagger singing happy birthday to me." M. C. read that Mick Jagger, Kim Basinger, and Jessica Lange were three of the hardest autographs to get in the world, "and all three of them, very graciously, signed autographs for me."

Galatoire's remained open late one night to accommodate the band U2 after their performance at the Superdome. Their group of twenty included Ashley and Wynonna Judd. Although the kitchen closed earlier, the party went on until 2:00 A.M., with only the sconces on the walls providing illumination due to a request for dim lights.

Bernadette Peters, a friend of Leon Galatoire III, is a frequent patron of the restaurant. About ten years ago, when Leon was still manager, she was playing at the Blue Room and came in with her entourage after the restaurant had closed. One couple had finished dining but refused to leave and just sat there and watched her eat. Understandably, that made her nervous, so rather than Leon asking them to leave (which he said he could not do) her manager went back to the restroom and put on a chef's outfit, then came out and told the dawdling couple to say goodnight. When Leon finally opened the door to let the actress and her party out, there were at least 150 people outside on the sidewalk waiting for her to appear. "Miss Peters didn't expect it and was absolutely surprised," Leon said. "She was very nice and signed autographs."

The paparazzi would have been ecstatic during the Tennessee Williams Literary Festival in the spring of 1997 when actor Alec Baldwin was a special Festival guest. Baldwin had told a reporter who asked if he had any plans for his visit: "I love Galatoire's. Obviously, when I go to New Orleans I want to eat." One frolicsome Galatoire's evening, Baldwin and some of his Hollywood cronies were dining with much hilarity in "do-rags"—napkins tied in knots at the corners and worn on their heads. This custom was begun in olden days by slave women working in plantation kitchens. The locals watched the celebrity goings-on with bemusement, for they had all seen "do-rags" worn here before. Usually, however, it was by very drunken lawyers on the Friday before Mardi Gras. Nowadays rumor has it that the old Galatoire's embroidered napkins taken from the restaurant as souvenirs are being used all over the world by film crews as "do-rags," even as far away as Australia and New Zealand. Dennis Quaid, Kathleen Turner, and Alec Baldwin may have begun the fashion in film land, but now everybody wants one.

Artist LeRoy Neiman at his table

Lynette Stilwell and artist LeRoy Neiman met one Friday when Neiman and his secretary Lynn Quayle were seated next to Stilwell, who was sitting alone downing Martinis and waiting for the rest of her party, the Quarter Rats, to arrive. The Rats are a group of French Quarter friends who lunch at the restaurant loudly and frequently (Nina Tyler, Carol Allen, Gloria Amadee, Beth Mazur). Neiman always makes sketches for paintings while at Galatoire's and the stylish Stilwell found herself the subject of one. Not short on hospitality in the convivial style of Galatoire's, she introduced herself and invited Neiman and Quayle to join her table. The artist complied and, when the rest of the party arrived, became the first and only male Quarter Rat.

When Neiman comes to New Orleans for his openings at Hanson Gallery on Royal Street, the Rats always make the scene and gather for gala lunches at Galatoire's. As a result, they all have the artist's framed likenesses of themselves on their walls. The Rats also own T-shirts sporting mice with rhinestone eyes, but they would not be caught dead wearing a T-shirt to Galatoire's. "It's a Beverly Hills wear-hats-to-lunch-stay-all-day thing," Neiman told celebrity-watcher and columnist Chris Rose. "Nobody ever told

Brenda Lee, right, with favorite waiter, Lee McDaniel

me Galatoire's was the best, but it is," Neiman said. "*The New Yorker* describes the restaurant as a combination of Maxim's and the 21 Club."

Local celebrities often make the scene, too. In his famously fractured English, flamboyant artist and furniture designer Mario Villa, originally from Guatemala, calls Galatoire's an "oasees of pice." "I go there when I want to feel like a reel New Orleanian," he said. "I put on my leetle coat, and it's yust a magical place." Villa was present in 1995 when *Vogue* writer Julia Reed put a Friday lunch party of ten people together for the magazine's European editor-at-large Hamish Bowles. "It was a gret, gret, GRET lunch," said Villa; "they crown a Galatoire King and he parade around and around the restaurant. It was a day of famous pipple!" Exotic entertainer Chris Owens has been coming to Galatoire's for years from her club down the street. Another flamboyant local celebrity, now deceased, was present in effigy for Valerie Cahill's fortieth birthday on the evening of Friday, December 13, 2002. Cahill's friends, along with musician Ernie K-Doe's widow, Antoinette, brought his wax likeness—colorfully and spectacularly attired and bejeweled—to sit at Donald Lambert Sr.'s usual Friday table, which was extended to accommodate the large party. As the evening progressed, Cahill's celebratory group left Galatoire's and returned to K-Doe's big white limousine driven by his personal chauffeur for the trip to the Mother-in-Law Lounge (made famous by K-Doe's hit song "Mother-in-Law") where some two hundred guests waited to continue the party.

"Galatoire's is my absolute favorite restaurant in the world," says entertainer and song writer Rich Look. Married to real estate broker Cassandra

Sharpe, Rich performs often at Le Chat Noir. About Galatoire's Cassandra says, "Every time I walk into Galatoire's I am flooded with memories. Old World is what Galatoire's is all about. It has been left behind, and thank God for that. We really don't know what we have—the last little bit of Paris in New Orleans."

Béchamel Sauce

4 cups milk
1/2 teaspoon salt
1/2 teaspoon white pepper
Pinch cayenne pepper
1 bay leaf

1/2 cup white wine
1/2 cup butter
1/2 cup flour
1 cup heavy cream (if needed)

In a sauce pan, heat the milk to a simmer. Reduce heat and add salt, pepper, cayenne, bay leaf, and white wine. Simmer for a few minutes.

In a separate pan, melt the butter over low heat and add the flour, constantly stirring the roux with a wire whisk.

Strain the milk through a fine sieve and pour it into the roux pot, stirring constantly in a circular motion until the sauce thickens.

Add heavy cream, if needed, to enrich the sauce or to thin it out if it becomes too thick.

Simmer for 5 minutes.

MAKES 4 CUPS.

Stars from the entertainment world are not the only celebrities to dine at Galatoire's, of course, for there have also been numerous politicians and statesmen through the decades, including several U.S. presidents, a bevy of U.S. senators, and an equally impressive number of governors, among them the irrepressible jokester Edwin Edwards. Gilberto Eyzaguirre remembered having served three presidents from Central American countries in one day. After Hurricane Betsy in 1965, when frequent customer and New Orleans mayor Victor Schiro went on TV to reassure the city, "Don't believe any rumors unless you hear them from me," John Fontenot said "the whole joint was talking and laughing about it the next day." Fontenot also recalls the visit of President George W. Bush during the Republican National Convention of 1988 along with "the President's daughter, old man Bush's daughter—they all came and ate here, it was pretty neat." More recently, on New Year's Eve, 2002, George W.'s twin daughters, Barbara and Jenna, dined upstairs with six friends and were served by Andi Knox and Sunny Holliday. David Gooch had provided everyone with party hats, and the group remained for a long, leisurely dinner, with plenty of drinks and celebration.

In March of 2004, First Lady Laura Bush dined at Galatoire's with, among others, developer Joe Canizaro and shipbuilder Boysie Bollinger. According to the *Times Picayune,* an Acme Oyster po-boy found its way into Mrs. Bush's hands as she stepped out of Galatoire's, presented by Acme personnel waiting on the sidewalk outside. Writer Chris Rose wrote that the stunt came about because Mrs. Bush had once expressed a preference for oysters over king cake.

Antoine's got into the act when actress Savanna Smith asked for Baked Alaska, a specialty of Antoine's, not Galatoire's. Leon Galatoire (then manager), Roy Guste (then manager of Antoine's), and Steve Hogan arranged for a large Baked Alaska to be hand-carried down Bourbon Street from Antoine's to Galatoire's and presented aflame to the actress with lights lowered and a lineup of Antoine's and Galatoire's waiters standing by. This showy caper made up for the time when a lady came to dine at Antoine's and was dissatisfied with her table location. "Where would you like to be, madam?" asked the Antoine's waiter. Her answer: "Well, really, I'd like to be at Galatoire's."

Sunny Holliday remembers the night that Madeleine Albright, President Bill Clinton's Secretary of State, dined at Galatoire's with her entourage of seven or eight people. They had called ahead to reserve space upstairs, but only the downstairs was open that night. So they were seated at table 22. Secret Service men secured the place before Albright arrived, and while she was in the restaurant, one Secret Service man was on the roof, one by the door, and several inside Galatoire's. "She reminded me of my Guatemalan grandmother," said Sunny, who usually prefers not to wait on the famous because "most of them expect special treatment." Her exceptions are "very nice" comic Jeff Foxworthy and Lauren Hutton, who sits at table 35 downstairs.

During the Clinton/Lewinsky scandal *New York Times* syndicated columnist Maureen Dowd skipped a panel at the Investigative Reporters & Editors National Conference in favor of the famous Friday lunch at Galatoire's, where "lawyers in seersucker are smoking big cigars and drinking champagne and telling tall tales. Blondes in flowered chiffon dresses and strappy heels are doing business on cell phones and drinking white wine and flirting with gentlemen at nearby tables." The gist of her column the next day (*Times-Picayune* June 9, 1998) reflected her belief that today's public is "numb" to political corruption and that "the rest of the country has taken on Louisiana's tolerant and bemused attitude."

That tolerant attitude, at least when it came to New Orleans District Attorney Jim Garrison, did not apply to the popular head of the International Trade Mart, Clay Shaw, who was acquitted of what most consider a trumped-up charge of conspiring to assassinate President John F. Kennedy. Shaw was an everyday diner at Galatoire's ("he always sat at a side table") and, according to his many supporters, "a wonderful man and a strong force for good in the community until the sensational trial that ruined his career and his health."

The unflappable maitre d' since 1991, former boat dealer Arnold Chabaud, is a master of the celebrity game. While being completely the gentleman, he makes it clear that famous people do not get special treatment at Galatoire's— "at least any more special than the usual service that everybody enjoys."

From left to right, Cesar Rodriguez, Zachary Richard, musician;
maitre d' Arnold Chabaud

Special parties could be handled with panache, however, when the restaurant was closed or at times when it was not busy. When A&M records first signed renowned Cajun musician Zachary Richard, they celebrated the occasion at Galatoire's one night after most of the customers had gone. Chabaud and his wife Shannon, business manager for the Neville Brothers, were invited. "Everybody was tired from Jazz Fest, and we were just transfixed when the door opened and there was a table that took up almost the entire side of the restaurant, the longest table anyone had ever seen. It was all set with wine glasses and silver that reflected in the mirrors. The vision was wonderful—a beautiful sight," said Chabaud. That was the night Zach rose and sang a Cajun lament, "Aux Natchitoches," in tribute to his late waiter, the inimitable Nelson Marcotte, who had died the week before. He sang it a capella in French," said Chabaud. "You could sense Zach's emotion. Everybody felt it. It was a touching and memorable moment."

Kenneth Holditch and Kim Hunter dining at
Tennessee Williams's favorite table

In March 1999, Kim Hunter was in New Orleans for her first visit in decades to participate in the Tennessee Williams Literary Festival. She was taken on a literary tour of the French Quarter during which events seemed to conspire to make it an enchanted afternoon for the actress, the guide, and the other tourists. On Dumaine Street, near the house Tennessee Williams bought in 1962, three young men, slightly intoxicated, saw a woman on a third-floor balcony and began to yell at her, "Stella! Stella!," without having the vaguest notion that the actress who had first created Stella on stage and in the movies in *A Streetcar Named Desire* was within hearing range. As the group stopped in the two hundred block of Bourbon Street, the guide turned to Miss Hunter and asked, "Stella, do you remember taking Blanche to Galatoire's for dinner?" She replied that she did indeed remember the fictional scene, but that she had never been to the restaurant. The next day, two NPR radio producers from San Francisco, Davia Nelson, and Nikki Silva, took the original Stella and the tour guide to Galatoire's for a memorable drinking and eating experience. The restaurant staff presented Kim Hunter with a glass inscribed "Galatoire's" and one of the old menus as souvenirs of her remarkable experience. Seeing the woman who first and most memorably brought Stella to life on stage at Williams's table was yet another of those unique and marvelous Galatoire's time warps.

Actress Carrie Nye, center, with two friends from the Mississippi Delta

During the 2002 Festival, Richard Thomas, a fine actor who gained fame as John-Boy in *The Waltons,* did a staged reading of letters by the young Tennessee Williams and dined later at Galatoire's with Rex Reed and a few others. Friendly customers came by the table to speak to him as though he were really the small-town neighbor he played on TV and he responded in kind. Another night Rex Reed came in with Elizabeth Ashley, Patricia Neal,

LOFTY PRAISE FROM JOHN-BOY WALTON

So, I figure that since all good folks want to get into heaven, all folks who love good food want to get into Galatoire's. For if the streets of one are paved with gold, the tables of the other are laden with Oysters en Brochette, Trout Amandine, and Cup Custard. And, since conversation in the heavenly city must be between like-minded souls and joyous—Mark Twain and G. B. Shaw—so the act of being gathered together over the snowy linen of Galatoire's, and under the gaze of one of her ministering angels, likewise must inspire that conviviality which makes life here below worth the waiting until our reward.

RICHARD THOMAS

and Stephanie Zimbalist. Dick Cavett and Carrie Nye were Reed's companions at Galatoire's during the 2003 festival.

Reed recalled a visit to New Orleans in 1966 during the filming of the Williams play *This Property Is Condemned*. He was assigned to interview its star, Natalie Wood, for *The New York Times*. "Natalie was so enamored of Galatoire's that she virtually turned it into the studio commissary," said Reed. "She went to lunch there every day, often with Robert Redford, her costar, and Sidney Pollack, the director." One day Ruthie the Duck Girl, a beloved street vagabond who roller-skated around the French Quarter in a full-length net Alice in Wonderland gown followed by a gaggle of ducks, was standing at the entrance to the restaurant selling postcards of herself. "Three for a quaaataa," Ruthie brayed to Wood in her deep voice, and was invited inside by the movie star, who did not want to attract unwanted attention standing on Bourbon Street negotiating for postcards. Wood was thrilled with the images, and immediately sent them to some of her best friends, Herbert Ross, Nora Kaye, and Elia ("Gadge") Kazan. The next day the actress wanted more postcards, and sure enough, Ruthie was back. This time: "Three for a dollaaa." "I think I'm getting schnockered," said Wood.

Tennessee Williams's brother Dakin frequently holds court at Galatoire's with local friends and out-of-town fans during the annual festivals. Dakin is always dressed in bright silk Armani jackets with precious rings sparkling on his fingers and a large jeweled pectoral cross that had belonged to his and Tennessee's grandfather, Reverend Walter Dakin, dangling from his neck.

Mel Gussow captured it all in *The New York Times* in May 2001. "While Stanley Kowalski and his friends have their 'poker night' (the original title of '*Streetcar*'), Stella takes Blanche to supper at Galatoire's. That restaurant, one of Williams's personal favorites, remains as it was in his lifetime, a sea of white tablecloths and tuxedoed waiters, the noise level as high as the conviviality. Williams's table is in a corner by the window, with no plaque commemorating its most famous guest but with memories wafting through the room."

Cesar standing, and favorite customers,
Bob Edmundson and his wife Cathy

CESAR RODRIGUEZ

Latino Superstar

*F*or more than twenty-five years Cesar Rodriguez was one of the most popular waiters at Galatoire's, with a long list of customers and a unique personality. His Latin good looks and ironic, off-hand sense of humor pleased both women and men. Cesar was a favorite of Miss Yvonne's, who, one of his fellow waiters recalled, could always follow whatever kind of joke he was carrying on.

Although Cesar passed on into the Great Beyond June 3, 2002, none of his preferees will ever forget him, and stories about him are legion.

The Peruvian native came to work at Galatoire's in 1974 when the restaurant where he had been working had a major fire and was closed temporarily. As is customary, he acquired the new position because another Galatoire's waiter recommended him. From the beginning, Cesar was a stand-out in many ways, not the least of which was his weekly commute from Orlando, where his wife lived and worked for Delta Airlines. With spousal privileges, on Thursdays he jumped on a plane for the hour's flight to New Orleans and was homeward bound Monday mornings. He was known by his regulars as "our jet-set waiter."

To learn English, Cesar attended Delgado Community College and later studied business at the University of New Orleans, but he found his real calling at Galatoire's where his pampered customers included Jimmy Buffett, Ed Bradley, and dozens of local devotees. "I'm spoiled," Cesar told a newspaper reporter in 1991. "Ninety percent of my customers are regulars. With regulars you don't have to work so hard; you already know what they like." Cesar's regulars never bothered to look at the menu. He would either tell you the best choices and let you select or, depending upon his mood, just bring on the meal he knew you wanted. As far as some were concerned, Cesar could even be a chef. On occasion he went into the kitchen to grill steaks himself, and those were said to be the best steaks of all. Once he was standing in the door of the restaurant and saw one of his regulars, a guide, standing across the street with a literary tour. Cesar came out and called to him, "You left your doggy bag last night when you were here." The guide and his group laughed and proceeded up the street, stopping here and there to see a site associated with an author. They were two blocks away when Cesar caught up with them, held out a bag of hot fried shrimp, and said, "See you soon," and headed back to Galatoire's. The tourists were astounded, and one asked, "Do waiters always treat you that well." The guide laughing, said, "What can I say? This is New Orleans, that was Galatoire's, and Cesar is Cesar!"

One of Cesar's regular customers, Julia Reed, came in late one evening and after Cesar brought her usual drink, he asked what she wanted to eat. "You know what I'd really like is a Krystal hamburger," she said. "Cesar sighed and shook his head and shrugged his shoulders, as only he could do, and dashed out of the restaurant. He came back shortly thereafter with a paper bag full of four small Krystal burgers. "Now here's your dinner," he announced to Reed. "Eat it, I'm ready to go home."

Among others of his hundreds of customers, the Moores from McComb, Mississippi, developed a strong friendship with Cesar, and would always call ahead before making the trip to New Orleans to be certain that he was working. The couple still keeps a bottle of Old Taylor behind the bar, not a popular brand for most bourbon drinkers, and Cesar would bring their bourbons out to the line, if necessary. Ophelia Moore remembers occasions when Cesar would simply grab the Old Taylor bottle and place it on their table, saying that it was easier to cut out the middleman. The Moore daughters proudly display Cesar's gifts of carafes and engraved sugar bowls on their dining tables.

Former Miss America Lee Meriwether joined a group of New Orleans friends at Galatoire's for lunch, three of whom were Cesar regulars. The usually blasé waiter was so overjoyed to meet the actress— Meriwether was his mother's favorite star (in her ongoing role in *Barnaby Jones,* at that time still playing reruns in Peru)—that he asked for her autograph for his mother and brought her a gift bottle of wine, whereupon one of the party, Nancy Huls, took great issue with the starstruck waiter. "You've been my waiter for twenty years, great tips and all," she complained, "and you never gave me a bottle of *anything.*" Huls added in an especially aggrieved voice: "I know Lee was Miss America, but I was Meridian's Miss Hospitality." Another of the group chimed in: "Me, too; I was Miss Laurel." So Cesar went back to the kitchen and returned with another bottle.

Exotic entertainer Chris Owens is another of the glamorous women who adored Cesar. She recalls taking a group to Galatoire's for dinner. "Cesar greeted me like a star," she says. "He brought a bottle of my favorite champagne to the table, but when he uncorked it, the liquid bubbled and spurted everywhere. 'Quick,' he said, 'splash some behind your ears. It's good luck!' And since Cesar said it, we did it."

At Cesar's wake, one of his long time preferees and friends spoke of the effect of the Cesar's passing:

"To me—and to hundreds of patrons of Galatoire's, Cesar was not just a friend, but an institution, a symbol and embodiment of the unique relationship that has existed in New Orleans for surely a century between waiters at great restaurants and their regular customers. If you were his customer, you were also his friend, and Cesar, like his colleagues at Galatoire's, knew not only your drink of choice and how you wanted it mixed, what fish you preferred, and how you wanted your shrimp or crabmeat or soft-shell crab prepared, but he also knew the story of your family, what projects you were involved in, any problems you were facing, and just what mood you might be in on any particular occasion. Cesar possessed a most acutely ironic sense of humor, and his words and antics often converted one from a bad mood into a renewed sense that life is, after all, precious and well worth living. He knew your birthday—and probably your age—and saw to it that it was acknowledged in whatever way you wished—some of us are not fond of being sung to; others are.

"Cesar worked at Galatoire's for almost a quarter of a century and became a very vital and integral spirit of one of the city's greatest institutions. With his passing, the institution, its customers, and the city have suffered a great loss. It is a blessing that we can still see his face smiling at us from the pages of a variety of magazines in which he appeared. Those of us who care, who cherish the tradition Cesar Rodriguez embodied, will perhaps some day join him in a gourmet's paradise in which he will be serving us Crabmeat Yvonne, Shrimp Clemenceau, Trout Amandine, his own special smoked filet, and whatever other culinary treasures appeal to our palates, and entertaining us with his delightful company. Ave! Cesar! We will miss you more than we perhaps let you know. God bless."

KENNETH HOLDITCH

Act Three
Rituals & Ceremonies

Scene Seven

Street Pageant
The Line

"Everyone has his Galatoire's line story, because anyone who likes good food has waited there to eat it."
—Harriet Cortez, *New Orleans States-Item*, June 1, 1972

One of Galatoire's most enduring customs was the long line out front, a result of the persistent refusal of the restaurant to take reservations. One local wag dubbed it "the white man's food line." A mixture of melodrama, curiosity, and anticipation always swirled around the well-dressed people queued up on raunchy Bourbon Street to wait for a table. Who was standing in as a proxy? What celebrity would try to jump the line? What colorful character would saunter by? How did that group of eleven get in before us? Can I offer you a pre cocktail cocktail from the bar across the street? Give those little tap-dancers a dollar, dear. Wow, check out the see-through undies in the window next door! "Even the line is fun at Galatoire's," said a regular, "it's like a separate little social event outside." The Bourbon Street theater was always a titillating preview of the show inside.

Before World War II the restaurant's private dining rooms upstairs could be reserved; but during and after the war—because of the shortage of waiters—those dining rooms were closed and the legendary line began in earnest. Gordon Maginnis, realtor and member of an old-line New Orleans family, recalls that his grandmother, Mrs. John B. Hobson, did it her way, line or no line. "Her chauffeur would drive her to Galatoire's and she would march through the delivery entrance to the back of the restaurant and enter the dining room to take her place at a table." However, for everyone else, until the renovation from 1998–99 when the upstairs dining rooms were

It is always a party in line at Galatoire's

reopened with a bar added, the line was an inflexible yet weirdly cherished fact of life for Galatoire's patrons. Standing in line could lead to some interesting conversations with a variety of people, a few of them wanting to know, "Have you eaten here before?" and "What's the food like?" or "Is it worth waiting?" to which one answers, of course, "Yes, many times, but never often enough" and "Great, unlike anything you'll find anywhere else" and "If you like good food, it's worth waiting. If not, there's a lineup of fast food chains on Canal Street a few blocks that way."

Loyal regulars were usually not annoyed by the line and, indeed, when it was gone, some even felt nostalgia for it. It was, after all, a restaurant line of distinction—the only one in which New Orleanians would ever dream of standing. It is noteworthy that when Galatoire's was undergoing renovation, some of the patrons who groaned the loudest about the line and the inconvenience of not being able to reserve a table were troubled that the practice

NO RESERVATIONS
Please Go to the End of the Line

would be discontinued. For diehards who yearned for the status quo, the abolition of the line seemed to herald the final apocalypse. "Not having to wait outside in rain or cold weather is appealing," said a wistful Betty DeCell, a French Quarter resident and Galatoire's regular since 1962. On the other hand, she'll miss it, too. "I've met so many interesting people over the years, standing out there in the line."

Perhaps one of them was the nicely-soused lady from Chicago who came down Bourbon Street in 1995 with two bourbons in go-cups, wanting to dispose of one of them. As she chatted up the people waiting to get into Galatoire's, she offered her extra drink to everybody, but nobody in line would take it. She lurched off, saying: "Well, hell, you can never find a drunk when you need one." Or maybe it was the braless, over-endowed woman who swung pendulously by saying, "Some people just shouldn't wear hot pants." Or the two Chevron Oil executives that J. Wilson Jones III met, who had fired up the corporate jet and flown over from Houston just to take their wives to dinner "at their favorite dining spot." Or the dapper old Frenchman in white linen Shirley Ann Grau wrote about: "I remember when this place wasn't so famous but what you could get in. We advance backwards!"

Unbeknownst to those standing in it, one day the Galatoire's line changed a life. A young man who had wasted his life to the point of standing in line every day at the Ozanam Inn soup kitchen in the Warehouse District was ambling into the French Quarter one day. He approached Galatoire's and passed the long line of people standing out front. He noticed that they all looked happy and smiling and well-dressed—they were having fun—and the people in line at the Ozanam Inn looked sad, depressed, and down-at-the-heels—completely the opposite. At that moment, he had an epiphany: He'd rather be in the Galatoire's line. He resolved then and there to become the sort of person who could stand in the Galatoire's line. He made something of himself, has a family, and is now successful. Of course, he eventually returned to New Orleans to take his place in line and dine at Galatoire's.

As genteel and friendly as the line was, it did not allow for line jumpers of any ilk or fame, or those who were perceived as being line jumpers. People have been known to get downright rude. One Sunday evening after a business meeting at the Fairmont, Temple Brown instructed an out-of-towner joining their table to "walk around the line, come on in, and don't make eye contact. Look like you own the place." The man arrived much later, looking disheveled, and said, "They're real hostile out there, kicking me in the shins and pushing me around." The man had tried to jump the line by shaking hands with everybody, "but that was the worst thing he could have done" said Brown.

Because the line had already started forming, Yancy Jones had a hard time getting inside one year when her father was hosting an Ole Miss vs. Tulane football brunch before Galatoire's opened. Late arrivals, she and two friends tried the front door, but it was locked. A man in line told her that the restaurant was not open yet, but she began to knock, which annoyed him further. "Honey, this is the line. They aren't open yet." She tried to explain about the party, but the man growled at them to get to the back of the line. In the nick of time, her father opened the door. "We smiled at the mean man and his party and walked inside," she said. "We had the entire dining room to ourselves, and we felt like royalty."

One regular attempted to buck the line in a spectacular way, a notable exception to all those—locals, tourists, and even pampered celebrities—who generally accepted and respected the line tradition. It seems that the *Times-Picayune* carried an announcement in its social column that a Galatoire's regular had reserved the entire restaurant for a Friday luncheon party. In addition to regular Friday customers who had also read the article with dismay, Miss Yvonne was annoyed enough to ask, "Who does she think owns this place?" On the appointed day, the woman arrived before opening time to discover the usual long line waiting at the door so she proceeded to go through the service entrance, the kitchen, and into the dining room. She announced to the staff that she wanted all the tables for her party. When they refused, she continued to insist upon having her wish and as time passed and the argument intensified, she was asked to leave. When she refused, two waiters were instructed to escort her out of the restaurant, which they did, one grasping each arm, back through the kitchen, the service alley, and out to the sidewalk, and thus the contretemps ended. Steve Hogan also earned Miss Yvonne's disapproval for attempting to jump the line, and on at least one occasion succeeding. Finally he got back into her good graces after going out West to pan for gold and bringing her back a vial of gold dust.

Through the years the line has become so much a part of New Orleans lore that it has taken on a mythic quality—so much so that often it is difficult to separate myth from reality. Nevertheless, when regulars bring in out-of-town friends unfamiliar with the restaurant's unique traditions, they love to

OH, MY HEART

People are very possessive about their place in line at Galatoire's. One day a couple had inched their way almost to the front when the gentleman began to exhibit signs of a heart attack. An ambulance was called, and an emergency vehicle soon arrived. The man was placed on a stretcher inside the vehicle, the wife accompanied him inside it, and the doors closed. But instead of the ambulance moving on down Bourbon Street toward the hospital, it remained parked in front of Galatoire's, its lights flashing. Alarmed patrons watched with trepidation for about fifteen minutes, only to see the ambulance doors open regale their guests with line stories without regard to their veracity. For example, many a New Orleanian has dined out on the tale, which may be apocryphal, that the Duke and Duchess of Windsor, during their 1950 visit to the city, stood in line for a table. Others of the famous who braved the line, presumably without a whimper, included numerous movie stars and musicians, the Shah of Iran, Henry Kissinger, presidents Roosevelt, Eisenhower and Carter, and presidential candidate Gary Hart, who before his fall from grace—and after standing in line for a half hour—entered to a standing ovation from those dining on Super Bowl weekend. When the distinguished English actor Charles Laughton grew testy standing in the lunch line, Justin Frey placated him by explaining the system. He suggested that if Laughton came back that evening at five, he was likely to be seated at once. Not only did Laughton return that night, but he did so several times within the next few days.

Captain Clarke Hawley ("Doc"), retired captain of the *Natchez*, which operates out of New Orleans, asked President Gerald Ford when he was on board the steamboat if he had eaten at Galatoire's. The president responded that he had not because he refused to stand in line, thus joining Charles De Gaulle in the ranks of those forever outside the doors. David Gooch commented that "The feeling was that if you're that important, send somebody to stand in line and hold the table for you. Lots of people did that." Dwight Eisenhower left a Secret Service man to stand in line and waited for a table in his nearby limo. In February 1994 *Worth Magazine's* Global Chic "checklist of cool for status seekers in New Orleans" listed "Paying someone to wait in line for you at Galatoire's on Friday afternoon, then having Imre as your waiter." The other two were "Shooting craps with Governor Edwards" and "For whites, riding with the Zulu Krewe during Mardi Gras; for blacks, riding with the Rex Krewe."

A local maneuver was to send a member of your group to stand in line early, with the rest coming later, a device made easier after the advent of cell phones. The lawyers who always lunch on Fridays were known for sending

and the couple emerge to reclaim their advantageous place in line.

"What happened?" everybody asked as the ambulance left. "Are you okay?" "Yes, it was a false alarm," the man replied. "I'm not having a heart attack, just a bad day."

"But you were feeling terrible. Don't you think you should go home and go to bed?" asked someone. "Are you kidding?" he answered. "It would really be a bad day if I had to give up my place at the head of the line."

their minions to stand in line. Or one could avoid the long lines by arriving during off hours, not during peak times, which are 11:30 A.M. to 1 P.M. for lunch or 6 P.M. to 8 P.M. in the evening. "I won't stand in line," declared Judge John Minor Wisdom in the *National Law Review*. "I go Sunday afternoons, about 2:30. That way we can feed at the trough for hours. It's like a club. I've had the same waiter there for years." In a 1998 *Time* magazine article, Calvin Trillin wrote about a businessman who expressed concern years ago when a new industry was announced for New Orleans. Rather than reacting with the usual boosterism, he was afraid the influx of new executives into the city would cause longer lines at Galatoire's.

Chicken Financière

1 (3 1/2-pound) chicken, cut into 8 pieces	3 cloves of garlic, peeled and minced
Salt and freshly ground black pepper	4 medium white mushrooms, chopped
4 tablespoons of vegetable oil	2 1/2 cups beef stock
4 chicken livers	1 cup red wine
4 tablespoons of butter	2 tablespoons tomato paste
4 tablespoons of flour	1 teaspoon finely chopped fresh parsley
1/2 cup minced scallions,	Pinch cayenne pepper
white parts only	1/2 cup pitted sliced large green olives

Rinse chicken, pat dry, and season with salt and pepper. Heat oil in a large skillet over medium-high heat. Working in batches, brown chicken for about 6 minutes per side. Remove and set aside. Add livers to skillet and cook for about 30 seconds per side. Remove and set aside.

Pour off fat, add butter, and melt over medium-low heat. Add flour and cook, stirring constantly with a wooden spoon, until mixture turns golden brown, about 10 minutes. Add scallions, garlic, and mushrooms and cook, stirring, until fragrant, 2 minutes more. Whisk in stock, wine, tomato paste, and parsley. Increase heat to medium, bring to a simmer, and cook, stirring occasionally, until sauce is thickened, about 15 minutes. Season to taste with salt, pepper, and cayenne pepper.

Add olives, chicken, and livers to the sauce. Reduce heat to low, cover, and cook, stirring occasionally, until juices run clear, about 25 minutes. Divide chicken and livers between 4 plates, coat with sauce, and serve. Garnish with additional parsley if desired.

SERVES 4.

One distinct advantage Galatoire's has over many other distinguished restaurants is that after it begins seating for lunch at thirty minutes before noon Tuesday through Saturday and noon on Sunday (a concession to church-going patrons) they do not close until the dinner crowd has departed in the evening, which can range from 10:30 P.M. to midnight. "I don't believe we've ever asked anyone to leave because of the hour," Miss Yvonne told William F. Diehl Jr. in 1966. "It's a real pleasure to find people who are willing to take the time to really enjoy their dinner."

The keeper of the door was the hero or the villain of the day, depending upon which side of the door a customer was standing. Because he must always do his job with finesse, he was always on the spot to manage the line diplomatically, yet firmly. Arnold Chabaud, assistant manager and maitre d' since 1991, was often called the most powerful man in New Orleans. Now, instead of being out on the sidewalk in an orderly line-up, diners are packed in upstairs at the bar or in the tiny entry hall waiting for their names to be called. Chabaud still finds his task demanding and even more chaotic on Fridays. The line still exists, but only as names on paper. The same seating rules apply. "It's still first come, first served," he says. "Most people want to sit downstairs, and downstairs only holds about 120–130 people." The down-

The line in hot summertime—men are carrying their coats, which they will don just before they enter the door; Bill Borah, center, talking to pass the time

stairs dining room is narrow, but optically expanded by the run-on wall mirrors. The arrangement of the thirty-nine tables is crucial, with long rows of two-tops that cannot be pushed together standing against mirrors and forming narrow aisles.

"People get distraught when they have been waiting a long time and no tables open up. They don't understand that I have no control over how long people stay. Some people think a game is going on (regulars call the supposed game a "fix"), but if nobody leaves, nobody can come in." Even now, when there is a bar upstairs and people have a place to wait, it seems they get even more distraught. "Oddly enough, they used to be more patient waiting in line outside," says Chabaud. "Now they come storming down and raise a fuss, but there's nothing I can do. I tell them to wait for their name to be called. Don't come down every ten minutes. I don't ever get mad, but I can't let even one person step over me. I have to be firm and not lose control."

Some considered the line to be Galatoire's best and cheapest way to spread the word about its quality. Certainly passersby wondered why so many people so often stood in front of this particular restaurant, and, with any degree of perspicacity, figured out that it must be a place to get an excellent meal. One wonders if perhaps it did not occur to the original Justin that he need never take out an advertisement—which he never did—because he often had a long line of devotees outside who might as well have been carrying sandwich boards proclaiming, "Eat here for a good, good meal!" "Monsieur Galatoire steadfastly refuses to advertise because 'the lines are too long now,'" wrote Diehl in the October 1966 *New Orleans Magazine.* In her book, *New Orleans* (1973), Sarah Seawright, commenting on the line one often saw in front of the restaurant and "the unpretentious decor," notes that "New Orleans' best restaurants have preserved the tradition that it is the food that counts."

Justin I's philosophy was that, given the number of patrons his establishment had and the number of them who returned again and again, he must be doing something right, so there was no need to change. Surprisingly, in a century in which change per se is extolled, he persisted in the old ways. It was he who established the "no reservations" policy during World War II when the shortage of waiters forced Galatoire's to close its upstairs private dining rooms. The policy remained in force until recently, becoming in the course of time one of the venerable traditions that distinguished Galatoire's from other restaurants. "My father used to say that if you take a reservation and the party arrives to find for some reason their table is not available, you have failed them, disappointed them, failed to fulfill your obligation to your customer," Miss Yvonne said. Consequently, Justin vowed never to make promises he was not certain he could keep; ergo, no reservations. She remembered her father, whom she affectionately called Popsy, as being a true democrat, who said, no doubt remembering his own early desire for a military career, "A poor soldier gets just as hungry as a rich banker. From now on we will operate on a first come, first served basis." He felt that everyone should be treated equally, from commoner to royalty, from laborer to captain of industry or elected politician. This he proved when Oklahoma State played St. Mary's in the Sugar Bowl back in 1946. The line was long when the Governor of Oklahoma showed up to dine, expecting his usual preferential treatment. Popsy went out to greet him and chat briefly, then asked, "You believe in fairness, don't you, Governor." "Certainly I do," he responded, as any astute politician would. "Then you will surely understand having to stand in line like everybody else." The governor smiled and nodded and the crisis was averted by the good will and diplomacy of the even more politic restaurateur.

Waiting in line at Galatoire's, where everyone is equal

Years later, in 1988, waiter John Fontenot came out to an extremely long Friday-before-Mardi-Gras line to tell J. Bennett Johnston, another political figure, who was at the time senator from Louisiana, that there was a telephone call for him from Ronald Reagan. As he escorted the senator into the restaurant, the maitre d' heard someone in the line say, "Well, he won't be back out," obviously assuming that after a call from the president, a table would be found for the senator. "It's a fix," someone else said, believing the call to be a ruse. To the surprise of the other standees, however, Johnston emerged from the restaurant a few minutes later, escorted by Fontenot, and dutifully returned to his place in line.

Even members of the family were not exempt. Carolyn Frey Rodman, a granddaughter of Justin, the patriarch, remembers standing in line when she and her friends went to the restaurant for her birthday parties. "You didn't cut in front of the paying guests," she said. Chris Ansel Jr., a Justin grandson, served for a while as maitre d' at the family restaurant. On a day when he was off duty, his grandfather invited him to "Come to the restaurant and I'll treat you and your wife." When Chris and his wife Sonja arrived, they took their place in line as if they were only another couple of customers awaiting their turn for a fine dining experience, and there they remained until their turn to enter. Justin Frey, another grandson and namesake of the original Justin, remembers bringing a girlfriend to Galatoire's and taking his place in line. The man behind him, annoyed by the wait and not knowing who Justin was, said, "I wish I was a member of the family; then I could get in." Justin said, "Well, I'm a member of the family, and I'm in line." The man said, "Yeah, sure." When Justin and his girlfriend went in, the man asked the maitre d', "Who is that?" His reply, "The grandson of the owner."

So world leaders, celebrities, senators, judges, royalty, celebrities, regular customers, newcomers and relatives all stood in line in equality and no one received special treatment. "That's what's great about the place; that everybody's equal," said Phil Brooks, whose cousin Phillip Schoen married Denise Galatoire and still had to stand in line. Trillin wrote: "There are people who believe that the line at Galatoire's Restaurant, which does not take reservations from anyone, is the only aboveboard operation in all of southern Louisiana."

Curtis Wilkie, at right, discussing the line with Kenneth Holditch, at left, and Marda Burton, center

"'TWAS THE FRIDAY
BEFORE CHRISTMAS ..."

'Twas the Friday before Christmas and in the hour before dawn, the only creatures stirring on the upper end of Bourbon Street were a dozen hardy souls holding a place in line outside Galatoire's.

Dressed in their windbreakers, sweatshirts and jeans in the dark and cold, they looked like supplicants at a soup kitchen. In fact, they represented the vanguard for one of the most fashionable lunches of the season. Yet when the restaurant finally opened at midday, none of them would get to go inside.

Instead, they would be paid for their duty and drift off, as one said, to buy "a bike for the kid" with the money. Those who hired them as stand-ins would actually sit down to the feast.

In a city that thrives on tradition, the overnight vigil has become an essential part of a unique festival: lunch at Galatoire's on the Friday before Christmas and, later, Mardi Gras.

Around 11 P.M. Thursday, Kirk Gros staked out the first spot and said he intended to keep his place around the clock. Just before the doors opened for lunch at 11:30 A.M., he said, he would yield his position to the party of eight paying him ten dollars an hour to ensure they would be seated.

Tables are coveted for Galatoire's long, leisurely lunches, where the meal usually spans five or six hours as elegant New Orleanians loosen up for the holiday weekend with endless rounds of Shrimp Rémoulade and Pouilly-Fuissé.

A listing in the social register does not guarantee a seat at Galatoire's, however. Since the restaurant takes no reservations, the beautiful people must find someone to wait for them before the maitre d' assigns someone to wait on them.

"This is the first year I've done this," said Gros, a security worker. "One of the ladies at the place where I work was trying to find somebody to stand in line, so I decided it was a way to earn a little extra Christmas money."

Louis Molina, behind Gros, said this was his fourth time to stand in line "for a lady who used to live here. She flies down from New York every year to do this party with about ten friends."

Albert Bryant, his face almost obscured by a bundle of wraps, said he was holding a place for ten people on behalf of an antiques dealer from nearby Royal Street. Ronnie Porter, a courier by day, said he had been hired by the president of an insurance company to claim title to twelve seats for Friday's lunch.

Because of the size of the groups that would come, and with seating limited in Galatoire's, there was no assurance that anyone without an overnight representative would be seated.

"Next year we're forming a union to make more money," said a man who was seventh in line and had brought his own folding chair.

Though the job entails spending the night on the sidewalk, it has its side benefits. A camaraderie develops among the stand-ins; they fetch one another coffee and doughnuts. And Bourbon Street offers a carnival of distractions for much of the night.

"We talk amongst ourselves and get to be one big family," said Troy Jones, whose sister-in-law is housekeeper for the folks who would pay him one-hundred dollars and eventually take his place. "And if you stay here long enough, you'll see almost anything, some pretty weird things."

During the wee hours Friday, the group witnessed two fights that spilled out of the Voodoo Lounge across the street, a parade of transvestites in slinky dresses and high heels, and finally, a flow of strip-tease artists heading home before dawn.

As the sky lightened, the stand-ins talked about how they would use the extra Christmas cash. They planned to buy presents for their children or their wives, they said, or to keep enough for a bottle or two of liquor for themselves.

But Ronnie Porter was more wistful. Gesturing toward Galatoire's, he said: "Someday, if I could afford it, I might like to see what it's like inside."

CURTIS WILKIE
"THEY ONLY SERVE WHO STAND,"
BOSTON GLOBE, DECEMBER 24, 1995

Act Three

Rituals & Ceremonies

Scene Eight

Friday Matinees
Friday Lunch

*"Lightheartedness as well as lightheadedness
is the mode of the day as time and rules are suspended."*
—Brenda Maitland, *Country Roads,* August 1998

In 1996, a young woman, newly arrived in town to take a job as public relations director for a major hotel, was told by local friends that she must dine at Galatoire's and that she should go on a Friday. "You're not going to believe it," they said. They told her about the long lines, the unusual and convivial mix of diners, and, of course the meals—meals that could last all afternoon and into the evening, lunch blending seamlessly into dinner at some point in the early evening when all consciousness of time had been erased by a succession of Martinis or Old-Fashioneds or Sazeracs or wine and the face of the beautiful old clock over the counter faded dizzily into a pleasant haze. She was not disappointed.

"When it's rolling on Friday afternoon, there's not a bar on the planet that is as wild as Galatoire's," said photographer Louis Sahuc. Nobody seems to remember the facts surrounding the origins of the now-famous ritual known as Friday lunch at Galatoire's, exactly when it became such a fixed lodestone in New Orleans life, or how it evolved into the on-going and often outrageous party that it is today. A party where Doc Hawley once "got so schnockered" that he walked outside and "got into an argument with a hitching post." A party where normally sedate businessmen have been known to smear on lipstick and kiss the tops of bald heads. A party that seems to get more rambunctious as the years go by.

145

Perhaps it is because New Orleans itself in its hedonistic way has always been in the habit of beginning its weekend revels at mid-day on Fridays—or even earlier. Those with an aversion to waiting never show up at all on Fridays, when the restaurant is crowded with hell-bent-on-a-party-groups beginning their weekend revels. Back in the mists of time, deal-making businessmen and lawyers began the Friday lunch tradition. Because standing in line was never one of their favorite things to do, it was not uncommon for bosses to send their secretaries, legal clerks, or other employees to stand in line for them, sometimes for an hour or longer.

In certain circles, especially legal ones, no business is transacted in offices on Friday afternoons. "Entire law firms are known to empty for the afternoon for lunch at Galatoire's," wrote Curtis Wilkie in the *Boston Globe* (October 17, 1994). One law firm suffered through great arguments when the decision was made to move their office to the Entergy Building on Poydras Street because it wasn't within walking distance of Galatoire's. Craig LaBan, who was the *Times-Picayune* restaurant writer in 1997, called Fridays at Galatoire's the ultimate power leisure lunch. "I doubt many deals get cut on one of those famously boisterous Friday afternoons at Galatoire's," he wrote. "But if you need a lawyer or a judge, just look in the corner and holler." The *National Law Journal* once warned its legal eagles, "If a bomb falls on Galatoire's on Friday, watch out."

Conducting business at Friday lunch

One local lawyer went so far as to ask for and get Friday lunch at Galatoire's for the remainder of his life as part of his retirement package. Another prominent lawyer, Jack Gordon, even chose his new Place St. Charles office so that he could monitor the Friday lunch line on the sidewalk in front of Galatoire's from his desk and know exactly when to send a stand-in. Fellow attorneys strolled down the hallway to look out his window and that of his colleague, Walter B. Stuart IV—also situated for a good view of the 200 block of Bourbon Street—and those in other firms telephoned them to get a clue about the Friday line. Gordon's friends and partners have filled table 22 for almost fifty years, so long that the waiters have taken to calling him "Il Supremo."

From the first, the four partners have had a pact: the minute they sit down they always order four Martinis and if one is absent that day, Jack drinks his Martini for him. One day Jack came to lunch, but his partners did not. He ordered three Martinis instead of the usual four. Cesar, their waiter then, said, "That's not enough Martinis," but Jack said, "No, that's enough." "Why, did somebody die?" Jack replied, "No. It's Lent; I'm not drinking."

According to Lacey Wood writing in *St. Charles Avenue,* when a court runner finally complained about being sent to stand in line, the law firm wrote it into the job description. As a reward, the paralegals and secretaries were sometimes gathered up and taken to lunch. One law clerk, Patricia Goodwin, whose sister owns "a wonderful restaurant in New Orleans but understands my love of Galatoire's," was in law school at Loyola from 1980–83 and, needing money, began clerking for a local firm. "Almost immediately I became the main Friday-go-wait-in-line person. What self-respecting lawyer waits in line in ninety-five degree and ninety-five percent humidity heat on Bourbon Street? Not many. That's what law clerks are for. We were half-way presentable and decently dressed and expendable."

After several of the Friday stints, one of the lawyers invited her to stay for lunch. "Near faint from heat and hunger and eager for something wonderful instead of the drudgery of law school and long hours as a clerk, I practically ran into Galatoire's. There it was—the white tablecloths, the waiters deceptively casual in recognizing 'their' customers, the mirrors and the people. Women with blue hair, women with blond hair, women with hats on but due to the dress code, no women with pants and no men in Levi's no matter how dry cleaned and pressed they were—men with stereotypical lawyer suits, men with the then-cutting edge of brightly-colored-striped shirts with white collars and suspenders under their very well-cut and beautiful suits. The older men visited with one another—having practiced in New Orleans for years. The traditionalists and wannabes had on their summer white linen or seersucker suits. So this was Friday at Galatoire's." After graduation, Goodwin's law-school study group, called the "Fan Club" (fans of Galatoire's, of course) continued to meet once a month at their favorite restaurant.

Kim Sport's regular Friday birthday group, the "Galatoire's Gals," originated at Jack Gordon's table, via an employee who invited Sport to lunch some ten years ago. "I thought, 'Wow! Galatoire's is really fun.' So we lived happily ever after." In 1995 Sport celebrated her fortieth birthday at Galatoire's first-ever Monday night party—"A Great Gatsby Gathering At Galatoire's." "Everybody wore Gatsby white," she said. The "Galatoire's Gals" became friends while working as volunteers for the Jefferson Dollars for Scholars program on the West Bank. They celebrate birthdays on the nearest Fridays, and the birthday "Gal" chooses the color everybody wears that day, including hats. "My August birthday is so hot we call it 'Little Black Sundress Day,'" says Kim. The group has coined the phrase "Doin' the turn"—for those times when one goes for lunch and stays for dinner, too.

Friday lunch at Galatoire's was the beginning of one writer's slide toward procrastination. She moved to the French Quarter because of its perceived literary inspiration, but found its work ethic left something to be desired. As the story goes, she came to town with good work habits, but they eroded night by night and day by day after Friday lunch at Galatoire's caused her to cease work on Fridays. Then she lost two more days—Thursdays at the Napoleon House and Wednesdays with the lunch-bunch at Tujague's, leaving only Mondays and Tuesdays to work—prompting one wag to say, all too truly, that for New Orleanians work was what one did between meals.

Artist Philip Sage has made two etchings of Galatoire's; the first, a sold-out limited edition, "Lunch at Galatoire's," was done as part of a series on eating and drinking in New Orleans. Karen Solomon and Susan Villere then convinced him to memorialize "Friday Afternoon at Galatoire's," and that print depicts a number of their friends, including Richard, their waiter.

The *Gourmet* article on the best restaurants in America, 2000, describes the peculiar ritual of Friday lunch: "Women in floppy hats, men in seersucker suits, politicians pressing the flesh, businessmen who have no intention of going back to the office, a few tourists—all settle in for an afternoon of eating, drinking, talking, and table-hopping that sometimes continues into dinner. The atmosphere is more cocktail party than restaurant lunch. . . ." In truth, the festivities can sometimes get out of hand, and the behavior of some of the regulars takes on more the quality of residents of *Animal House* than customers in an established restaurant.

Louis Sahuc looks at the restaurant as an entity all its own, a place where a customer and his waiter could both clown around in pink feather boas. "The pretty ladies in big hats—pink, yellow, blue, white—come in to ooohs and aaahs and proceed to get snockered so they can flirt with impunity with every man who stops by their table to admire them," he says. "Patrons seldom cross the line of decency because getting banished from the Galatoire's party would be akin to being black-balled from the club. The locals dress; you come in as a proper lady and gentleman, and you leave the same way. The surface gentility is in inverse proportion to the outrageousness lurking in the psyche. This all gives Galatoire's an extra dimension lacking in other places. This might as well be the history of one big one-hundred-year-old party, with the patrons and waiters as stars and the family trying to keep control of the party." Waiter M. C. Emmons says, "Fridays, people come early and say they're going back to work but they never make it." Bridget O'Brien wrote in the *National Law Journal* (1987), "Time seems to stop inside the restaurant. Just sitting down for coffee or a drink can last as long as a lunch should take. Tables for six become tables for twelve in the course of an afternoon."

For at least one local, Friday lunch at Galatoire's began what he called "Lovers Day." Furniture dealer Aaron Mintz recalled it as "very, very laid back and relaxed. You went there about 1:30, after all the hubbub had subsided and you have a very leisurely lunch and you have a couple of drinks and then you and your companion retire." In his case back in the 1940s, he and his companion had only to retire upstairs next door, where he had a not-so-secret *pied à terre* during his bachelor days.

Sixteen years ago, Galatoire's served as matchmaker in a much different way for David and Beverly Anderson Walker of Rosebank Plantation in St. Francisville. Having met under quite proper circumstances, Beverly, then a French Quarterite, agreed to meet David for lunch at Galatoire's on Friday. "I knew that I would be safe, as I would be among friends," she said. A large number of her friends came and went from the table during the afternoon, leaving her as "treasurer" with their "guesses" as to their share of the bill. Her new friend, David, had only a salad and a Scotch, but when only the two were left at the table and the bill came, it amounted to $800 without tip. "I had collected only $500," she said. "Without hesitation, he said 'Give me the bill' and wouldn't even take the $500. I thought to myself, 'I won't let him get away.' We have been married for almost fourteen years, and Galatoire's is still our favorite restaurant."

In 1991, realtor Dorian Bennett's wife, Kell, had recently given birth to their daughter, Delia, and he called to check on her. "Kell was supposed to be home in bed, but I get no answer, just a message saying 'It you're looking for us, we're at Galatoire's.' I drop everything, alarmed, and rushed to Galatoire's. This was not in my picture of the way things should be. Given that it's Friday, there may be spilled drinks, hot coffee, maybe even flying objects. But there she is with friends from Aspen—they were all higher than kites—and this newborn baby tucked away in a corner fast asleep. And nobody thought a thing about it but me. I simply didn't see the logic of it. But Kell was 'get over it, chill, give him an Old-Fashioned.' So all my appointments were cancelled, and that was the rest of my day."

One Super Bowl Friday, a national sports magazine called a local professor and freelance writer whose specialty was New Orleans life and literature. The sports reporter said that he would like to interview the professor, who quickly informed him that he had a strong aversion to sports. That didn't matter, the reporter insisted, since he was writing an article about what else there is to do in New Orleans other than attending the game. The two agreed to have lunch at Galatoire's. The professor, a long-time habitué of the restaurant, arrived early and got in line in order to secure a table—it was Friday, after all—and was seated at eleven-thirty with the rest of the horde. When the sports reporter arrived, thirty minutes later, the professor had already finished his first Old-Fashioned and they both ordered more. Their waiter that day was the late, great Cesar. Without prodding, Cesar kept the drinks coming, and after three hours, the reporter suggested that they order some food. "Bring us something, Cesar," the professor said, and soon soufflé potatoes, fried eggplant, and the Gouté platter, arrived—with more drinks. Finally, at four o'clock, the sports writer insisted that they must order entrees, which they did. When the meal was finished, Cesar arrived with cognac for both, and the sports reporter said, "We didn't order these." "Don't worry," the professor said, "I'll pay." "No," the reporter said, "I'm on an expense account. This is on me." When the cognac had been properly disposed of, Cesar suddenly appeared with a bottle of champagne. "This is for your birthday, Doc," he told the professor. "You remember I told you I had one for you and you couldn't drink it on your birthday?" After appropriate thank-yous to this estimable waiter, the champagne was enjoyed until suddenly the sports writer looked at his watch and said, "Oh, my God, it's five o'clock. I have a dinner engagement at six." Suddenly he looked up and across the table. "I never did interview you," he said. They both laughed and parted. The article never appeared in the magazine.

French Fried Eggplant

1 large, long eggplant	Flour
1 egg	Oil for deep frying
3/4 cup of milk	Powdered sugar
Salt and white pepper to taste	

Peel eggplant and cut to the size of large French fries. Soak 30 minutes in salted water. Rinse and pat dry. Make a batter with egg and milk and season well with salt and pepper. Dip eggplant into batter, roll in flour, and deep fry until golden. Sprinkle with additional salt and serve with powdered sugar.

SERVES 4 AS AN APPETIZER WITH COCKTAILS OR AS A VEGETABLE WITH ENTRÉE.

Similar and even more extreme "forgetfulness" has been recorded. One Friday, as a major socialite tells it, he and his aunt went to Galatoire's and partied from noon to full dark. They headed home, but then realized they had never gotten around to eating at all. Another typical scene is a collection of older ladies sipping their cocktails and checking out other patrons. Anne Preaus recalls her mother complaining about their Martinis being so strong after one lunch that she had kissed a woman she could not stand. Friday customers too numerous to document are "over-served," the waiters say, and Friday nights at the restaurant are often late. The couple holding the record for the longest stay at Galatoire's is Bill and Lynn Watkins Kearney. They were almost first in line for lunch one Friday and by the end of the night, about twelve hours later, were one of the last parties to leave. "They'd been socializing the entire time because they knew everybody there," said Ken Solis, then maitre d'. "That was a great party night!"

The decibel level in the dining room mounts in direct proportion to the potables served, but the waiters keep glasses filled and mouths shut. Discretion is everything. Imre says, "Nobody is drunk, they're just on medication." M. C. Emmons served one Friday customer "his few Martinis and his Shrimp Rémoulade and his Trout Amandine and then he called me over and said, 'Excuse me, waiter, are you going to serve my lunch today?' I said, 'Sir, you've already eaten.' He got really caught up in the Galatoire's spirit that day." Another memorable remark, this one overheard in the men's restroom: "For a sit-down bar, Galatoire's serves the best food in town."

The wages of sin—pardon me, Friday lunch—are not always predictable. As the day winds its way toward evening, some patrons, including the "Galatoire's Gals," traditionally adjourn to the Absinthe House down the street. "I got shouted at last week for standing on a barstool," said Sport. At Galatoire's, each birthday "Gal" is allowed, even expected, to stand on her chair during the Happy Birthday singing. "We are not a shy group." But they don't approve of vulgarity and "there are lines we don't cross." Often their husbands show up later on. "The worst thing for our husbands is for us to call them to join us late in the evening, because they show up cold sober, and we're just having a great time by then," she said, laughing. "It's oh what have we gotten into?" The "Gals" have all had their "little problems with car dings," said Sport. "Now we're more into designated drivers and taxis."

After one Friday lunch, appropriately enough, yachtsman and attorney Dwight LeBlanc merely stepped into a boat coming down Bourbon Street. What the heck was a boat doing on Bourbon Street? "Who knows?" LeBlanc said. "There was a boat being pulled slowly down the street, so I just hopped into it and rode along while the 'uptown swells' walked."

Once during their "budget" days, Pat and Lee Mason met a young couple from Maine standing in the line, dined with them, then, many drinks later, partied their way around the block to an opening for a Russian artist at Hanson Gallery. "We found ourselves in a special room in back where, in the state we were in, we couldn't resist buying a huge wonderful painting, budget or no budget," said Mason. "Galatoire's gets the credit for that painting, which we still love."

If the ordinary Friday is a boisterous affair at the restaurant, think quadruple boisterous for the Fridays before major holidays such as Mardi Gras and Christmas. Lunch on the Friday before Mardi Gras is the year's most famous meal and the one when the most outrageous goings-on are logged. It's the last chance to party at Galatoire's before the excessive and intemperate holiday that ends at Midnight on Fat Tuesday. After the bibulous Friday lunch crowd leaves—frequently late at night—the restaurant closes down until Ash Wednesday when patrons slowly drift back into Galatoire's in a hangover daze. Devout Catholics and Episcopalians are marked with ashes on their foreheads; the rest are marked with the less visible, but still telltale signs of too much Mardi Gras. Ash Wednesday is a quiet day, but one must eat.

As for Mardi Gras itself, various family members recall occasionally going to the balcony of the closed restaurant to watch parades before they were banned from the Quarter in 1973 (the same year that Justin Galatoire died). "One year there was such an overflow from Mike Anderson's next door that they climbed over onto our balcony," said David Gooch. "So the next year we hired a guard, but he got drunk and let his own family come up. So nobody at all uses it now."

Nonetheless, in honor of the holiday, Galatoire's recently created the Mardi Gras Martini, a blend of vodka, crème de menthe and Triple Sec. It was unveiled at a party co-hosted by Rain Vodka. Can a Mardi Gras Old-Fashioned be far behind?

According to David Gooch, the famous Friday lunch before Mardi Gras began developing back in the seventies when Krewe of Momus members "would come with their hangovers from the parade and ball the night

REVENGE DINING

At a Friday before Mardi Gras lunch in 2001, diners at our table were intrigued by a mysterious lady in black sitting alone at a table for two. She wore a huge, swooping black hat and on the opposite chair reposed a giant hatbox. We asked our waiter to find out about her. Quickly a romantic though macabre rumor swirled around the room that she came here to dine once a year and always brought her husband's ashes in the hatbox.

Summoning up our courage, we approached her, and she graciously told us the real story. She always dines VERY expensively at Galatoire's, alone but for her hatbox, as before." Another krewe, Hermes, rolls Friday night, causing some to call that day "Hermes Friday." Some who have long kept the tradition become incensed if they are unable to secure a Friday lunch table, and occasionally animosity can be observed in the line. The maitre d' is often hard-pressed to control the confusion, but somehow he always does it. Groups lucky enough to be seated often decorate their table with the traditional Mardi Gras beads, doubloons, and confetti and sometimes don outrageous hats or other articles of clothing as the event increases in its Bacchanalian intensity. Some men have been known to place brassieres on their heads, and a few young women have danced on tables, sometimes with disastrous results.

Waiter Richard Smith tells of a memorable lunch on Mardi Gras Friday nine years ago when a party of sixteen people came in to find only one table left, a two-top way in the back. The group's leader, Bill Metcalf, said, "I'll take it." Then he turned on a boom box he had brought with him and started ordering champagne and appetizers. His guests would come and go and mill around the tables all over the restaurant and sit down with other parties and come back and drink champagne and eat. They played musical chairs all day long because there were not enough chairs to go around. When the party was over they had had a great time, twenty bottles of champagne had been consumed by the group of sixteen, and the bill was $1200 for a two-top.

Rather titillatingly, Galatoire's Bourbon Street location is between a sex apparel shop and a club showcasing exotic dancers. One year in the mid-nineties such proximity to the world's oldest trade inspired four young matrons, regulars all, to disguise themselves—with the assistance of wigs, makeup, and outfits considerably different from their usual frocks—as Bourbon Street ladies of the evening rather than Uptown ladies who lunch. With some success, they scandalized and thrilled those of the Mardi Gras Friday clientele who had had enough time to dampen their cognitive skills with liberal doses of Martinis and Manhattans. Perhaps due to this influence, the gathering seemed even more unrestrained that year. The ersatz hookers

revenge on her now-deceased spouse, an ungenerous man who not only pinched pennies until they howled, but told her she was not attractive and that women who wore eyeglasses should never wear hats or earrings. Worse, he left his estate in such disarray that she had to fight his mother and siblings for years to get her share. In the hatbox is always a brand-new hat for which she has just paid a fortune at Fleur de Paris. On her head is always last year's hat she bought for this year's revenge dining at Galatoire's.

eventually took their lipsticks around to various tables where many of the gentlemen allowed their faces to be garishly made-up. The celebratory gentlemen chased around the restaurant kissing everyone, often leaving bright red lipstick imprints on the tops of baldheads. Those lacking baldness obtained forehead imprints. Too bad that impressions left by the well-known artist George Dureau could not be preserved and framed. Other gentlemen, mostly lawyers, merely climbed upon tabletops to toss Mardi Gras beads and make speeches. In later years, the original four "hookers" grew into a rollicking group of ten or more, the costumes became even more outrageous, and the Cosmopolitan was added to the usual drinks.

George Dureau, right, leaves his mark on Arthur Pulitzer, left

One year in the even-wilder-than-now eighties, the Mardi Gras Friday antics became so obstreperous that a reveler sneaked up behind Miss Yvonne and crowned her with an unmentionable style of hat. Someone snapped her photo, in full smile, not realizing what was perched atop her head. When she glimpsed her chapeau in the mirror, she was not amused. History does not record if the perpetrator was eighty-sixed. "Back then, the group was almost out of control," says David Gooch. "They would drink a whole lot and go around and find a pretty girl and crown her Queen of Galatoire's." M. C. had trouble one Mardi Gras Friday when the crowd was so dense he was unable to get food to table 11, so he took the trays down the alleyway and came in the front door. "I live for that day," he says. "Some people don't want to deal with it, but I love it!"

One group of pretty, proper, beautifully-dressed Uptown ladies, Dathel Coleman and friends, went next door and bought fake bosoms to wear on a Mardi Gras Friday. They had their photo snapped and artist Beth Lambert did a life-size painting of the scene that once adorned a restaurant on Magazine Street. "My mother saw it and thought the Mardi Gras bosoms were real," said David Gooch. "I suggested they buy another set and hold it over to the side before having their picture taken, so people would know those bosoms weren't real."

The raucous Mardi Gras Friday meal has become so ritualized over the years that tables, always scarce on Fridays, are at such a premium that regulars hire people to stand in line for them. Tommy and Dathel Coleman started the trend more than ten years ago, and soon Mickey Easterling took up the challenge. As many began hiring surrogates it became necessary for them to stand in line all Thursday night, then Thursday afternoon, and then earlier and earlier in the week. The surrogates are so well paid, however, that family members of waiters or of kitchen staff often scoop up the jobs. If Galatoire's regulars thought the new upstairs bar would make the overnight line obsolete, saving them many dollars on surrogates, they were wrong. Now, stand-ins begin staking their claims around 3:00 P.M. Wednesday (forty-four hours with two overnights) and the price for a surrogate had risen to $350–$600 in 2003. M. C. lost a number of tables of Mardi Gras regulars. "They didn't get in this year."

Of course, none of the overnight surrogates literally stand, or even lean. They spend the long hours sitting and lying on Bourbon Street in all kinds of contrivances. They camp out with chairs, lounges, and blankets and even take turns as teams. Until 11:00 A.M. on Friday, the sidewalk in front of Galatoire's resembles a convention of amiable street people, actually apropos for the second block of Bourbon Street.

David Gooch remembers the first time he noticed the phenomenon. On a Thursday before Mardi Gras in the late 1980s, he opened the door as accustomed to find at the head of the line a lady sitting in a chair reading a book. Rather than waiting to come in for lunch on that day, however, she said "I'm waiting for tomorrow." She was so determined to be first in line on Friday that she sat and read her book, paid someone to take her place overnight, and returned the next morning to claim her chair by the door.

After the upstairs was renovated, the "Arthurians," a group of about thirty men who organized as an offshoot of the Round Table Club, began to meet on Mardi Gras Friday at Galatoire's for their annual luncheon. For their 2003 event, the group had ordered hand-chopped ice to be delivered from the icehouse. "I urged everyone I knew to tell their waiters to take their ice from our bowls," said Gordon Maginnis, "but it didn't do much good; our tables were completely covered with bowls of ice—the minimum order was three hundred pounds."

The Friday before Christmas has also become a riotous festivity, complete with overnight stand-ins, costumes, jingle bells, Santa hats, and gifts. One of those Fridays in the late 1980s, Patricia Goodwin's Fan Club convened to "celebrate our friendship" and exchange gifts. "We ate and drank and opened presents and ate and drank and spoke to every lawyer we knew." Mid-afternoon, when the restaurant was only half-filled, they began singing "The Twelve Days of Christmas" ("I promise you, none of us are very good singers."), and the other customers and staff joined in "with great gusto and enormous enthusiasm." Whenever Goodwin returned to the restaurant, Cesar would talk about "the best Christmas he had in all the years he'd worked at Galatoire's, when Pat and her friends sang Christmas carols with the whole restaurant." She tried to repeat the experience the next year after she had moved to Alexandria, but "it was the only time Galatoire's ever closed due to snow," So she turned back and went home. "I drove for eight hours and went nowhere—just to get to Galatoire's."

Waiter Gerard Beasley enjoys working the night (one week before Christmas) the Brennan restaurant family takes over the upstairs for a buffet-style Christmas party. "And Christmas Eve is the best of all days to work," he says. "A lot of locals come in and give you little Christmas bonuses; it gets real crowded. It's always a real nice day." According to maitre d' Arnold Chabaud, Christmas Eve tables are completely filled up for the night by 5:00 P.M. "If holidays fall on a Friday, the scene gets even wilder," he says.

Halloween calls for festivity, whether it falls on a Friday or not. One recent Friday Halloween, a big upstairs party of costumed women were making merry, calling themselves "Witches & Bitches." In the next room gamboled numerous guys adorned with blinking horns on their heads. The juxtaposition of the two groups was extraordinary, and soon the two noisy parties noticed each other and merged. "But all costumes still must adhere to the dress code," Chabaud warns. Just so, art dealer Bertrand Delacroix came in on another Halloween Friday night accompanied by the elaborately costumed "Pope" Vic Sarjoo. Delacroix appeared to be dressed totally up to code and was led in with handshakes all around. From the front, his jacket, shirt, tie, and long pants were perfectly proper. However, as he turned to greet acquaintances, his half-suit (or "coffin" suit) from the rear exposed him completely, neck to ankles, so rather than giving him a Salvation Army jacket, the management gave him the boot.

Celebrating Christmas the Friday before; seated, left to right, Burt, Byron,
Red, Brad, and Ben Adams; standing, left to right, Bruce Adams, and
Nelson Marcotte, the family's favorite waiter

"Easter Friday"—known to most as Good Friday—although ostensibly a
religious holiday, is also occasion to dress up and party down at Galatoire's.
Charles Mayer, Anne Strachan, Leonard Parrish, and various friends have
been going to Galatoire's every Good Friday for thirty years. The ladies wear
their Easter bonnets and decorate the table with flowers and all sorts of
Easter objects. "Once a friend from Ft. Worth came in with a huge box. I
opened it and there was a live rabbit in a cage," relates Parrish. "I thought
Yvonne was going to have a hissy fit. 'Get that thing out of here', she said. Of
course, you can't bring live animals into a restaurant; it's against all the
health rules. So Imre, our waiter, said 'I'll take it' and off it went. Months
later, Imre told me, 'I've got so many rabbits now at my house you can't
believe it.'" Waiter Reynard Lavigne played a live rabbit on Easter Friday 2002
when "I had a big table of hat ladies for the first time." This was Reynard's
first introduction to the "Galatoire's Gals." "They put ears on me, tail, too.
Then they called me Reynard Cottontail instead of Peter."

No matter what Friday, lunch that day is a theater of the spontaneous.
Only occasionally does a bit of planning show through, as when the "Gals"

come in all dressed up in the same color. Yet through it all, despite the furor and noise and hordes of revelers moiling about in the narrow aisles, the kitchen staff always seems able to turn out the same great cuisine; the waiters always move efficiently among the milling throngs, rarely exhibiting any sign of the strain all this confusion must be on their nerves. Considering that, Friday lunch at Galatoire's is something of a miracle.

Bacalao

Mémère's Recipe for Codfish Served on Good Friday

Clarisse Galatoire, wife of Justin I, was called Mémère. She cooked this dish for her family on Good Friday and it was served on that day at Galatoire's for many years. This recipe was provided by the late Leona Frey, who carried on the tradition and prepared Bacalao at home.

3 large filets of salted codfish	8 tablespoons of minced garlic
10 pounds of potatoes	1 1/2 cups of olive oil
1 pound of butter	

Run cold water over fish and soak until all salt is removed (takes 7 or 8 hours).

Boil fish for 5 or 8 hours until tender. Bake the potatoes until tender; do not overcook. When cool, peel and cut into medium-size pieces.

In a large pot, melt 1 pound of butter, add the garlic and olive oil and cook over medium heat for a few minutes.

Add codfish and blend well, then add potatoes. Cook until mixture is well blended.

Serve and enjoy.

SERVES THE ENTIRE FAMILY.

Helen Gilbert, left, and Alice O'Shaughnessy enjoying the Friday Matinee

ALICE O'SHAUGHNESSY & HELEN GILBERT

The Two Sisters: Birds of a Feather

From time to time, an old faithful will expire at table, and when that happens, friends consider it fitting, a *belle mort*—beautiful death. When Alice O'Shaughnessy, after a long and richly full life, keeled over in 1996 at Ruth Chris Steak House, where they faithfully dined on most Sunday nights, her younger sister Helen Gilbert said she was sure Alice would rather have died at Galatoire's instead, where the two sisters had held constant court every Friday for more than twenty years and Helen still does.

"We were known there as 'The Ladies with the Hats,'" Helen said proudly. They loved holding court at Galatoire's at a table where admirers took turns paying their respects and kissing the sisters' rose-petal cheeks. "We know all the young boys," Alice once remarked to the *Atlanta Journal-Constitution*. "They can't kiss the twenty-year-olds because their wives wouldn't like that at all." They chose Friday, Helen said, because then they would see many of their friends, including the usual gaggle of attorneys who claim that day as their own. One of their favorites always came over when he finished lunch to say that "he had saved Alice and me for dessert" and tell people to "leave them alone, they belong to me." On another occasion, a young stock broker told his friends that the only reason he was still single was that Helen wouldn't marry him.

Alice and Helen always arrayed themselves dramatically, in large hats, turbans, bright colors, and elaborate jewelry, often of their own design. Once Helen wore a feather duster pinned to her hat. Both sisters "loved dressing up and we got to be known because of fashion." On one Friday before Mardi Gras, a man borrowed Helen's hat and wore it around for the rest of the day. "If this was a low class restaurant," she said, "that would be low class, but in Galatoire's, its elite."

One memorable Friday at lunch, when Helen got up from her table of lady friends to air-peck an ancient gentleman, her skirt slipped off and landed on the floor around her ankles. Luckily, she was wearing panty hose and not walking around. Blasé about the entire incident, she insisted, "As far as I'm concerned nobody was looking at that, they were looking at my outerwear." An observer remembered the incident differently, saying that Helen seemed regally oblivious to the fact that her panty-hosed derriere was aimed at the next table, leaving it to a companion to hastily retrieve and pull up the offending skirt. No other notice was taken of this occurrence whatsoever until later, when Helen turned around to the next table and said, "You'd think a goddamned Romeo Gigli skirt would stay up, wouldn't you?"

Another humorous fashion episode occurred when Helen was wearing a loose jacket on a warm day and decided to unzip it a few inches to cool off. Ever ready to titillate, she told her lady friends, "You know, I don't have anything on under this jacket." Whereupon Sheila Davlin challenged Helen to unzip all the way, promising her thirty designer pillows (from Davlin's business) for her favorite charity. Helen complied, "but luckily the table reached up high" on her short frame. Laughing, she recalled: "I was exposing myself for charity at Galatoire's."

The sisters, who were always known as gadabouts, delighted in telling people all about their glamorous past and present lives. Alice once told her friend H. M. Vanderhoeven "There are only two times in your life when you are completely honest: when you're a child and don't know any better and when you're old and don't give a damn." They loved to gamble and when New Orleans finally opened a casino, they were frequent VIP guests. Now that Alice is gone, but certainly not forgotten, Helen carries on the show in fine style with her many friends and with her daughter, artist Jan Gilbert, and son-in-law Kevin McCaffrey, a writer and culinary activist.

Neither of the sisters was ever shy, and Helen made it a practice to order her drink (Jack Daniel's Black Label on the Rocks) and then begin to "work the room," talking to everyone—friends and strangers. "I often said that Alice and I could have met the Boston Strangler and thought he was nice."

One day they talked to a man at the next table who revealed that he was very depressed because he had just lost his wife. He decided, he said, to "get myself to Galatoire's and that will lift my spirit." The two sisters included him as part of their day. Years later, Helen was there with friends who had finished their bottle of wine—she stuck to her Jack Daniel's, of course—and Richard Smith brought over a new bottle of wine and began to open it. "This is from one of Mrs. Gilbert's admirers," he said, then refused to tell her who it was.

When the meal and the wine had been consumed, Helen asked another waiter, Imre, if he knew who the benefactor was. He pointed out a man in dark glasses. When she went over to thank him, the man said: "I just wanted to let you know that you and your sister were so nice to me the day I was here and so depressed." For Helen, "This was part of Galatoire's." As she was leaving the restaurant, she told her friend: "You see, you can get things by being nice," and the friend wanted to know if she got the man's address so that perhaps she could date him. "I said, 'No, thank you.'"

On a recent occasion, Helen, who never met a stranger, was making her tour of the tables, greeting and being greeted, when a lady she did not know asked her what was going on at her table and said, "We looked about and decided you were the best." Helen was so pleased—"All the younger women around, and yet she chose me!"—that she took off her hat and gave it to the woman, who asked, "What is this?" Helen replied: "Well, I've got a lot of hats but you gave me a compliment that really registered with me." The woman got Helen's address and wrote later to say that if she ever came to San Antonio, she must stay with them, and "That's typical of the reception I get from people."

Galatoire's has no better advocate than this remarkable habitué. Helen began going there with her husband, who had been with the

Brooklyn Dodgers. After both sisters' husbands died, they began to look on Galatoire's as a second home and a comfortable place to restore their spirits. "It's really unbelievable how much it will salvage your life if you let it," she said. "It's the ambience that nobody else has and the fact that Galatoire's doesn't change." She believes that one of the charms of the establishment is that "they have not opened twenty restaurants. They have stayed with their own restaurant and this is a part of their family and they've maintained a New Orleans tradition."

She has been friends with all the Galatoire family members, among them Miss Yvonne and Clarisse Gooch, who used to call her "Miss Galatoire," and their descendants. She speaks with affection of friends, living and dead, whom she associates with the restaurant, including June Perkins Bailey, another lady who loved hats, and now lives in Florida. June had worked for *Women's Wear Daily* before moving to New Orleans "and enjoyed the idea of Alice and me being dressed up." She thinks fondly of the restaurant as being "like a performance of the locals. We represented the city, and we knew it." Going to Galatoire's, she insists, teaches people what New Orleans is all about.

Being in Galatoire's was "like heaven for Alice and me." She told her sister that their late husbands would look down at them and think of them as "delinquents." She recalled with a twinkle in her eye that Alice did not like to go to church, but after being widowed, she began to accompany Helen. If it rained on Sunday, however, she would call and say, "Helen, it's raining. Do you think we ought to go to church?" And I would say, 'Alice, we go to Galatoire's when it rains, why not church?'"

When Alice died, there were four or five hundred people at her wake and funeral, many of them with Galatoire's associations. The officiating priest said, "I think I was chosen for this service because I was the last priest to go to Galatoire's with the two sisters." It was a tribute worthy of Alice O'Shaughnessey, a woman who was herself a New Orleans tradition, a tradition that is kept alive with élan by her beloved sister.

Marda Burton
Kennteh Holditch

Act Three

Rituals & Ceremonies

Scene Nine

Extravaganzas
Other Special Occasions

> *"Galatoire's . . . a special, almost magical place where*
> *Orleanians have been dining on special occasions since right after*
> *the turn of the century—and not the one that just turned."*
> —Angus Lind, *Times-Picayune,* February 7, 2003

*G*enerations of New Orleanians have celebrated the significant events of their lives within the nurturing mirror-lined walls of Galatoire's. Author Patty Friedmann is no exception. She was granted her own VIP booksigning at Galatoire's when *Eleanor Rushing* was published. It includes a Galatoire's scene in which an angry Eleanor yanks off a tablecloth full of drinks and dishes, and a Martini olive goes flying across the room. "I had Eleanor Rushing go to Galatoire's for the special times in her life, because that's what New Orleans people always do," Friedmann said.

During her booksigning, Friedmann "flashed back to my first memory there sitting at a table in a highchair. I'm not sure it was really a highchair— I've never seen a highchair at Galatoire's—but I remember sitting up high." Friedmann's grandfather who was born in 1898 always sat at a back table next to the bar. "He went there every day and ordered a lamb chop and six Scotch-and-sodas," she said.

Family has always been important at Galatoire's, and Sunday has long been a quieter "Family Day." By now, no one knows why; it seems that it just always was. The menu cover was once blue and regulars called it the "Blue Bible." It is not uncommon to see three generations of one family seated at a table on a Sunday, from the youngest, drinking their "Shirley Temples," to the oldest, often drinking Old-Fashioneds, which seems to be favored by the

163

more mature Galatorians. Late in the afternoon, anyone who knows New Orleans "Society" will recognize the "royalty" of Uptown, ex-kings and queens of the old established Carnival krewes, interspersed with newer, often younger locals. In "No Place for You, My Love," Eudora Welty described it: ". . . a party combined in a free-and-easy way when the friends he and she were with recognized each other across Galatoire's. The time was a Sunday in summer—those hours of afternoon that seemed Time Out in New Orleans."

On a recent Sunday, for example, high school graduate Jennifer Mains, her family, and five of her best friends dined upstairs to the strains of Patti Adams's string quartet, the same musicians who had entertained for her sister Heather's graduation and wedding to Giovanni Cafiso. "This is our tradition, and it's always a great event," said her parents, William and Lynda Mains. Downstairs at a table for fourteen, Brucie Rafferty hosted a family reunion to commemorate the wedding anniversary of Rafferty and her late husband, and people table-hopped and sang to two birthday tables, one with small children on their best behavior. Upstairs at the bar, Milly Barranger and daughter Heather Case waited for a friend, reminiscing about Case's first visit to Galatoire's at age seven in the company of two impressive *grande dames,* her grandmother, Miriam Barranger, and Mayo Godchaux, colorful widow of the owner of the department store around the corner. "I was feeling sick, and our waiter cured me with a drink made with bitters," said Case, "I'll never forget that day." The bartender, Rich Reichbach, was telling them about his honors thesis, positing Galatoire's as a sociological microcosm of New Orleans, when waiter Bryan Casey came up the stairs to ask for the restaurant's only bottle of Angostura bitters. "It's time to go downstairs, Mother," Case said. "The professor has arrived."

In the days when Canal Street's posh department stores flourished, so did the ritual of Saturday lunch. Football games in the old Tulane Stadium and later the Superdome swelled the customer roster for Saturdays. Hoards of fashionable shoppers descended upon Galatoire's before or after their shopping expeditions to D. H. Holmes, Godchaux, Maison Blanche, Krauss, Kreeger's, or other stores once lining Canal Street. During the week, employees at those establishments frequented Galatoire's, where they could have lunch in style, with a bottle of wine, for less than ten dollars a couple. The restaurant was obviously aware of the devotion of the department store staffs and customers, since through the years it created several salads named for the stores.

From surrounding towns came weekend shoppers by automobile, bus and train. Dress-to-kill Uptown ladies found Saturdays perfect for exciting expeditions to wicked downtown. One did not have to penetrate far into the sins of Bourbon Street to reach the respectable haven of Galatoire's. Dry-state Mississippians came to town on their liquor runs (most patronized

Schwegmann's grocery store), plus whatever French Quarter fun they fancied. Dodging the Mississippi Highway Patrol, their cars usually returned to Mississippi with trunks dragging low. One prominent family would depart by train, laden with giant wicker baskets filled with intoxicants packed in straw. Largely unscathed by the law, most found the occasional fines and confiscations a smaller price to pay than the exorbitant ones charged by Mississippi bootleggers—plus, there was the added spice of breaking the law to add zest to the trip. (It is worth noting that when the controversial Mississippi local option liquor law was passed in spite of well-financed opposition led by a coalition of bootleggers, sheriffs, and preachers, then-Governor Paul Johnson told columnist Bill Minor that he was offered a three million dollar bribe to veto the bill. Rumor had it that the offer came from a group of Louisiana liquor wholesalers, who stood to lose millions in sales.)

By the time Mississippi finally passed a local option law in 1966, the Galatoire's habit was already so firmly entrenched in their lives that innumerable Mississippi families still found their Galatoire's "fix" just as necessary as did their Louisiana counterparts. In *Dining and Dynasties,* one New Orleans resident, transplanted from Mississippi long ago, asserted that "We Mississippians feel that Galatoire's is at least half ours." Indeed, many of the house accounts of long standing are held by natives of the Magnolia State, whose families have been coming to New Orleans for decades and habitually crown their visit with a meal at the restaurant. Often as not, there are as many Mississippians in the restaurant on a Sunday or special day as there are native New Orleanians.

The Moore family of McComb is one of those families; they have celebrated countless special occasions at the restaurant, including Ophelia's and Melton's fiftieth anniversary in 1994, and Melton's eighty-fourth birthday in March, 2003. They call Galatoire's their "family room," and bring their entire three generational clan to Galatoire's every December 26, "to shop, to visit, and to eat." According to family member Thomas Hewitt, they "use their Saints season tickets as an excuse to visit Galatoire's." The gregarious Ophelia, who is "prone to introduce herself to anyone she fancies," was given engraved social cards to present to her new-found Galatoire's friends; so she presented them to Terry Bradshaw, Archie Manning, Willard Scott, local celebrities, and "scores of other good-natured Galatoire's guests."

A special birthday or anniversary treat was an excellent reason to trek to New Orleans and Galatoire's from nearby Louisiana cities, as well. One day, an entire family arrived from Baton Rouge to celebrate the birthday of the matriarch, who was in her nineties and was accompanied by her children, grandchildren, and great-grandchildren. It was difficult to get the frail woman's wheelchair in the door, but the staff managed. She had insisted on coming to Galatoire's even though her family had tried to talk her into going somewhere closer to home. Although she was unable to talk, she had written down her wishes in great detail.

Over the years the waiters, with their own simple but often hilarious ritual, have contributed to thousands of unforgettable birthdays. First, they bring a cup custard with a candle and try to quieten the din by tapping on glasses. Then comes an announcement of the person's name followed by ah-one, ah-two, ah-three, "Happy Birthday To You," in whatever accent is most prevalent that day. Most of the diners join in the song and applaud loudly at the end, when the celebrant is given a Galatoire's pen, once presented by Miss Yvonne, but now by David Gooch or Justin Frey. Although nobody is counting, the birthday ritual takes place probably hundreds of times a month. It is not unusual on a Sunday for it to occur a dozen or more times. One Saturday night after several off-key Happy Birthdays had been sung, Frank Purvis called his waiter Richard Smith over to ask him a question: "What is the proportion of people who really have a birthday and those who decide after they get here that they have a birthday?" Richard answered, "About fifty-fifty."

The Villere family always observes its members' birthdays at Galatoire's. Pierre Villere, whose mother has been a Galatoire's patron since 1944, has been a regular all his adult life, and now his two children follow the custom. CeCe, age twenty-one, and her brother Pierre, age twenty-three, have collected dozens of Galatoire's pens which their father is saving for them. A favorite family tale concerns his daughter's eighth birthday when father and daughter went for lunch *a deux* and CeCe was introduced to *Pomme Soufflé* for the first time. She bit into one and exclaimed, "Wow! Empty French fries! But, Daddy, how do they get the middle out?" Villere explained the procedure, "assuring her that there was not a poor soul in the kitchen laboriously scooping out the middle of the French fries." Parish, daughter of Daniel Edmond Sullivan, too, always has birthday parties at Galatoire's, with Imre doing the honors as both waiter and leader of the singing—"ah-one, ah-two, ah-three."

GALATOIRE'S SPECIAL

Clarisse Galatoire Gooch (Mrs. John Barr Gooch), the oldest living member of the Galatoire family, celebrated her ninety-fourth birthday on October 11, 2002, with a party at the restaurant complete with toasts and birthday singing. Rather than the usual cup custard with candle, the doyenne of the family blew out candles on a fancy layer cake. Mrs. Gooch is a tiny stunner of a refined Creole lady, who could easily be mistaken for a woman in her seventies. When we interviewed her at her home she not only showed us

Villere birthday party; "Frog" White, seated fourth from right,
Pam Renoir, second from right

Attorney Keene Kelley and his wife Christel began a family tradition early with a first birthday party for their daughter Camille on June 22, 2000. "Of course, we intend to continue the tradition in future years," said Keene. On the other end of the spectrum, five years ago Cokie Rathborne took over the entire restaurant for his sixtieth birthday party. Becky Breithoff, who is now a college student, went along for her mother's birthday at the "family store" when she was five or six years old. Becky's mother, Sally, is a granddaughter of Justin Galatoire, and at the party Becky's great-aunt Yvonne joined the party and told many stories of days gone by. "As the entire restaurant sang 'Happy Birthday' to my mom," said Becky, "she grabbed me, sat me on her lap and whispered in my ear, 'Becky, you can blow out the

her exquisite collection of silver (she is a recognized expert in English silver), regaled us with tales and gave us recipes, she introduced us to her own "Galatoire's Special." Her son David Gooch makes up a batch of Sazeracs for her each week, pours them into a whiskey bottle and delivers them to her house. She, in turn, often passes them along to her doctor. As she poured "specials" for us she confided, "They all say, 'Hello, Mrs. Gooch,' but they don't look at me, they look to see what I'm bringing the doctor."

candles.' I was so excited because my birthday was not for another month and a half!" Becky's cousin, Simone Galatoire Nugent, comes to Galatoire's once a month to have lunch and celebrate birthdays with three of her oldest friends in New Orleans, Jeannie Simmons, Patty Corales, and Claire Simno. "We are like the Ya-Ya Sisterhood," Simone said. When Simone's fiftieth birthday party was held upstairs in the new dining room, as a gag, black mourning was the attire for all the guests except Simone.

Monthly lunchers at Galatoire's—from left to right, Simone Galatoire Nugent, Jeannie Simmons, Patty Corales, and Claire Simno

The family of W. Paul Andersson, the Honorary German Consul, celebrates many notable events at Galatoire's, and a special memory is his daughter Lise's eighth birthday on the day after Valentine's Day. "After all the festivity with the customary singing, which she greatly enjoyed, on the way out we passed a table of two lovely elderly ladies, who stopped Lise to give her one last and very personal birthday wish. With obviously genuine affection, one of the women removed her small silver necklace on which hung a single red heart worn for the holiday. She fastened it around Lise's neck, gave her a kiss on the cheek, and asked her to remember this birthday for many years to come. "Lise is now twenty-four and works in Manhattan, but she still treasures the necklace."

In order to initiate customers to the second floor dining room, Galatoire's gave a series of parties for the regulars before closing the first floor for renovation. Some long-timers were at first leery of the changes, but gradually the convenience of the upstairs bar and the private dining rooms worked its charm. One of the first of the old-line patrons of Galatoire's to avail himself of the upstairs space was Dr. Victor Chisesi, who booked all three of the private dining rooms for his sister Rose Annette's birthday party. Eighty-five guests imbibed lavishly at the open bar, ate an abundance of soufflé potatoes and fried eggplant, and then dined on some of the most classic Galatoire's dishes. Wine flowed during the meal, and champagne was served afterwards with the birthday cake. Clearly, New Orleans was willing to accept the changes that had at first seemed extremely alien to them.

"We do love the new bar and the eating area upstairs, but our first choice is that lovely downstairs dining room," said Pat Green of Birmingham, Alabama. "It makes you feel as if you are in another time frame, as if you have been transported back in time. We are so fortunate to live so close." Green's husband asked what she wanted for her fiftieth birthday on July 2, 1998, and "it only took me a second to say that I would like to celebrate with a few close, fun friends in New Orleans at Galatoire's," she said. Eight friends joned the Greens in New Orleans and partied for three days, beginning with a gala birthday lunch at Galatoire's. "I always seem to order the same thing when we go there because it is so good and you can't get it anywhere else," said Green. "From the best brandy milk punch in the world to Oysters en Brochette to the 'to die for' Trout Amandine to 'funny coffee' at the finish, the lunch, the service, and our friends all 'clicked' to make this a party I will always remember," said Green. "My husband will be sixty in another year and I know that he will try to celebrate that milestone at Galatoire's, too."

Trout Amandine

4 (6-8-ounce) filets of speckled trout	Oil for frying
Salt	1/2 pound of butter
Pepper	4 ounces of sliced, toasted almonds
Milk	Juice of 1 lemon
Flour	1/2 tablespoon of chopped parsley

Dip salted and peppered fillets in milk, then roll in flour. Fry in hot oil in shallow pan until golden on both sides.

In a separate pan, melt and continuously whip butter until brown and frothy. Add sliced almonds and lemon juice and pour over trout. Garnish with chopped parsley.

SERVES 4.

Matriarch Helene K. Deadman, born in 1899, longed to survive until the year 2000 so that she could have the distinction of having lived in three centuries. However, she celebrated her last birthday at Galatoire's on September 6, 1998, and died three months later at age ninety-nine, not quite attaining her wish. Her son, Webster Deadman Jr., who escorted his mother to the restaurant almost every Sunday for lunch during the last years of her life, reports that on her last birthday she ordered her favorite meal: two Southern Comfort Old-Fashioneds, Shrimp Rémoulade, Trout Amandine, and Crepes Maison, accompanied by two glasses of wine and two snifters of brandy—then, as her son pushed his mother out of Galatoire's in her wheelchair, said, "Well, it's a good thing I can't walk."

Margarita Bergen, New Orleans' most highly visible Latina, has many of her birthday feasts at Galatoire's. During one memorable birthday luncheon for twelve, Margarita spied a "gorgeous-looking young mans, so I followed him to the men's room and waited for him to come out so I could invite him to my table and find out all about him." Actor and Hugo Boss model Gary Moore was flattered and remains a Margarita fan. Diane Sukiennik and Michael Reiss, Los Angeles food, wine, and travel writers also met Margarita at Galatoire's. "We were invited to a wonderful wine dinner shortly after the upstairs opened, and we just happened to be sitting across the table from her," said Reiss. "You can't sit across from Margarita and not have a fiesta." The pair described their experience. "The event was filled with locals who exuded the spirit of New Orleans and you felt as if you were a member of a large extended family. By the end of the evening, we had exchanged cards with probably twenty people. We felt a great sense of conviviality and welcome from the moment we stepped in the door."

Numerous marriage engagements begin at Galatoire's with a glass of champagne in which a diamond ring reposes, so far always noticed before being drunk down. Mark Green remembers his first dinner at Galatoire's when an engagement occurred at the next table, the show enhanced by the petitioner dropping on one knee to propose at tableside. As she said yes, the bride-to-be burst into tears and then loudly lamented the fact that she was not prepared for this. She was not wearing waterproof mascara. At Mark's first lunch, the original Stella in *A Streetcar Named Desire,* Kim Hunter, was being interviewed by NPR Radio and he was introduced to her by her luncheon companion. At Mark's second lunch, artist Fredrick Guess was there sketching the scene, and a fellow diner was Lena Horne. Since Mark at that time had lived in New Orleans only six months, and these were his first three meals at Galatoire's, no wonder he believes "this place is always a happening!" (Another artist who finds Galatoire's an irresistible subject is Rise Delmar Ochsner, who now lives and works in California. Her large painting of diners reflected in the big mirrors adorns a popular postcard. Known for his architectural drawings, artist Jim Blanchard has also portrayed the newly renovated façade of the restaurant on a postcard.)

Arnold Chabaud's son Steve and his bride, Rushell Bertucci, the latter now a popular waiter at Galatoire's, chose the restaurant for their rehearsal dinner in 1994, taking over the middle of the dining room, leaving the side tables free for customers to enjoy the show. In December of 2002, Laura Bayon was dating Max Reichard, who, like Laura, had youthful memories of Galatoire's. He had taken a Fulbright to teach in Croatia for a year and returned to the city because one of his sons was getting married in New Orleans. "Max asked me to dinner at Galatoire's, knowing it was my favorite place. That night over coffee, Max asked me to marry him. I happily accepted, and we were married in November of 2001."

Stephanie Haynes's favorite story about Galatoire's concerns the day in 1947 that her parents, Poche Waguespack and Patricia Goodwin became engaged. He invited her to dinner, but before they went into Galatoire's, they stopped at a fortune-telling parlor across the street, where Goodwin was told that she would marry "a tall, dark, and handsome man." In the restaurant, Waguespack proposed, "so of course Galatoire's is my mother's favorite restaurant in the world!"

A romantic dinner at Galatoire's in 1994 was also "a wonderful way to start a friendship," according to Meredith and Bailey McBee of Greenwood, Mississippi, who invited a gentleman sitting alone to join them for drinks. "We were in such a happy state—we had decided to marry that night and we had each consumed two Martinis and a whole bottle of wine—we could not let the gentleman spend the evening alone," said Meredith. The three became fast friends and the couple invited their new friend to their wedding; he returned the favor when he wed and the two couples, one living in south Mississippi and one in north Mississippi, still get together at Galatoire's as often as possible.

As far as can be determined only one wedding ceremony has been performed at Galatoire's. On the morning of Friday, May 24, 1996, Darleen Hingle and Jerry Carlisle tied the knot before the big desk behind which stood "the marrying judge," Dominic Grieshaber, at Miss Yvonne's usual post. "We wanted to get married there because of two sentimental reasons," said the bride. "One because it's where Jerry and I met on a crazy Friday before Mardi Gras, and also because my father, Joseph Pierce, was chef there when I was growing up." Along with her father preparing Trout Amandine and Cherries Jubilee for her at-home birthday parties ("I was the only little girl with such fancy food at her parties."), Carlisle remembers riding with her mother to pick him up and having ice cream in Galatoire's custard cups brought out to her. "When the doors opened after the ceremony it was like a movie and somebody had shouted, 'Action!'" Carlisle said. "People just poured in, scurrying for their favorite table." Later, after the wedding lunch for family and

Wedding of Jerry Carlisle and Darleen Hingle at Galatoire's, May 24, 1996

friends, M. C. and Cesar served everyone in the restaurant pieces of wedding cake, and the newlyweds took off for a honeymoon on the island of St. Lucia.

According to Jeanne Nathan and artist Bob Tannen, their minimal at-home garden ceremony in June 1982, was simply the appetizer for the main course—prodigious fun at Galatoire's, where their fifty luncheon guests met outside in line for the first seating and took over a front-to-back table in the middle of the restaurant. Flower trees from Dathel and Tommy Coleman and a wedding cake from La Marquise decorated by artist James LaLande provided the entire restaurant with an unforgettable tableau. "Since we were honeymooning at the Royal Orleans, it was easy for the Galatoire's party to crash our suite afterwards, which they did, under the leadership of Chappy Hardy," said Nathan.

Lynn Kearney's favorite memory is "the night they closed Galatoire's." Her husband, Bill Kearney IV, had approached David Gooch about having their rehearsal dinner at the restaurant, and "we had our hearts set on being downstairs." Upstairs supposedly would be renovated by then and it was agreed that Galatoire's would serve its guests upstairs while the rehearsal dinner took place downstairs. However, the renovations were not finished in time to open the upstairs to diners, so the restaurant closed for the Kearney's private party, and "we had a marvelous time. All of our dearest friends and family members were around us. I just wish we could have been married right then." Recently, her husband gave Kearney a surprise forty-fifth birthday party with her parents, twin sister, and thirty friends in attendance "to give me the surprise of a lifetime. What a night! Galatoire's just breeds a joyful atmosphere!"

The age-old rites of romance and marriage have their inevitable outcomes, among them a new generation with their own Galatoire's stories. French waiter Michel Virrolet was the favorite of Judge and Mrs. J. St. Clair

Favrot, who had dined at Galatoire's decades before their daughter, Michelle Heidelberg of Hattiesburg, Mississippi, was born. "When my mother found out that she was pregnant with me, they celebrated at Galatoire's and informed Michel of the good news," Heidelberg said. Several months later Michel was told Madame Favrot had had a little girl and named her Michelle. "'Oh, mon Dieu!' he said, 'Drinks for everyone!' I may be the only baby ever named after a waiter, and he took excellent care of his namesake." Heidelberg pulled her first tooth with Michel's help upstairs in the ladies' room, and "appropriately, soft dishes followed." Heidelberg had many birthday parties there, her parents driving to New Orleans "with as many little girls as would fit into the backseat of the car." While at Newcomb and Tulane, Michelle used her father's house account at Galatoire's for numerous significant events, including introducing her parents to Webb, her future husband. "It is still *the* place in New Orleans that I choose to dine for a special occasion," she said.

"It is so important at special family times to celebrate at Galatoire's— marriages, anniversaries, graduations, birthdays, baptisms and divorces," said Bridget Kramer Balentine. (The latest phenomenon is people coming in to commemorate a deceased loved one after the funeral is over.) Balentine was on hand when Mike and Fran Utley had their two boys christened at St. Louis Cathedral with a party at Galatoire's afterwards. "Jimmy Buffett and Ed Bradley were altar boys; Rita Coolidge and I were godmothers." Mick and Slade Utley are both musicians in Nashville now. Those who know Balentine best say she can make a party out of a new haircut. She and Louis Sahuc were even there to salute the last day of hand-chipped ice.

Wedding anniversary stories are legion. Lisa and Tommy Thames from Laurel, Mississippi, dined at Galatoire's while honeymooning in New Orleans. "We were young and in awe," she said. "There was a family at the next table from Texas, celebrating their parents' twentieth anniversary, and it was a magical lunch." The Thames came back to Galatoire's to celebrate their twentieth anniversary in 1996. This time, at the next table was another anniversary couple with their boys, ages ten, eight, and six, all in their ties and finest Sunday dress. "This was their boys' first trip to Galatoire's and they were on their best behavior," said Lisa. "They were very impressed by all the grown-ups and the white cloths on the tables and John Fontenot, their waiter. The father told us, 'I hope my children will come to Galatoire's on their anniversaries,' and they all nodded solemnly and promised they would."

The beginning of a new year is always cause for revelry, and large parties on New Year's Eve began in earnest after the upstairs renovation. According to David Gooch, when the twentieth century turned to the twenty-first in 2000, "We had a big private party upstairs, so it was packed." But oddly enough, it was a relatively slow night downstairs "because most people didn't think they could get in. We closed up before midnight." New Year's Eve 2002 proved to be more memorable; the restaurant served a record nine-hundred diners.

Chicken Bonne Femme

2 chickens, cut up for frying
1/2 cup of oil
4 potatoes, sliced thin
1 large onion, sliced thin

1 toe garlic, minced
Salt and pepper to taste
Parmesan cheese to taste
1 tablespoon minced parsley

Sauté chicken in oil to desired doneness. While chicken is frying, cottage fry potatoes. After chicken is browned but not entirely done, add onion, garlic, and salt and pepper to taste. Before serving, drain all oil from chicken and top with potatoes, Parmesan cheese, and parsley.
SERVES 4.

An earlier New Year's Eve provided a singular memory for longtime patrons Ginger and Tom Ford from Mandeville, who were visiting their friends Ronald and Karen Corkern in the French Quarter. Ginger wore her tennis shoes for the six-block walk from their apartment to the Galatoire's line, then changed into party shoes and put the tennis shoes into her large purse. That night, several New Year's toasts were offered, and a nationally acclaimed opera singer was introduced and persuaded by applause to honor the restaurant with a song. Although her oddly off-key performance fell far short of her buildup, her male companion made the grand gesture of removing her shoe and, treating it like Cinderella's glass slipper, poured champagne into it and toasted her magnificent voice. "At this point all the others in the restaurant were biting their lips trying very hard not to laugh," said Ginger Ford. Saying "I can do better than that," Ronald Corkern "pulled out one of my tennis shoes, stood, and poured champagne into it for a toast of his own, wishing all a very Happy New Year. After the theatrics of the previous toast, this brought down the house."

Billy Broadhurst was born on New Year's Eve, and he and his wife Nancy always celebrate with a New Year's Eve lunch. "New Year's Eve at Galatoire's is the best of all worlds," he says. Because Café Brûlot had always been a favorite of the couple, in 1994 when they married, their waiter Harold gave them a Brûlot set from Galatoire's. Broadhurst first went to Galatoire's with his Crowley parents as a young child. "When Canal Street was beautiful we'd come to New Orleans at Christmastime and walk the streets and look in the windows like people do in New York. We'd stay at the Monteleone, where all of South Louisiana stayed."

Pirate School spring break at Galatoire's—from left to right, Ned Hémard, Reynard LaVigne, Dick Meyers, and Chip Tilton

David Gooch himself commemorated a few noteworthy times at the "family store," including a party for about eighteen of his fellow high school graduates in 1961. He is also a member of the "Pirate's School," a loosely-formed club of thirty-three men who took their name and membership ritual from an old Cajun joke told by Roger Boynton of Abbeville, the official joke-teller. The only thing the men do is party twice a year, wearing eye patches and other pirate regalia, either on Avery Island the third weekend in October or Galatoire's on the third Thursday night in April. "We all wear eye patches to dinner, but we have to take them off to see," said Dick Meyers ("I'm the crazy fool who put this organization together ten years ago"), "but one of our waiters, John Fontenot (the other is Endre Toth), runs around all night in an eye patch."

Another quirky club is the "Momus Mourners," which always meets at Galatoire's during carnival season on the Thursday night of the Momus ball to mourn the 1993 politically-based demise of one of the last of the old-line parades. "We loved this carnival parade and refuse to watch anyone else roll on Momus night," said Lynn Kearney. "Where better to go than Galatoire's to 'mourn' the loss of a beloved friend?" The dozen members attire themselves in formal black mourning clothes and veils, bestow black beads, and "make a toast at the striking of the 'Second Bells' at 9:00 P.M." Each member goes by the name of a different size of champagne bottle to keep their identity "a secret." Out of town friends send funeral wreaths to the restaurant, which remain hanging on the wall for a time. One year a certain professor ended up crowned with one like a laurel wreath.

Seated to far left, Buddy Watkins; standing in back, second from left,
Bill Kearney; middle in back, David Gooch; seated to far right,
Mrs. Marilyn Watkins

MOMUS MOURNERS TOAST
(Delivered on the striking of the "Second Bells" at 9:00 P.M. on the Thursday before Mardi Gras.)

The Lord of Misrule has been banned from the street,
so Thursday before Carnival our Krewe will meet.
From all o'er the city or from wherever we roam,
on this night of nights we'll call Galatoire's home.
We gather together and mourn all en masse,
a great parade that no longer will pass.
We'll always remember his wit and his charm,
his love to poke fun, but do no one harm.

Born to celebrate summer at Galatoire's "sans kids and husbands," the White Party began as an engagement festivity for one of seven good friends from Natchez. In honor of the bride-to-be, white dresses and fancy lingerie were worn, and still remain the traditional apparel of the group, now enlarged to twenty-five. Cammie Wood Dale, now of Lafayette, and her sister-in-law, Patricia Dale Roberts, now of Houston, began the White Party and over the years have enjoyed the services of waiter M. C. Emmons, who,

The White Party, July 2000; from left, Cammie Wood Dale,
Kenneth Holditch, and other revelers

We stand here and honor his glorious reign,
with one thought alone to ease our pain.
That on this night we can welcome his son,
Lord Chaos rolls on to remember his fun.
So please won't you join us, and all lift a glass,
to Momus who stands alone in his class!

LADY NEBUCHADNEZZAR

Dale said, "can read our every whim—from what champagne to chill and appetizers to tempt us to the freshest fish and our triumph, *Le Café Brûlot*." In 1997, one member flew in from Los Angeles for her fortieth birthday, and so the White Party lives on in an ever-widening circle of celebration.

Such clubs, both tongue-in-cheek and serious, have a long history of fun at Galatoire's. The restaurant still has a few artifacts, such as a menu from a 1910 meeting of the Knickerbocker Club, and a mildly risqué flyer from a "Hard Times Supper" (dedicated to Harry A. Wilmer) given by the Knuckler's Club on January 31, 1914. Courtney-Anne Sarpy's father, Leon, told her about accompanying his mother in the early 1920s to a gathering of l'Athenee Louisianais in a private upstairs room at Galatoire's, where French was the language of the evening. "As he was the thirteenth guest, he was relegated to a small side table, so that there would not be thirteen at the principle table." A few patrons can recall the member of the "Martini Club," who came to dinner with friends after having drinks elsewhere. The man fell into his soup, and someone raised his head up by the hair. "Oh, he does that all the time," said his friends. "Call his wife." He was taken outside in a chair to wait for her, and kept falling out of the chair—but survived to dine another day.

Galatoire's staff Christmas party with the Rebirth Jazz Band and Santa Claus, 1994

Twice a year, Galatoire's staffers have a party of their own. The parties began around 1995, and always include a mid-year picnic in the Peristyle at City Park. Their yearly Christmas event began in the main dining room on

Monday nights at the restaurant, but now plays out in various venues, "because most of us are homebodies and like to go to other places," said a waiter. They have been entertained by Charles Neville and his trio, Bill Davis of Dash Rip Rock, the Rebirth Jazz Band, and Santa Claus in a mule-drawn buggy. "Everybody remembers that party; it was such a happening."

Before the renovation, large parties at Galatoire's were often tricky to arrange. In December, 1980, for the one hundredth anniversary of Waldhorn's Antiques, Stephen Moses hosted a dinner for forty by sending his secretary and three friends at 5:30 P.M., each to get a table for ten. Other customers were furious, but the party went on as scheduled. Now that the upstairs is available, Christmas parties at Galatoire's are convenient and popular. December restaurant decorations are simple and elegant with pine garlands with red bows downstairs and gold ribbons upstairs.

Of course, some events at Galatoire's are more unusual than others. Take New York City author and food authority Jessica Harris, for example, whose mother, the late Rhoda Alease Jones-Harris, was so fond of the restaurant that Harris took her ashes to lunch at Galatoire's. ("Going through airport security with a box of ashes is another saga," said Harris.) "Mama absolutely adored Galatoire's; it was something we did every time we came to New Orleans, and I wanted her to have a walk through the Quarter and one last meal at Galatoire's." Harris bought two backpacks to hold the box with her mother's ashes: one for everyday (Gap) and one for dress (Louis Vuitton). "Mama wore her Louis Vuitton to Galatoire's with one of her Hermes scarves tied on," said Harris, "and she had her own chair at the table." Imre was their regular waiter—"he adored Mama"—and he brought her usual glass of champagne. "As always, we had Café Brûlot, and she had her own cup."

Harris also entertained the very-much-alive Leah Chase for a memorable seventy-ninth birthday party (January 6, 2003) and "the nicest thing about it was that for some uncanny reason it was my first visit to Galatoire's," said the famed restaurateur. "It was wonderful! I loved most of all those waiters; they look like they have been there a zillion years. I was just amazed by them. They made you feel so good; they treated me like a queen! If anybody wants to feel like a king or a queen, just go sit there!" Among the dozen guests were writer Lolis Elie, artist John Scott and his wife Ana Rita, John and Lynn Fischbach, Michele Jean-Pierre, antiquarian Kerry Moody, Kenneth Holditch, and Chase's namesake daughter. "We had such a good time, and the food was great. We sat there for hours and it was just a beautiful thing. I like Galatoire's, and I've been back since."

Another landmark occasion took place when Dollye and Ingersoll Jordan's family mansion on Third Street was sold to Shirley and Frank Sinclair and the closing took place at Galatoire's. The documents were signed

Sheila Davlin, center, and Barbara Spencer, right,
every day is an extravaganza

at a separate table from the party (which also included the Sinclairs, Keene and Christel Kelley, Buzz Harper, and Les Winnegar), but then it was "back to the champagne!" This was a triple-occasion party, celebrating the closing on the mansion, Dollye's birthday, and the purchase of her new condominium.

THE CHRISTMAS MINK

One Christmas Eve a lavish gift backfired. On duty that day as a reserve police officer, Galatoire's regular David Oestreicher was called to the restaurant to handle a theft. The party was in full swing as officer Oestreicher walked in wearing full uniform to the surprise and loud greetings of many of his friends who were not aware of his volunteer post and thought his attire was a joke.

The aggrieved victim was a lady he knew named Colleen Foley, who proceeded to relate her tale of woe. The night before she had been at the Absinthe House, where her mink coat was stolen when she had her back turned. "I'm afraid I can't do anything about it now," he told her. "Yes, you can," she said, "my mink coat just walked in on the back of that blonde over there." Oestreicher turned to see the woman, who was with a married man whom Oestreicher knew.

Dollye remained Uptown, but her brother Ingersoll moved across the river to the West Bank. When a friend lamented his moving so far away, he assured her: "No, it isn't. It's only fifteen minutes from Galatoire's."

Even natural disasters can turn into a party at Galatoire's. According to waiter Dorris Sylvester, "during the flood in 1995, we had just a skeleton crew here, but the air conditioning was working and the joint filled up with customers. People came and had a great time anyway." Every year James A. Koerber from Hattiesburg, Mississippi, rewards his CPA firm's employees with a trip to Galatoire's on the first Friday after April 15. They travel by limousine ("to avoid any DUIs"), and "everyone talks about it all year." Koerber's "natural disaster" story concerns the November 16, 2002, fire at Mena's Palace on Iberville Street, when all the electricity in the French Quarter went out while he and business partner Tom Wofford were ending their Saturday night dinner at Galatoire's. "Of course, we were not going out on Bourbon Street during a blackout, so the waiters and staff made us all feel right at home," he said. Waiters put baguettes on everyone's tables, and stuck birthday candles in them. "When the candles burned down, a waiter came around and said, 'Looks like you need more wattage' and put another candle in the roll. Everyone sat around having drinks by 'candle-roll' for at least an hour and a half." One of the busboys was stuck in the elevator, and people were concerned about him, but the waiters said, "we just dropped a Heineken down to him, so he is doing fine." Even without the electricity, the entire Galatoire's staff was "friendly, professional, and most importantly, fun to be around," said Koeber. "I have been dining at Galatoire's for years but this was my most memorable dining experience."

Such friendly ambiance as that found at Galatoire's is often described as "comforting," and it has never been more apparent than during the dreadful

The blonde woman was called outside to the small vestibule and Oestreicher told her that her coat had been reported stolen and asked her where she got it. "Why my boyfriend gave it to me just this morning for my Christmas present," she answered. Oestreicher's next interview was with the boyfriend, whom he informed that this small world would get even smaller for him if he did not return the coat to its rightful owner. After a bit of blustering, the perpetrator turned over the coat to Foley and the matter was dropped, although the entire restaurant was agog as the unlikely drama played out.

Oestricher's wife, Tiffany, explained it: "All world's meet at Galatoire's!"

week following the Tuesday, September 11, 2001, attack on the World Trade Center. That day, as everyone in the restaurant sat stunned in grief and shock, David Gooch was asked to say a few words, which he did; and the assembled diners, including Dr. and Mrs. Roy Hock, longtime regulars, observed a minute of silence and sang "America the Beautiful." The next day, the ritual was repeated with "God Bless America." Gary Smith from Nashville, who often visits the restaurant when in New Orleans, was there the following Friday when only a few stranded people from out of town lingered in the restaurant. "Most of them were singles and they seemed very sad," Smith said. "My waiter asked if those visitors could join my table, and perhaps my guests and I could cheer up their evening." The invitation was promptly extended and the resultant camaraderie made a doleful situation much better.

When stockbroker and Army National Guard Special Forces Major Geary Mason and his unit were called to active duty in February 2003, he celebrated his birthday with a grand going-away party at Galatoire's. As a cup custard with candle arrived at his table, his waiters Reynard Lavigne and Tom Bockhaus led the singing, adding an announcement that the honoree was leaving to fight for his country. After a standing ovation, Mason's brother Tommy and one of his brokerage partners Beau Mire softly began singing "God Bless America," which was taken up by the entire dining room in a moving tribute. "It really sent chills down your spine," Mire told Angus Lind, who wrote about the evening in the *Times-Picayune* (February 7, 2003). Visitors from San Diego "said they had never seen anything like this in their lives" wrote Lind. "In special places, special things happen. Welcome to New Orleans and Galatoire's, folks."

Happy Birthday, dear Marc

MARC TURK

Happy Birthday to Marc

𝒜 birthday celebration at Galatoire's is not an unusual event, except for this one related by Marc Turk, developer, former restaurateur, and originator of the Bombay Club.

"It was a Wednesday in 1995 and Mom had early surgery scheduled at Touro Infirmary, so my day began at 5:00 A.M. About noon, after seeing Mom in the recovery room, I was told to go away for at least five hours as she would be sleeping. So off I went to the bank, where I realized it was September 6, my birthday.

"It seemed to me a good idea to celebrate this important occasion at the Big G—known to others as Galatoire's—but the friend I called so late had other plans. Although I can't remember in my thirty years of living in New Orleans ever eating there alone, I thought why not; and I opened the double doors into—I couldn't believe it—an absolutely empty restaurant! The only occupants were the waiters taking a break beside the cashier's desk and Miss Yvonne, the matriarch of this grand family. As I walked in the door, the most amazing thing happened: all the waiters jumped up and began putting their jackets back on. A diner/customer had arrived and the sophisticated ambience had to be maintained!

"David Gooch rushed to greet and seat me, assuring me that yes, of course, Galatoire's was open. I told him I wanted a late lunch and I wanted to smoke. No problem; he sat me dead center, promptly moving the table's "no smoking" sign to the next table. I told David it was my birthday, but I didn't want any fanfare or singing. Again, no problem.

"I ordered my Beefeater Martini (and the ones at Galatoire's are double by most restaurant standards) and those divine soufflé potatoes. Another Beefeater came with my Oysters en Brochette, compliments of Miss Yvonne. When I told my good friend, Leonard Parrish about that, he huffed, 'I've been going there for fifty years and no one ever sent me so much as a glass of water.'

"Later, with my stuffed eggplant I ordered my third Beefeater (I remind you they are doubles), and it came to me that a Martini is like a woman's breast: one is not enough and three is too many. Dessert! A Crème Brûlée and a Grand Marnier!

"All this time, not another soul had entered—Galatoire's had been my private dining room. But by this time I was blind, stinking drunk. When I asked David for the check I added: 'Please ring up United Cab for account 852, and ask that they pull up as close to the curb as possible.' When the taxi arrived, David came to escort me to the curb, and as I went out the door and was poured into the cab, I heard the entire wait staff singing 'Happy Birthday, dear Marc.'

"So impressed was the taxi driver that he refused to charge me for the ride home."

MARC TURK

Act Three
Rituals & Ceremonies

Scene Ten

Costumes
Dress Code

*"Women with blue hair, women with blonde hair,
women with hats on . . . men with stereotypical lawyer suits,
men with summer white linen or seersucker suits . . .
so this was Galatoire's."*
—Patron Patricia Goodwin

The Galatoire's dress code has provided a great deal of humor over the years, usually at the expense of those who came to dine while dressed inappropriately and tried to be seated anyway. The traditions of dress, which have been recently relaxed, are still greatly revered by the regular diners who consider dressing up for Galatoire's an obligation that dates back generations when the ladies who lunched always wore hats, gloves, and their prettiest frocks, and gentlemen would never dream of appearing without coats and ties. In the spring, seersucker and white linen suits still fly off the racks at men's stores in New Orleans. The spring 2004 J. Peterman's catalog bragged about a pair of their pants: "These particular seersucker pants are worthy of someone whose family has dined early at Galatoire's every Friday since 1905." ("Don't bother," said one gent, "those pants are not really seersucker, they're just cords.") Proper dress is a big issue with locals in general, since New Orleans has always held high its standards as a French outpost, and the French have always been considered fashion plates. Once Uptown ladies even dressed up to buy groceries. Their grocery store of choice was Langenstein's on Arabella Street, an Uptown establishment that is still popular today. Consequently, according to Ann Mahorner,

185

who got this information from her mother, Stella Mahorner, every Uptown lady owned "a Langenstein's dress and a Galatoire's hat."

Ladies still wear hats to Galatoire's. "Galatoire's is one of the few places left you can still really get dressed up for lunch," said Kim Sport, the "Galatoire's Gal's" head cheerleader. "Galatoire's was where women always dressed elegantly and gentlemen always wore coats and ties, and I would like to see this maintained. I think it makes the restaurant and the city special." The "Gals" always appear wearing the same color, "at least from the waist up because that's what shows." Bridget Kramer Balentine is also a hat person. "Before I come in the door, I peek in my sunglasses to be sure I look just so," said Balentine, "because there you have to make an entrance." When Leon III was manager, Balentine said he put fruit on her big hat "every time he passed my chair, and Louis Sahuc said, 'When the flowers and fruit begin to fall off ladies' hats, that's when you leave.'"

For many years, even as most of the French Quarter restaurants relaxed their dress codes in the interest of tourism, Galatoire's still held firmly to its coats-required and no-jeans policy, to the chagrin of many movie stars and Henry Kissinger. As just one example, in 1984, when patron Anne Moore's male guest, a visiting Viennese painter with long flowing curls, was denied seating, the waiter said, "The lady will not be allowed to be seated wearing denim." "I never knew whether the artist had been aware that he was identified as a lady, as his English at the time was limited," said Moore, "but the next time he came to visit he had cut his hair."

According to Ken Solis, maitre d' at the time, the first jeans wearer to come inside was Designer Oleg Cassini in the mid-nineties, in jeans made of velvet. When the *Times-Picayune* printed the story that the restaurant had regarded his attire as "dress denims" and let him in, jeans in their dress-denim disguise slowly inched their way inside. Eventually even ordinary jeans came to dinner, although not without scorn from the regulars. When the requisite tie for dinner was abandoned in the early eighties, a furor erupted, echoing the one caused by the relaxation of the coats rule in the late seventies—coats were no longer required for weekday and Saturday lunch.

There was also a time, as recently as the early eighties, when ladies were not allowed in unless attired in skirts. One visitor remembers being sent back to her hotel to change from a designer pantsuit to a skirt—any skirt—and, even more remarkable, actually doing it. Skirts are still the preferred attire for many female diners, but for most women the abolition of the dreaded "skirt rule" around the mid-eighties was a welcome milestone. Some amusing happenings came about because pantsuits were still not acceptable dress at Galatoire's for several years after the style was in vogue around the country. Various items of apparel were donned and removed to

Dressed in style and meeting code, from left to right,
actor Bryan Batt, Nina Gensler, and Jay Batt

get around this rule, from sarongs purchased in a sleazy Bourbon Street shop to buttoned-up coats with nothing much underneath. Around the corner, D. H. Holmes Department Store was handy for quick skirt purchases. A few daring young ladies even took the "no pants" rule literally, wearing skirts but on occasion leaving off their underwear. Of course, the group planned such occasions in advance. "It wouldn't be fun unless somebody knew you were doing it," one said.

When Patricia B. Mitchell, of Foodways Publications, and her husband Henry lived on the Gulf Coast, he was an Air Force lieutenant at Keesler AFB. In October 1969, they made their first visit to New Orleans. Jim Wilson, the director of Beauvoir and his wife, Sandra, had insisted that they must go to Galatoire's so they parked in the D. H. Holmes garage around the corner and took their place in line. "For the occasion we were dressed in our best," Patricia recalls, "I in a fairly elaborate faux-snakeskin pantsuit from Deedy's Boutique in Biloxi—by far the most expensive outfit I'd ever owned." When the maitre d' came out and informed her of the skirt rule, a determined Patricia hurried back to their car and discreetly changed into a dress she had brought along. "I was back in line by the front door in time to startle the maitre d' when he made his second appearance."

G. Espy Reed recalls an occasion around 1960 when he and his wife were at Galatoire's and two couples entered and were confronted by Paul, the maitre d', with the skirt rule because the younger of the two women was wearing a pantsuit. They left, only to return after the young lady had removed the offending garment. She now wore her jacket as a dress. "Galatoire's had no requirement as to hemline," said Reed. "New Orleans streetwalkers had longer dresses than that one. That dinner should have been on the house."

Perhaps dinner should also have been on the house for the woman who went to the ladies room and came back through the restaurant—twice—with her dress tucked up into her panty hose. Sophisticated out-of-towners were especially surprised by the rule. When she was a fashion coordinator for the home fashions industry in New York City, Andrea Sonfield and her future husband, Bob, president of Maison Blanche, went to lunch at Galatoire's where she was turned away in her new Yves St. Laurent pantsuit. Sonfield, too, then wore her pantsuit jacket as a dress to dine at Galatoire's. "Fortunately, the jacket was just long enough to pass," she laughed. This same scenario was played out many times, to the great delight and amusement of male patrons. Perhaps this highly visible part of the show caused the infamous skirt rule to remain in force longer than it ordinarily would have.

The men also danced around the rules with ingenuity. Most donned with good humor the Salvation Army jackets and ties hanging on hall trees beside the front door. (If you notice, you'll see the ill-fitting jackets still hanging on coat hooks ready for the dinner crowd, but ties are no longer necessary.) Those who strenuously objected usually were wearing jeans, an item of apparel de rigueur in Hollywood, but not allowed in Galatoire's at that time. Since men do not wear panty hose underneath their garments, they found it highly impractical, not to say embarrassing, to do as the ladies did and walk about in their jackets and skivvies.

However, there are always exceptions. When told he could not be seated without a coat and tie, one man went to the men's room and came out wearing the Salvation Army coat and tie but NOT his shirt and pants. Customer Mikki Pfeffer took an artist to the restaurant who hated wearing jackets and tried to remove his coat once he was seated, but "a waiter came

DEAR DOROTHY DIX

The "Dear Abby" of her day, Dorothy Dix (Elizabeth Gilmer, 1861–1951) began her syndicated advice column in the *Times-Picayune,* and at the height of her fame her readers numbered some sixty million people.

A New Orleans restaurateur asked Dorothy Dix what he should do about customers who turned up in clothes inappropriate for the establishment's dress code. Her response in a letter is indicative of the extent to which New Orleanians valued proper attire while dining out.

by and waggled his finger, saying 'No, no, no!'" Another customer was allowed to dine without a jacket because he was too large to fit into any of those available. According to longtime customer Leslie Schiff from Opelousas, sometimes ingenuity knew no bounds. When there were no loaners on the coat rack, Las Vegas attorney Joe Brown left and quickly returned properly attired, but two hours later a jacket-less gentleman entered Galatoire's and requested the return of his coat. Brown had gone to a corner bar and rented his jacket from the man, who had drunk his fill and was ready to go home.

Hollandaise Sauce

6 egg yolks	1 teaspoon lemon juice
2 tablespoons solid butter	1 teaspoon red wine vinegar
Pinch salt	2 tablespoons cold water
Pinch cayenne pepper	2 cups clarified butter

In a double-boiler, combine the egg yolks with the 2 tablespoons of solid butter cut into small pieces, salt, cayenne pepper, lemon juice, and red wine vinegar. Using a wire whisk, slowly blend the mixture over medium heat, allowing the butter to melt into the mixture. Whisk until the mixture takes on a thick, almost coarse, texture.

Remove from heat and add 2 tablespoons cold water. This will prevent curdling.

Using a ladle, slowly pour in the clarified butter, whisking the mixture constantly with a circular motion. The sauce should achieve a nice, thick consistency. Keep at a constant temperature and do not refrigerate.

MAKES 2 CUPS,

"Of course to do proper honor to your artistry, people should dine in full dress . . . but this is a free-and-easy day and one can't insist as much on the conventions so here is my suggestion. Let the matter rock along this winter without taking any actions for the shirtsleeve period is about over—Then next summer open up the small dining room for the coatless—advertise it as a convenience for them—and keep the main dining room for your patrons who prefer to be dressed like ladies and gentlemen. I confess I would not enjoy a meal when the men were dressed like roustabouts."

"Elie Nastase was thrown out of a tennis match in New Orleans for giving a referee the finger, so we were expecting fireworks when he came to Galatoire's and didn't have on a jacket or tie," said Leon Galatoire III, who was manager at that time. "But he was very nice. He put on our jacket and he picked out a tie that had a design that looked like aspirin or something. He picked that one he said, 'because it looks like Quaaludes.'" Incidentally, Leon was famous for his own sport—pitching. "He could pitch a cigarette pack to anyone in the dining room with uncanny accuracy," said Bryan Begue. "All you had to do was hold up your hands, one with your empty pack and the other one open, and WHAP! There were your cigs right in the palm of your hand."

Once a scheme was hatched to provide more attractive jackets than the relics from the Salvation Army. A group having Sunday lunch decided to supply coats bearing their own name labels as donors. Some present offered seldom-worn designer coats, others, jackets formerly belonging to deceased relatives. Since the subjects of his art are often the physically challenged, artist George Dureau indicated that he would provide coats especially designed for amputees and dwarves. Ann Mahorner had labels embroidered for each of the group, but the plan was put on hold during the renovation.

The former ties-after-five o'clock rule, too, offered occasions for laughter. One January afternoon at two minutes past five a friend of Tom Maher's came in with a group but without a tie. No loaners were available, so Maher suggested his friend make a fast trip to Woolworth's on the corner. Grumbling that he was colorblind, he returned from Woolworth's with a garish tie on which he thought something was "written in Japanese." Instead, as his tablemates were only too happy to inform him, this usually strait-laced and impeccable dresser had picked out a tie patterned with the letters YCDB-SOYA, which stood for "You Can't Do Business Sitting On Your Ass."

Recently, in a letter to the Tom Fitzmorris Dining Forum website, the writer, "JCG," recalled a Los Angeles friend, going to Galatoire's in 1980 without a tie, and receiving "an ancient black tie that looked like it once belonged to a fired or expired waiter." He learned from locals about the collection of such ties kept "specifically for visiting Los Angelinos and other uncouth male aliens who showed up for dinner in a state of gastronomical undress. Legend has it that if one boiled one of those old ties from Galatoire's it would yield the best gumbo in town!"

Two "best friends for life, fraternity brothers at LSU, best men, and god-parents for each other," Amiss Kean from Baton Rouge and the late Neil Nehrbass from Lafayette, particularly enjoyed trips to New Orleans for lunch at Galatoire's, which they always called "white suit days." Their customary attire of white suits and shirts, colorful ties, and Panama hats earned them the attention of a "wonderful older lady with the look and ease of a long estab-lished regular." "Young men," she said (the men were well into their sixties)

"Do-rag" creativity that still meets the dress code

"I just want to say that it's nice to see that someone in this city still knows how to dress."

With some diners, it's not what they're wearing when they come in, but what they're wearing when they come out. At some point in the nineties, the exchange game became popular. One day at lunch, a couple went into the ladies room together, puzzling fellow diners. When they came out they had exchanged outfits. She was wearing his suit, shirt and tie, shoes and socks. He was wearing her clothes and being a rather slight man, he was even able to wear her jewelry and high-heeled shoes. It was such a perfect switch that other diners stood and applauded.

Once a table of three couples was having so much fun that the women decided to surprise their husbands by going upstairs to the ladies room and trading outfits. This they did amid much hilarity and anticipation, but when they returned to the table, none of the husbands acted surprised at all. In fact, none of them even noticed. The socialite Dollye Jordan confessed to exchanging clothes with a girlfriend one night when a large table of her friends caught the spirit. "I had never done anything so daring in my life," she said. Another time, a large table of couples decided an exchange of outfits should be made between husbands and wives. This caused quite a sensation in the dining room. One can only imagine the confusing chaos in the restrooms.

However, when one well-sauced gentleman on another occasion replaced his clothes with a tablecloth that he draped around him like a toga, the maitre d' had to tap him on the shoulder and say it was time to put his clothes back on. This may have been the same man who stripped down to his Calvins to shinny up one of the dining room's support columns.

The night of the 2002 Krewe du Vieux parade, Will Erickson, a Tulane student from Yazoo City, Mississippi, was in Galatoire's. The enormous Mardi Gras marching club specializes in hilarious and outrageous parodies and that year the theme was "Brave Moo World." After the parade a trio of Erikson's marching friends (Byron Seward and John and Sakiko DeCell) crashed Galatoire's—cold, hungry, broke, and attired in cow suits. They chose Galatoire's because they could charge their meals. Not only were they allowed to stay, but they were the hit of the evening!

These days, when cows, jeans, and shirtsleeves are approved, the only dress code that still stands is jackets after 5:00 P.M. and all day on Sundays. Oh yes, no T-shirts, please (collared shirts only), and no shorts. Not even Bermudas.

Keeper of the Flame

VIVIEN RUFF

"It was from her [Vivien Ruff] that I learned this was not just a restaurant; it was an institution in New Orleans."
—Gilberto Eyzaguirre

If you ever dined in Galatoire's late in the afternoon or early evening in the 1980s or 1990s, you would have seen her, sitting with a friend at a two-top against the wall. She was an elderly woman, frail, worn, sometimes on a bad day looking as bedraggled as a character out of a Charles Dickens novel, her appearance belying the fact that she could well afford her daily meals at the restaurant. One Sunday a young man shook his head in disgust and remarked to his companions, "That old woman over there looks like a bag lady. Who let her in here?" One of his friends, who knew Vivien Ruff, said, "Sir, that *lady* has been coming here for over seventy years. She belongs. The question is, do you?"

When she died in 1998 at the age of ninety-seven, Vivien Ruff had indeed been a fixture for decades in Galatoire's, where she had first dined when she was eighteen. An only child, she had lived much of her long life in the 4200 block of Burgundy Street. Jeff LaFleur, one of the former waiters and a cousin of waiter Harold Fontenot, recalled that when she was younger, she was "beautiful, with red hair, a thin waistline, a beautiful figure, and a wonderful personality." Physically, the years had not been kind to her, but her spirit had survived, with the help of Galatoire's.

She earned a master's degree in music and was an accomplished pianist and singer, but rather than pursue a career in that field, she became an executive secretary for one of the owners of Godchaux's department store. At some point in time she formed the habit of coming to Galatoire's every day after work about 5:30 P.M. and staying until 7:30 or 8:00 P.M. Often in those early years, she dined alone but was not lonely, for she knew all the waiters and family members—she and Miss Yvonne early on became friends—and many of the old-time regulars, several of whom would come by her table to chat. Across the room from her sat another Galatoire doyenne, Marian Atkinson, with whom she always exchanged greetings.

Like Marian, Vivien seemed perfectly content in that milieu, and clearly the visits to her favorite restaurant were the highlight of her day. She always began her meal with a whiskey sour, and her taste in food was eclectic; she dined on a wide variety of the restaurant's specialties, but was particularly fond of the stuffed eggplant. Through all those years of her devotion, a number of different waiters served her, including Ralph Lonera, known as "The Mouse" among the other staff members. After his retirement, she was searching for a replacement and asked Cesar if he would serve her. With his typically ironic humor, Cesar replied in fake hauteur, "You can't afford me," and her quick and ever more acerbic retort was "I can buy five m———— like you!" Nevertheless, they became friends, and he often waited on her. Ultimately, Gilberto became her waiter, attending her in her last years, introducing her to other customers as if she were some beloved elderly relative. After Vivien, Gilberto, the legendary busboy Linzie, and a few of the regulars discovered that they were all fellow Virgos—she had been born on August 31 and always celebrated her birthday in Galatoire's—and they would greet each other like members of some secret society.

Cordial as she could be, however, there was another side to Vivien's personality that made her a "keeper of the flame" if you will, determined to preserve the customs and traditions that had helped make the restaurant unique. "It was from her," Gilberto said, "that I learned this was not just a restaurant; it was an institution in New Orleans." Although she could be very explosive when she witnessed what she perceived to be a desecration of that institution, she never raised her voice (though her tongue sometimes dripped acid), but she did not hesitate to act.

A self-appointed "fashion policewoman," Vivien was a stickler for the dress code, and when a man wearing a cowboy hat sat at the table next to her, she arose in righteous indignation and demanded, "What kind of man is this to be here with a hat on his head?" The man blushed as Vivien went up to his table, jerked the hat from his head, and threw it to the floor, thus eliciting laughter from the startled customers around them. Similarly, she did not hesitate to scold those who were smoking in the nonsmoking section and on one occasion as she was leaving the restaurant, she removed a cigar from a man's mouth and dunked it into his drink.

Her particular aversion was to men who were not wearing the required coats on Sunday. Once after a coatless man and his party were seated, Vivien went to his table and announced, "I have been coming here for sixty-five years and I've never before seen a man without a coat on Sunday." The man explained to her that all the spare coats provided for those uninformed about the dress code were in use and that the maitre d' had gone to find another one. Unfortunately, since the waiters who kept the key to the supply room did not care for that particular maitre d'—long since gone from the restaurant—they refused to give him the key. The offending customer finished his meal, coatless, under the stern glare of Vivien Ruff, who telephoned Miss Yvonne on Tuesday to complain, and the maitre d' was almost fired as a result.

One episode especially demonstrates Vivien's love of the restaurant. Starting down the stairs one afternoon when the ladies room was still on the second floor, she tripped on a top step, fell all the way to the bottom, and was unconscious for fifteen minutes. An emergency vehicle took her to the hospital, where five lawyers who had witnesses the episode—the accident must have occurred on a Friday—contacted her to offer their services, but Vivien did not take them up on it.

Not long thereafter, however, one of her favorite waiters was standing in the front door, eating a piece of cheesecake, when one of the restaurant's owners drove past. The waiter was suspended, and when Vivien discovered that he was not there to serve her the next day, she asked Doug Wynne where he was. "He's got problems," Mr. Wynne said, to which Vivien replied, "He has problems? You've got problems. I've got a pending lawsuit I may file against you." The waiter was reinstated post haste.

Despite her occasional volatile temper—she once exploded into profanity when one of the managers would not cash a $250 check for her—her character was distinguished by some gentler virtues, including a unique sense of humor. One Monday, while standing in a line at the bank, she saw in front of her David Gooch, who had come to make the weekly deposit for Galatoire's. She jabbed a finger in his back and said, "This is a stick up!" and a startled David dropped all the money on the floor.

Courage was another of her qualities, which was proven over and over again in the face of increasing infirmity. Like her fellow Galatoire's habitué, Marian Atkinson, she struggled to make her daily—later weekly—visits to her beloved restaurant despite the debilitating pains of age. She celebrated her ninetieth birthday and a few more at *her* table at Galatoire's. Then, alas, she was confined to a nursing home where, characteristically, one of her favorite waiters often visited her.

With the death of Vivien Ruff, the voice of one of the staunchest guardians of Galatoire's was stilled, but her spirit lives on in others who are equally devoted, if not quite so volatile and vocal in their determination to see that the show must go on!

KENNETH HOLDITCH

Act Three
Rituals & Ceremonies

Scene Eleven

Box Office
House Accounts

> *"The first fifty charge accounts at Galatoire's
> were held by probably the grandest families in town."*
> —Dr. George Harris, Galatoire's aficionado

Charge accounts at Galatoire's, known there as house accounts, spawned their own stories from the beginning. For most of the restaurant's history, almost all customers paid cash only (cash tickets were simply stuck on a nail), although there were a few private accounts for stockbrokers, department store owners, lawyers, and doctors. Like the waistlines of regular diners, the list of house accounts slowly burgeoned over the decades. Having a house account became, after a while, a status symbol: simply signing one's check denoted that one had "arrived," was now a part of New Orleans, even if one was a newcomer to the city. Whereas it was once rare for a diner to acquire such an account, there are now people from all over the country, some of whom dine at Galatoire's only once or twice a year, who pride themselves on being able to "sign and leave."

Left: Hand-written house account number on a business card; right: Laminated house account card used today

For many years patrons had no physical "charge cards," but according to David Gooch, in the eighties the restaurant began giving out Galatoire's business cards with an account number written on them by hand. It was not until the late nineties that the present laminated account cards came into use.

Each day in the early years, the restaurant's charge tickets were filed in stacks of envelopes held together by rubber bands (all the A's in one stack, all the B's in another, etc.) and stored in rolling cabinets. Each morning the family would sit down to breakfast at a table at the back of the dining room, roll out the filing cabinet (stored under the counter in the kitchen) and sort through and file the tickets from the day before. At the end of each month they would go through the files and write up a bill by hand on a regular waiter's pad that would include all one's tickets for the month with prices, tax, tip, and total. Often the bill would include a polite little note jotted at the bottom asking for payment. Quite a few prominent New Orleans families neglected to pay their Galatoire's bills for years and the restaurant was noted for its long-suffering tolerance of those patrons who were slow in settling up. One 1958 note signed by Justin Galatoire said, "We honor your name, please honor ours." According to David Gooch, twenty-five years later the man who received that note "came up to me and apologized, saying it had been on his mind all that time," then paid his bill with interest.

As the list of house accounts grew by the hundreds, this billing procedure became more and more unwieldy. "In the early sixties, I remember quite a few of my regulars started getting house accounts," said Harold Fontenot, the waiter who has been at Galatoire's for the longest time. "Everything was done by hand." By 1974 when David Gooch took over as manager he saw the need to improve the system to accommodate the large number of house account customers, up into the thousands. "By then there were a couple of thousand accounts, and it became a nightmare just to find each customer's envelope simply filed under the first letter of their name," said Gooch. "So I decided to keep the envelope system, but assign a number to each name." (A-1, A-2, A-3, etc.) Today's computer system is set up using the same numbering

WAITING FOR LOW DIGITS

One and two-digit house account numbers are still especially prized, so much so that some customers ask for lower numbers when they become available, sometimes waiting years for a progression of customers to drop off the list due to death and other causes.

In a notable case of one-upmanship, shipping executive Angus Cooper was given the number C-1/2 in pre-computer days. This came about when attorney Robert Kerrigan received K-1 when a Mr. Knight passed away. Kerrigan had been waiting for K-1 for such a long time that he bragged about it to Cooper. "Then Mr. Cooper wanted C-1, but it was scheme for the now more than seven thousand house accounts. Even today, the waiters call David Gooch "Rainman" due to his penchant for remembering regular customers' account numbers. "Sometimes I'll see them come in and remember their number but not their name," he said.

From the beginning, the accounts most often used landed at the top of the envelope stacks, so the most regular customers received the lowest numbers. Besides the cachet of simply signing your name to a ticket, largely a local honor, the number of your account placed you among the elite old families who had house accounts for generations and used them often. The lower your number was, the more cachet, and this became such a status symbol that some customers even willed their numbers to their heirs. Among them is Stephen Moses, who inherited W-2 from his grandparents, Sam and Eva Waldhorn. Stephen and Dee Moses' children are the fifth generation of their family to dine at Galatoire's.

Even today, when credit cards are readily accepted, one- and two-digit numbers are prized. Anesthesiologist Dr. George Harris was given H-86 a long time ago, when he lived in the slave quarter behind Lindy Boggs's Bourbon Street house and brought ship captains from Russia, Spain, and Greece to dine at Galatoire's. Harris was then a medical resident and the only doctor in town with a federal immunization stamp who could go aboard foreign ships to give immunization shots to the crews about to load grain. Dinner at Galatoire's with the captains was his reciprocal arrangement so he could enjoy copious officer's dinners aboard ship. "I frankly don't know whether I had a sequential account number or if they gave me H-86 as a subtle threat to eighty-six me if I got drunk and bad. (For the uninitiated, in the parlance of serious partiers—which reputation Harris enjoyed then and still does—to be "eighty-sixed" means to be thrown out of an establishment for bad behavior.)

Juanita Pradel, a French Quarter preservationist who once had a custom couture shop on Chartres Street, believes she was one of the first women to have a charge account, issued by Justin Galatoire in the late 1950s. John

taken by a Mr. Charles Colbert, so I fixed him up with C-1/2. Then he could brag to Kerrigan that he was the only 1/2 in the system," said David Gooch, keeper of house accounts. "When we switched over to the computer, the machine refused to take a 1/2, so the lowest C Angus Cooper could get was in the C-30s." What a comeuppance!

"Jack Gordon was G-9, but he made his way down the list and now he is G-1," said Gooch. "Seven people had to die before he got it."

Sullivan has lived since the late 1960s in New York, where he runs his own catering business, The Butler Did It. He recalls that since he was fifteen he has had a Galatoire's charge account "which I have treasured." Growing up in Baton Rouge and Lake Charles, he frequently came with his family to "the City, as I thought of New Orleans all my life—at least until the Big Apple." George St. George Biddle Duke writes, "I am now a rancher in Montana, but I still have my number at Galatoire's!" Hilary Hogan (daughter of Steve), who now lives in California, still has her own house account, too. Leon III gave it to her, complete with card, when she was born eighteen years ago.

Stuffed Eggplant Galatoire's

1 whole medium-size eggplant	2 tablespoons fresh parsley
4 level tablespoons flour	14 medium size shrimp, boiled
4 tablespoons milk	4 ounces crabmeat
4 tablespoons butter	2 tablespoons bread crumbs
1 scallion	1 tablespoon Parmesan cheese

Preheat oven to 375 degrees.

Halve eggplant, bake in pan with water for 30 minutes or until tender. Use flour, milk, and butter, to make a heavy cream sauce. Let cool.

After eggplant has cooked, remove the pulp from the shell. Sauté the chopped pulp, scallion, parsley, shrimp, and crabmeat together. Add the cream sauce and cook all together until heated through.

Spoon stuffing into reserved shells of eggplant. Sprinkle with bread crumbs and Parmesan cheese and bake till tops are brown.

SERVES 4.

Patricia Goodwin tells of the time one member of the Galatoire's Fan Club who had a house account charged the entire group's lunch to her Galatoire's credit card and each member paid her back. "Why hadn't I known about this little treasure of credibility and prestige—the Galatoire credit card? The next time in, I signed up," she said. "There was no card then—you just remembered your number or just signed. Clients, friends, associates, relatives, expert witnesses—all were then taken to Galatoire's until I moved at the end of the eighties to central Louisiana." Now Goodwin always pays by signing the check. "You'd be amazed at how impressed out-of-town friends are and how urbane they think I am—and all because I simply sign a ticket and walk out."

"By clinging to a conservative vision of dining, Galatoire's became a bastion of eccentricity," wrote Jesse Katz in the *Los Angeles Times* (2002), so when the restaurant began using computers to track customer accounts, this headline ran in *New Orleans Business* in July of 1986: "What's New Orleans Coming To? Galatoire's Now Has a Computer!" Columnist Joe Mizelle goes on to write: "I couldn't believe my eyes. I opened my statement from Galatoire's and found a computer printout instead of the usual hand-written statement. Next time I was there, I asked David Gooch if the next change would be accepting reservations. He said, 'No way, not as long as we are here,' and Miss Yvonne agreed." (That momentous change did come eventually, but in a limited way that still left sacrosanct the first-come, first-served rule downstairs.)

The next big culture shock to devotees of Galatoire's was the acceptance of credit cards in April 1992, which made local headlines and caused shock waves all around town. Lisa LeBlanc-Berry had written in a 1988 *Gambit* review, "No credit cards here—but selected locals have charge accounts, which has a certain style that American Express can't buy." For five more years, cash and style ruled, and waiter John Fontenot continued to tell customers, "In God we trust!—I loved to use that line." Since then, however, quick payment for the restaurant and frequent-flyer miles for the customers have evidently worked their charms. According to Gooch, since credit cards have come on the scene, not nearly as many of the house accounts are used.

For some customers, outsized liquor tabs provide bragging rights. Mickey Easterling once hosted a downstairs luncheon for her daughter's first marriage that came in at $10,000, much of it for bottles of Dom Perignon placed on each table at Galatoire's, whether or not invited guests were seated there. In the late 1970s, Ted Gugert and Charlie Carriere were having lunch on Friday. They had Martinis. They had Pouilly-Fuissé. They had Martell brandy. They lunched until 4:00 P.M. and then went to pick up their

BREAKING UP IS EASY TO DO

When Bridget Kramer (now Balentine) and her boyfriend Tom Regan broke up, "her heart was broken," so the couple got all dressed up and went to Galatoire's with their friends, including Jimmy Buffett and Ed Bradley, for a gala "Break-up Party." (Her father, Texan Armand Kramer, picked up the $600 tab for which only $200 was for food.) "It was during Jazz Fest 1989; Leon was holding court in back; John was our waiter," said Bridget. "I made the announcement that I was relinquishing everything. I told Tom, 'My Neiman-Marcus cards are yours, but I want my own charge account at Galatoire's.' Leon said you got it and gave me number K-203."

wives and started over. More of the same. When the check came it was considerable. Ted looked at it and said: "Damn it, Charlie, you eat too much! Twelve dollars of this check is for food!"

There have been times when a regular's house account bill includes more than food and drink. Consider the puzzle Leonard Parrish faced when he received a bill with an unexplained one-hundred-dollar charge. He remembered a day when he had joined Mickey Easterling at table after their respective groups had left the restaurant, and the two had consumed a one hundred dollar bottle of Vieuve Cliquot. But he was certain that Mickey had paid for the champagne, so he called and asked Leon, who was on the desk that day, if they had been double-billed by mistake. "You forget," said Leon III, laughing. "You were feeling no pain, and you walked up to the desk and said you needed a hundred dollars. Then you just reached in the cash drawer and took it out. So that was the one hundred dollars we charged you, not the champagne."

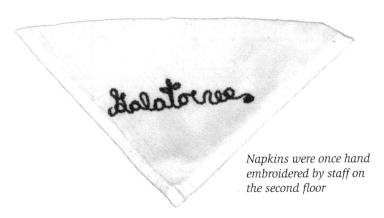

Napkins were once hand embroidered by staff on the second floor

"I used to keep track of all this myself until 1996," said Gooch, "then Libby Parsons and Zaida Garay became the first office personnel." Today, on the third floor where Gabriel Galatoire once lived in a palatial apartment, the busy office staff includes Jo Ann Nunnery, whose responsibilities are secretarial, taking reservations, and taking care of uniforms. Nunnery began working at Galatoire's twenty-two years ago as a "linen girl"—along with her mother Lula Mae Martin, her aunt Elizabeth Osbey, and her cousin Fanny White—sewing and embroidering tablecloths and napkins on three sewing machines set up on the then-closed second floor. Since 1995, the unadorned linens have been taken care of by a rental service, so the traditional patron perk of filching souvenir napkins (or taking leftovers home wrapped in them) is no more. "One lady has been coming here ever since she was a little girl, often with her grandmother, and leaving every time with a napkin. Her grandmother's house was filled with our linen," said Gooch.

Tableware is another story. "I can't tell you how many times people have mailed back a box of silverware, sugar bowls, and such, saying they felt guilty about swiping them," Gooch said. Collectors can now purchase at the restaurant Galatoire's-monogrammed wine and water glasses ($5), sugar bowls ($100), silverware ($6; $10 for knives), plates with the distinctive "G" ($30), and plain Hungarian crystal water carafes ($50). All you do is ask your waiter and take home your (paid-for) loot. At Adler's Jewelers, demitasse spoons, cocktail forks (six for $32.50), and gumbo spoons (six for $50) are wrapped into green felt packages with appropriate recipes. As proof of popularity, someone was such an avid collector that when Galatoire's donated monogrammed silverware, glassware, tablecloth, an old ice pick, and a bottle of Gooch's special Galatoire's cocktail to be auctioned for charity, several of the items, including the bottle, were stolen before the high bidder could pick up his $900-worth of the past.

There may be more treasures up in the attic. According to Gooch, along with "old journals and house account records and tons of unknown stuff," stand twenty-five metal spittoons, remnants of the pre-Galatoire's days when ducks and chickens hung in the restaurant windows and its name was Victor's. In those earlier days, obtaining a house account at Galatoire's, unlike today's standard credit application procedure, was largely a disorganized affair, especially if you ate there regularly. J. D. Cantey, a longtime customer from Baton Rouge with a low house account number explained just how he got his account at Galatoire's. "I was coming in a lot about thirty years ago, and I told Mr. Galatoire that I was a contractor and needed to bring my clients in and charge it off and the government wouldn't accept a record of cash. That's the only way you could pay in those days. So he brought over a plain slip of paper and said 'sign it.' I did, and he said: 'Now you have a charge account.'"

William Menge, whose father once lived upstairs over the old Victor's, had been a customer for years when he asked for a charge account form. He was informed: "Oh, you don't have to bother with that; just sign your name." Menge received in the mail a plain waiter's charge slip with his new account number on it.

Soon after receiving their own house account number, Bill Menge and his wife Sue invited out-of-town friends to Galatoire's for dinner. The visiting couple was astounded by Galatoire's customs, the husband observing: "This is the first restaurant I've ever been to where you walk in, the waiter hugs you, he brings you a drink before you order one, and then your food arrives but you've never seen a menu, and when you're finished, you just get up and walk out."

Gilberto Eyzaguirre

THE GILBERTO SUMMER

"Only in New Orleans"

$\mathcal{J}$f you want proof that New Orleanians are passionate about the dining experience, simply take for example the famous Gilberto brouhaha. When Gilberto Eyzaguirre, a favorite waiter for twenty-two years, was fired from Galatoire's in April of 2002 because of complaints from two female employees about sexual harassment, more than a hundred letters of protest ensued. With reinstatement the aim, they were copied, bound into books, and delivered by taxi to each Galatoire family member by physician Brobson Lutz, one of the ring-leaders of the customer revolt. Lutz was so upset by his waiter's firing that he telephoned a patient, Dr. Robert Barron, to tell him the results of his liver function tests, but began the conversation with the words: "Bad News!" "My heart dropped," said Barron, "I thought the worst; I was already having visions of chemotherapy." Then his doctor said, "Gilberto has been fired!" It took a minute for Barron to digest the fact that the bad news was not about him. "Yes, but what about my liver?" he asked Lutz. The answer came almost as an afterthought. "Oh, it's okay."

Devoted Gilberto customers boycotted and began a website that received thousands of hits. During one Friday lunch, restaurant doors were flung open by two gangsterish-looking, black-suited men in dark glasses who stormed inside and released a hundred helium balloons printed with the message "welovegilberto.com." All to no avail.

After a three-page *Times-Picayune* story about the controversy by restaurant critic Brett Anderson, the newspaper was deluged by "Letters to the Editor"—according to columnist Chris Rose, more than those generated by any other story in its history except September 11. Most were critical of the pro-Gilberto faction, many of whom also took his dismissal as an opportunity to vent their concerns about what they considered ominous changes at the restaurant during the last few years. Newspaper letter-writers considered their dining complaints frivolous in the light of world problems.

Anderson put it this way: "A waiter is fired from a restaurant, a nonevent most anywhere in America. But this is New Orleans and the restaurant is Galatoire's. A popular waiter's departure from the temple of French Creole cooking has the well-heeled regulars up in arms and longing for the past." Readers responded with what Anderson called "class rage." "I've never seen anything like it," he said.

Editorial letters particularly singled out those who complained about being served drinks with machine-made ice cubes rather than the old hand-chipped variety, a change made to great grumbling in 1994. This prompted Mickey Easterling, an especially colorful and vocal pro-Gilberto letter writer, to appear at the restaurant with her houseman bearing a silver salver holding a giant block of ice and an ice pick with which she and her entourage proceeded to hand-chop their own ice.

With cleverly-titled stories such as "Creole Contretemps," "Delicious Food Fight Embroils New Orleans," "Waitergate," "Fine Whining," "Tempest in a Saucepan" and the like, the press dined out on the story.

Wire services, *USA Today,* the *Los Angeles Times,* and other media giants found it the perfect example of how quirky life can be in New Orleans. Regulars scoffed that few understand the mystique of the restaurant and that they were defending its "soul." Treated to a plethora of waggish media coverage, most New Orleanians welcomed the long-running farce as excellent entertainment for a fiendishly hot summer.

Now a local celebrity, Gilberto landed at another fine dining venue, followed by his "regulars." His papier-mâché likeness was even the subject of a Shakespeare-themed float in the Krewe d'Etat parade during Mardi Gras 2003 ("He loved not wisely, but too well"). Unable to withstand their longings for such savories as Canapé Lorenzo and Shrimp Clemenceau, most boycotters came back to their usual tables at Galatoire's, albeit with different waiters.

Breaking his five-month fast during a September hurricane alert, Lutz staged a jazz funeral after an October Friday lunch at Galatoire's, saying, "It takes a jazz funeral to end the mourning." Carrying decorated umbrellas and a banner emblazoned with the ubiquitous welovegilberto.com, the large funeral entourage followed Bob French's Original Tuxedo Jazz Band to Gilberto's new venue. Even Galatoire's Vice President David Gooch joined the ranks for a drink. "I went back to Galatoire's when the year's first hurricane front approached New Orleans," Lutz stated. "I did not want to get washed or blown away without a stomach full of Godchaux Salad. Of course, the crabmeat is always superb at the end of summer and early fall."

Galatoire's had its best summer ever, having been the beneficiary of unimagined national coverage. "Galatoire's owes the *Times-Picayune* and the letter writers a million bucks in free publicity," food writer Gene Bourg said in *USA Today.* "That place is packed!"

Delivering the last word of 2002 on the matter was the Christmas Eve *Times-Picayune* editorial, a fable that portrayed Santa Claus having trouble at his restaurant, North Polatoire's. After he fired Filberto, his elves stopped hand-chopping ice and his customers revolted. Santa planned to fill the stockings of the "hand-chopped ice crowd" with mechanically-produced ice until they found "some real problems to get worked up about."

This "tempest in a Martini glass" (so-called by patron Marcelle Saussy) inspired *The Galatoire's Monologues,* a hilarious cabaret show produced at Le Chat Noir in New Orleans.

Backed by interpretive dancing, comic commentary, and jazz piano and guitar, selected pro-Gilberto letters were read by actors and a few letter-writers themselves, including Lutz, who treated the cast to lunch at Galatoire's on the day of the jazz funeral. So many of the letter writers enjoyed the performances that an attendee, Natasha Ramer, remarked that she didn't know whether to watch the play or the audience. Easterling took her block of ice to the show, in which she was portrayed grandly bejeweled, wearing a large hat with a giant chicken on top and with money falling out of her handbag. Another especially entertaining riff was a song by Peter Orr ostensibly written by Robert Zimmerman, aka Bob Dylan, a former resident of Audubon Place, whom the song imagines frequently dining at Galatoire's unrecognized by the "out of it" regulars.

The show proved so popular that it ran for many weekends to sell-out audiences, and still played intermittently more than a year later. Reviewing its performance in *Gambit,* critic Dalt Wonk spoke of the fear that "a barricade made of bales of seersucker would be thrown up across Bourbon Street in what threatened to become the second Battle of New Orleans," but came to the conclusion that the very nature of such an "outrageously eccentric situation" made him feel that "this oddest of cities" is not changing, but is "still essentially intact."

In Feburary 2003 the show was performed at Copia, the American Center for Wine, Food and the Arts in California's Napa Valley. Copia's description: "The facts of this 'theater of the absurd' are based on a true occurrence served up at the venerable Galatoire's restaurant, sanctuary of the Beau Monde of New Orleans."

The Galatoire's Monologues' producer Chris Rose calls the famous book of protest letters "the best publication to come out of this city since *A Confederacy of Dunces."* The one unarguable opinion in the long-running melodrama was the simple phrase on everyone's lips: "Only in New Orleans."

MARDA BURTON

207

Act Four
The New Century

Scene Twelve

Scenery Change
Renovation

"Change at Galatoire's during the past eighty-two years has been most remarkable by its absence."
—IVY Award Citation, May 13, 1987

*A*s Galatoire's goes into its second century and our world into the exciting whirlwind of the new millennium, the restaurant is more popular than ever as customers from near and far sample with enthusiasm the unchanging atmosphere and unfailingly excellent cuisine of a beloved and enduring New Orleans tradition. In 2001, *Gourmet Magazine* ranked Galatoire's among America's fifty best restaurants, the only one in New Orleans to make the cut. "It's the century-old, resolutely old-fashioned Galatoire's that makes us giddy with pleasure."

Such is the restaurant's reputation that Galatoire's was honored in 2003 with a prestigious James Beard nomination for our nation's most outstanding restaurant—one out of only five. The nominations go to restaurants in the U.S. that serve as national standard bearers "of consistency of quality and excellence in food, atmosphere and service." Although Zuni Café in San Francisco won, "just to be nominated for this honor is an unbelievable distinction," said Galatoire's manager Melvin Rodrigue. Coincidentally, before this nomination by the nation's leading food critics, Galatoire's chefs had been invited to cook for eighty-five invited guests at a gala dinner at the James Beard House in New York City, which took place a few weeks after the award ceremony. All in all, public and peer response to Galatoire's can be considered a glorious beginning to the new century.

Actually, the old restaurant began in earnest to launch itself into the twenty-first century in 1998. Galatoire's "new century" began with a total renovation, an update that many in the family felt had long been needed. Even after the death of the ultra-conservative family guru, Justin Galatoire, on December 4, 1973, at the age of eighty-seven, attempts to modernize and expand in the 1970s and 1980s were adamantly resisted by the older generation. Perhaps Monsieur Justin's experience in putting the restaurant's barbershop-style decor back to rights after the catastrophic fire of the late fifties had made him even more resistant to change. It is recorded in a 1969 cookbook that during the repairs some patrons asked him to take down the wall-to-wall mirrors so beloved today, saying they always felt like they were getting a haircut instead of a meal.

Celebrating the renovation: in background, from left to right, Michele Galatoire, maitre d' Jacques Fortier, Dorris Sylvester, and Louis LaFleur; in foreground, Melvin Rodrigue and Justin Frey seated, John Fontenot standing

In 1973, frustrated by the status quo, Justin's eldest grandson Chris Ansel Jr. left Galatoire's to open his own successful restaurant, Christian's in Mid-City; and eventually, in the late seventies, Galatoire's was refurbished. According to David Gooch, "We put up wallpaper to make it more elegant; it had been painted light green. We took down the fans that had been painted brown and

The upstairs opening; seated, left to right, Galatoire family members, Carolyn Frey Rodman, Leona Frey, Clarisse Gooch, and Brenda Gooch Bethea; standing, left to right, Leon Galatoire III, Chris Ansel Jr., Justin Frey, and Alfred Frey.

had them dipped and lacquered so that the brass came back. It was an important renovation for us, but not at all as extensive as the one twenty years later." The fans were decorative but wobbled, so they were no longer used. In fact, a waiter said they had never cooled much anyway, "they just kept flies away from the

food." The restaurant's unusual electric system remained the same; it had been noticed by patrons for years, but rarely remarked upon. Until the early nineties, Galatoire's, the city's pumping stations, and the streetcar lines were the only customers still served by one of the city's most antiquated power systems. "When the streetcars would start up, our lights would flicker," said Gooch.

When the younger generation came of age and influence in the nineties, expansion was inevitable. The family saw a burgeoning food culture on a national scale, enormous growth in New Orleans tourism, and only one small dining room. The physical improvements that Chris Ansel had wanted to make twenty-five years before were now a necessity. "I certainly wasn't interested in changing the cuisine," said Ansel, now retired as owner of Christian's and also as chairman of Galatoire's board.

When comanagers David Gooch and Justin Frey became vice presidents in 1997, a new manager was hired to drive the project forward. Twenty-four-year-old Melvin Rodrigue became the first non-family member to hold that position and began the new regime with such changes as new curtains, limited reservations, and final plans for remodeling. Joe Sevier, who has been lunching with friends every Friday at Galatoire's for thirty years, and his waiter Richard Smith joked with each other that Smith had been waiting on Sevier longer than Rodrigue had been alive. Even before he was hired, the board had instigated such measures as dispensing with hand-chipped ice and installing ice-making machines and relaxing the dress code for lunch—prompting the *Times-Picayune* restaurant critic to write: "Galatoire's and change do not sound right in the same sentence."

"We think of any changes we've made as great improvements," says Jack Gooch, chairman of the board since the summer of 2002. "The building required a substantial upgrade as well as needed improvements in the kitchen." Attorney Gooch is a grandson of Leon I. "I am confident that my grandfather and other family founding members would enthusiastically approve and be proud of the restaurant as it exists today."

When plans for total renovation went forward, the biggest improvement was rebuilding the second floor to include the first upstairs dining rooms in fifty years (doubling the restaurant's capacity) as well as a bar, a new upstairs kitchen, an elevator, and additional restrooms. This not only allowed the restaurant to take reservations for upstairs dining, but provided space for overflow. When the upstairs renovation was completed the three new dining rooms were introduced to the public on June 23, 1999, with great fanfare and, naturally, a party to which regulars flocked with great anticipation.

While the first floor was being stripped down to the plaster and subfloor and then reconstructed, regular diners accustomed themselves to the spacious upstairs rooms but avidly anticipated the *piece de resistance*. They

A SALON STORY

Once upon a time back in the nineties, in the beauty salon in the Royal Orleans Hotel—while my hair was being "conditioned"—all the chat was about Galatoire's no longer hand-chipping block ice.

"My dear, I HATE those machine-made cubes," one lovely said. "They're not cold enough; that's because they're hollow. My Old-Fashioned just doesn't taste the same anymore."

One of the city's "best blondes" chimed in: "I hear they're even thinking of taking reservations." A chorus of gasps followed, and then "I knew things were going downhill when they started taking credit cards."

"It was pure class when your doggy bag was a Galatoire's napkin; now it's just a tacky paper bag with a cartoon dog on it," complained a brunette having her long nails resculptured. "That was just the beginning," the blonde said, "do you *believe* that nobody is

Bryant Sylvester tending the new upstairs bar on opening day;
A. J. Capritto standing to the left and Coleman Kuhn sitting at bar.

missed their familiar downstairs haven. In a remarkable job of construction juggling, the restaurant experienced only two weeks of downtime. Davis Jahncke and Harvey Burns of Jahncke Architects, Inc., Armand "Ace" LeGardeur, CEO of the contracting firm Carl E. Woodward Co., LLC and project manager Legier Kuhner were the wizards who accomplished the feat.

upstairs embroidering *Galatoire's* on the napkins anymore? *The napkins are plain white!*"

After a moment of silence in which to contemplate the unthinkable, the conversation resumed. Expressions bleak, voices aggrieved, the ladies continued to top each other.

"Well, I hate those new curtains that open," said a smocked, silver-haired lady on her way to the shampoo room. Until a few weeks before, tightly curtained front windows contributed to the privileged, cocooned atmosphere, never allowing even a hint of Bourbon Street sleaze inside. "I don't like to see it getting dark outside," she added. "It reminds me that time is passing in the real world, and that I should be getting on home."

"I thought I saw someone in blue jeans Friday. I did. I *know* I did. We were all beside ourselves! We were just *wild!*" The redhead stopped for a moment to consider. "Well, actually, I didn't see him sitting down," she went on, eyes big and serious. "He was on his way out. Do you think he just came in to use the bathroom or something?"

Now that Galatoire's is completely remodeled, a staircase from the new foyer goes up to a big mahogany bar where people can belly up rather than stand outside in line on Bourbon Street. Interestingly enough, people still queue up outside before the doors open at 11:00 A.M. to be among the first on the written list in the foyer, which now takes the place of the line. The new century won't have many line stories to tell, since a reservation policy is now in place for upstairs dining. Although board/family member Carolyn Rodman has said, "People can certainly stand in line if they want to," the convivial bar has largely taken its place. Still, certain traditions don't completely fade away. Besides the maitre d' list, certain forms of the line linger on, including those for "holiday Fridays" when paid stand-ins are hired for over-night duty. In some cases, the maitre d' at Galatoire's can still be called the most powerful man in New Orleans.

When the downstairs dining room so beloved by so many was finally unveiled on October 5, 1999, a stream of apprehensive regulars was waiting. "Downstairs is theater and I love it there," says Leonard Parrish, who refuses to dine upstairs in the new space. "I always like the back table in front of the cash drawer because you can always see the show perfectly from there." In the *Washington Post*, Amy Culbertson wrote of "the biggest restaurant news in New Orleans this past year at the preserved-in-amber haute-Creole institution that still counts much of New Orleans society as its regular members." She told the wondering masses: "Since its reopening, regulars' fears have been assuaged: the main dining room remains unchanged, and the consensus is that the food has come through intact as well."

EVERYTHING NEW IS OLD AGAIN

Writer Lili LeGardeur dined at Galatoire's the night of October 5, 1999. With her were her father, Armand "Ace" LeGardeur, general contractor on the renovation project, his wife Wendy, his project manager, Legier Kuhner, and Kuhner's soon-to-be-wife Debbie. For them—and for us—it was an historic occasion.

"On an evening in October, the restored downstairs dining room opens without fanfare. My father and stepmother, Kuhner and his date, and I arrange to meet for dinner to celebrate. The job isn't actually completed—work crews will be busy on the third floor offices for two weeks yet–but the prospect of sitting in the completed dining room is too tempting.

"We gather in the new upstairs bar—just as we're supposed to. The bartender stumbles at my request for a Galatoire's Cocktail, but recovers quickly when I explain that it's a modified Sazerac. He pours out a triple.

"Riding down in the mahogany-paneled elevator, Dad lets out a little whoop and knocks at the wall, as if to assure himself it's really there. And then we're there: the dining room redone, brighter than remembered, only just beginning to fill with customers.

Kenneth Chabaud puts a fresh face on Galatoire's

The collective sigh of relief was almost audible. To most it looks exactly the same, if not better, the only change being a new entrance that knocked out tables 8 and 9. It encompasses the side carriageway and staircase rather than the old double doorway into the front of the dining room. The new entrance came under early fire until it was explained that it was not new at

"It's clean. The freshly stenciled fleurs-de-lis on the emerald walls are jewel-like, fresh. The velvet portieres gathered in the two front windows seem too rich, like something from a New York hotel—the Plaza, maybe. I squirm a little; I can see too clearly where the scaffolds stood. Sniffing the air, I wonder how they cleared the smell of paint.

"It's a moment of doubt, I admit it. But customers trickle in, among them an old friend and editor. A boy remembered from high school enters with his father and wife. Striding to the other end of the dining room to say hello, there's a familiar sound. It's the way high heels sound hitting this particular floor, and it's right.

"I miss that splotchy ceiling; the heads of the new sprinkler system are much less interesting to contemplate. But Galatoire's fills with such interesting people. All through the meal, I checked on them periodically, glimpsing in the mirrors unobtrusively, scarcely moving my head.

"Some things never change."

all, but the original entrance to the restaurant in 1905. In any case, the door's distinctive brass G still shines as brilliantly as ever, and the tiles on the checkered floor have been restored to the original one-inch-hexagon-size. The walls are fresh with golden fleur-de-lis, hand-stenciled now, and the beveled wall-to-wall mirrors reflecting the show look exactly the same, topped with rows of brass coat hooks and light sconces. Missing are the heavy velvet curtains over the front windows that shut Bourbon Street out and created a timeless world. Now floor-to-ceiling drapes cover the front walls—but not the windows—in a motion picture theatre effect. The faded awards and photos resting on their ledges have gone to their rest elsewhere. Women no longer need navigate steep stairs to get to the ladies room, prompting Joanne Sealy to complain, tongue firmly in cheek, that the climb was the only exercise she ever got. (The upstairs ladies room is much grander than the new downstairs one.) Unsightly acoustical ceiling tile is gone, along with its dubious benefits, leaving only the same old ceiling fans with bright lights to hover over the convivial din and clatter. In the back, the ancient desk and clock remain the focal point of the room, along with pretty women in hats. "It is sacred ground," said attorney and preservationist Bill Borah.

"We promised that nothing would change," said Rodrigue. "The fact that Galatoire's doesn't change is one of our biggest assets and part of our image. I think once our regulars saw the finished product they realized we weren't just saying that to please people, we meant every word of it." Bryant Sylvester, a Galatoire's waiter for fifteen years, put it this way: "New Orleans people, when they see something's going to happen, they get all excited. But when they see how it works out, they go with the flow." Attorney and longtime patron Patrick O'Keefe said, "There is a fabric about Galatoire's that is virtually indestructible." In *CityBusiness* Errol Laborde agreed: "There's still

LOOK AGAIN

You see wallpaper? Look again. Those French fleur-de-lis in the downstairs dining room are stenciled on the wall by hand. It just looks like wallpaper. Because nothing they saw quite suited the nostalgic look they wanted, Galatoire's family members and architects Davis Jahncke and Harvey Burns called in Sherry Haydel, a talented New Orleanian who specializes in custom designs and decorative finishes.

Haydel designed and made a master stencil ("the easy part") and then chalked out a grid on the walls. This was a challenge because the pattern had to come out even all the way around the room. Anyone from New Orleans knows that nothing old is even remotely even. Sherry and two associates painted the fleur-de-lis with a cream color, then sponged with metallic gold paint, followed by an application of brown glaze to add depth.

Look again. It's not wallpaper; it's more than 100 hours of meticulous work.

the mood and the feel in which people-watching is as much a part of the experience as the hot French bread."

"No doubt locals will hotly debate the qualities of the new Galatoire's versus the old for years to come," wrote S. M. Hahn in the *Times-Picayne*, November, 26, 1996. "In the end though, quibbling is pointless. Compared to Galatoire's every other restaurant is just a restaurant. Galatoire's is an embodiment of New Orleanian *joic de vivre* like no other. Which set of doors you use or where you choose to sit becomes irrelevant once you enter Galatoire's world, and the world of Galatoire's enters you."

Deirdre Stanforth's words written long ago in 1967 still carry the ring of truth: "Galatoire's almost seems to have been left on Bourbon Street by accident, a relic of what used to be in the gaslight days when Creole aristocrats in evening clothes arrived in their carriages at the French Opera House. All the turmoil and change swirling about its doors, however, have affected it not one bit." John DeMers in *The Food of New Orleans* described Galatoire's in 1997 "with its glittering dining room filled with high-society/wave-and-wink, its veteran wait staff, and a menu taken from a Creole time capsule. What Galatoire's does no one does better." It is interesting to note that, even in years since the turn of the new century, phrases such as "time-warp" and "time capsule" turn up constantly in descriptions of Galatoire's.

While still carrying a turn-of-the-last-century ambiance on its public stage, the changes backstage were extensive, especially in the ancient, outdated kitchen on the first floor, called "a hot hellhole" by food critic Tom Fitzmorris in *CityBusiness,* January 24, 2000. It was gutted and begun anew, with another complete kitchen constructed on the second floor. "They did wonders in the kitchen; it is immaculate," said waiter John Fontenot. "Everything is so plush."

Galatoire's continues to be one of the nation's signature restaurants, employing over one hundred workers backstage, who, like the melting-pot city itself, comprise a United Nations of cultures, including African American, Hungarian, South American, Cajun, and Yankee. The kitchen staff has expanded to twenty-five cooks and eleven porters. The wait staff currently numbers twenty-nine waiters, twelve busboys and six bartenders. Business has increased exponentially. "There's been a tremendous demand for private dining facilities and now we can supply it," said Rodrigue. According to Erin Barrilleaux, catering manager, in December 2002, they averaged five or six parties a day, mostly given by locals. "Galatoire's did not suffer as much as other French Quarter restaurants after 9/11, because we depend a lot on local customers," said Carolyn Rodman. Big firms do "buy-outs" of the entire restaurant on Mondays only, and often upstairs rooms are reserved for large dinner parties.

When the kitchen was completed, a new menu was introduced, including the traditional dishes along with a few new ones. Banana Bread Pudding, Pecan Pie, and Sweet Potato Cheesecake have been added to a dessert list that

THE GREAT FLIP-FLOP

Carl E. Woodward won the contract in February 1998 with an innovative plan to build a second floor kitchen, then 'flip-flop' kitchens to keep the restaurant up and running on the second floor while the first floor kitchen was demolished and restored.

Limited access to the site called for nineteenth century methods. All the materials for the second and third floors—literally tons of sheetrock, plywood and timber—arrived by truck on Bourbon Street, then were lifted hand-over-hand to the second floor balcony and through a window. Debris from demolition left the same way.

When dining shifted to the completed second floor, workers still had to bring everything in and out by wheelbarrow and bucket through narrow passages for the first floor construction. Twenty-foot steel beams were lifted to the second floor, and steel risers were transported in sections, then welded in place.

LILI LEGARDEUR, "RENOVATING GALATOIRE'S", *LOUISIANA CONTRACTOR*, OCTOBER 1999 once offered only K & B ice cream, *Pêche Flambe,* Cherries Jubilee, Caramel Cup Custard, Crepes Maison, and the nobly named *Coupe Princesse* and *Coupe Duchesse.* The *Princesse* is a scoop of vanilla ice cream topped with canned fruit cocktail and Cointreau, and the *Duchesse*'s ingredients are a canned peach half, currant jelly and port. Along with K & B ice cream and *Pêche Flambe,* the *coupes* have both disappeared from the handsome new menu presented in a thick padded-leather cover which few regulars bother to open. They still prefer to ask their waiter's advice, just as they have for generations. Writer Thomas Heard said, "A New Orleans friend tutored me on how to act like a regular. The first rule is 'Don't look at the menu.'"

Crepes Maison

8 tablespoons of grape jelly	Peel of one orange and one lemon,
8 (6-inch) dessert crepes	slivered
6 tablespoons of toasted, sliced	Powdered sugar
almonds	4 jiggers of Grand Marnier

Roll 1 tablespoon of grape jelly in each crepe. Place 2 crepes per serving on an ovenproof plate. Top with sliced almonds, orange, and lemon peel, and sprinkle with powdered sugar. Pass under broiler until hot. Pour 1 jigger of Grand Marnier over each serving.
SERVES 4.

In his turn-of-the-century review of the "new" Galatoire's, Fitzmorris noted that changes "have made surprisingly little difference in the dining room." He found most of the standard dishes "are just as they always were," and that "the chemistry is working as well as ever, and perhaps even better."

After a four-hour lunch in which five people consumed Crabmeat Maison ("just as fresh and generous"), Shrimp Rémoulade ("just as tangy"), Trout Amandine ("just as toasty"), Grilled Pompano Meunière ("still the best simple fish dish in town"), Chicken Clemenceau ("overpolished"), eggplant sticks, lamb chops ("still of fine pedigree and cooked simply but deftly"), Trout Marguery ("Galatoire's neglected old signature dish"), caramel custards, a magnum of Champagne and bottles of Puligny Montrachet and Gevrey Chambertin, the critic's altogether fitting conclusion was: "the place remains emblematic of the sybaritic abandon with which we Orleanians approach eating."

219

CURTAIN CALL
The Last Word

The talk at the beginning of the twenty-first century is of cloning and genetic tinkering, the Internet and solar power, space stations, global terrorism, and the war in Iraq. In New Orleans, tourism, not shipping, is the number one industry. Instead of yellow fever, mosquitoes are bringing West Nile virus. Legal rather than illegal gambling is in town to stay. Certainly a far cry from Gibson Girls and Model T's.

Yet, as always, Galatoire's customers still socialize and forget their troubles, gossip and talk politics, liberally imbibe and dine out on wonderful stories and some of the best and most dependable food in New Orleans—just as they have for a century. Change as the world has, and inevitably will, we don't see that changing.

MARDA BURTON

SECOND CURTAIN CALL
The Last, Last Word

We celebrate the past, with yearning, the present with nervous reactions, and the future with faith unlimited. The old French bistro has become something else, but it has survived; it will endure. For that, we thank whatever gods—culinary or otherwise, maybe Bacchus—who have made it all possible.

KENNETH HOLDITCH

221

ACKNOWLEDGEMENTS

We wish to thank the many people who love Galatoire's and shared their stories with us—so many, so often, and in so many places that we had to collect them on cocktail napkins, check stubs, scraps of paper, business cards, envelopes, whatever came to hand at the time.

We appreciate the assistance of those members of the Galatoire family who keep the flame burning, especially David Gooch and Chris Ansel. Thanks to Arnold Chabaud, the waiters, kitchen personnel, and other staff members and their families who treasure the scene and were so dedicated to our project. We are grateful to Jude Swenson, who so often dines at Galatoire's that she was able to help us identify many of the people in these photos, to Joanne Sealy, who so skillfully gave our proofs a final reading, and to Rosemary Daniell and Joe DeSalvo, who assisted us greatly with encouragement and advice. We thank Lili LeGardeur, Curtis Wilkie, Gene Bourg, Shirley Ann Grau, and all the other writers, both past and present, whose witticisms and insights live on again in this book.

This book would never have come together without a third collaborator —our talented Hill Street editor, Judy Long, whose patience and sense of humor endured when ours grew badly frayed.

Finally, we thank each other for the fact that we are still speaking after this collaboration, which one of us equated with "an excruciating form of punishment comparable to the pangs of eternal torment" and quoted from a T-shirt—"If a man speaks in the forest, and a woman is not there to contradict him, is he wrong anyway?"

PHOTO CREDITS

B. A. Adams Sr.
B. A. Adams Sr. and sons (157)

Bridget Kramer Balentine
Leon Galatoire and Jimmy Buffett (116); Ed Bradley (117)

Marda Burton   Milton Prudence (43); Louis LaFleur (78); Men's lunch
group (97); Annalee Jefferies and Bob Salazar (105); LeRoy Neiman
(119); Line at Galatoire's (132, 139); Curtis Wilkie, Marda Burton, and
Kenneth Holditch (141); George Dureau and Arthur Pulitzer (154);
Helen Gilbert and Alice O' Shaughnessy (159); Simone Galatoire
Nugent and friends (168); Sheila Davlin and Barbara Spencer (180);
Bryan Batt, Nina Gensler, and Jay Batt (187); Do-rag creativity (191)

M. C. Emmons
White Party (177)

Langdon Clay
Galatoire descendents (18); Marian Patton Atkinson (107)

George Dureau
Michele Galatoire, Mickey Easterling, and Leonard Parrish (92)

Galatoire Family
Jean Galatoire (7); Leon, Gabriel, and Justin Galatoire (8); Galatoire's
fiftieth anniversary celebration (9); Gabriel Rene and Rene Galatoire
(17); Justin Galatoire at table (27)

Galatoire's Restaurant
209 Bourbon Street (4); Menu and place setting (26); Lynn and Gloria
Mitchell (32); IVY Award (42); Waiters with wine salesman (70);
Momus Mourners (176); Staff Christmas party (178); Renovation celebration (210); Upstairs bar (213)

Nancy Lee Galkowski
Lee McDaniel (62); Lee McDaniel and Brenda Lee (120)

Leon Rene and Michele Galatoire
Leon Rene Galatoire (Leon III) (18); Michele Galatoire (18); Leon III
with alligator (41)

David Gooch
Cooks, circa 1940 (29); Lee McDaniel and fellow waiter (68); Waiter,
circa 1940 (76); David Gooch with staff (73); Galatoire family members
with staff (84) Villere birthday party (167)

Ned Hémard
Pirate School (175)

Lili LeGardeur
Kenneth Chabaud (215); Ladies room sign (217)

Kenneth Holditch
David Gooch and Yvonne Galatoire Wynne (17); Justin Frey and David Gooch (18); Kristina Ford, Rosemary James, and Julie Smith (58); M. C. Emmons and Gilberto Eyzaguirre (69); Becky Allen, Andre De Labarre, and George Dureau (92); Mimi Guste (104); Tommy Tune and group (113); Carrie Nye and friends (125); House account cards (197)

Wayne Isaak
Cesar Rodriguez, Zachary Richard, and Arnold Chabaud (123)

Nancy Moss
Willie Morris and group (59)

Rise Delmar Ochsner
Yvonne Galatorie Wynne (20); Don Lee Keith (51); Linzie Brown (86); Customers enjoying Galatoire's (99); Cesar Rodriquez, Bob and Cathy Edmundson (127); Line at Galatoire's (137); Men at Friday lunch (146); Gilberto Eyzaguirre (204)

Darlene Olivio
Jerry and Darleen Higle Carlisle (172)

Berenice Percy
Bunt and Walker Percy (55)

Earl Perry
Kenneth Holditch and Kim Hunter (124)

Louis Sahuc
Galatoire family members (211); Upstairs dining room (211)

Daniel Edmond Sullivan
Parish Sullivan birthday party with Imre Szalai (87)

INDEX

Index